ONE
HIS NAME SHALL BE ONE

Z.B. DAVID

Outskirts Press, Inc.
Denver, Colorado

The opinions expressed in this manuscript are solely the opinions of the author and do not represent the opinions or thoughts of the publisher. The author represents and warrants that s/he either owns or has the legal right to publish all material in this book.

ONE
HIS NAME SHALL BE ONE
All Rights Reserved
Copyright © 2007 Z. B. David
V 8.0
Cover Image © 2007 JupiterImages Corporation
All Rights Reserved. Used With Permission.

This book may not be reproduced, transmitted, or stored in whole or in part by any means, including graphic, electronic, or mechanical without the express written consent of the publisher except in the case of brief quotations embodied in critical articles and reviews.

Outskirts Press
http://www.outskirtspress.com

ISBN-10: 1-4327-0169-X
ISBN-13: 978-1-4327-0169-7

Library of Congress Control Number: 2006935937

Outskirts Press and the "OP" logo are trademarks belonging to Outskirts Press, Inc.

Printed in the United States of America

FOR ANTI-SEMITES:
WHAT IS JUDAISM ALL ABOUT ?

WHAT IS IT YOU HATE ?

WHAT IS THE DEFINITION OF A JEW ?

HIS NAME SHALL BE ONE

When all mankind

can rationalize,

clearly think,

understand, and acknowledge

that there is but ONE SINGLE GOD,

the ALMIGHTY CREATOR,

and when they all

worship only HIM

and obey all of HIS Commandments

then

the LORD,

the ONE SINGLE GOD

shall be KING over Heaven and Earth and,

on that day,

HIS Name shall be ONE

DEDICATION

This book is dedicated to the memory

of all men, women and children,

martyrs,

that for more than two millennium

were murdered only because

they had the belief

in the

ONE SINGLE GOD

This book is also dedicated

to all who live

and maintain

the belief in the

ONE SINGLE GOD

THE ALMIGHTY CREATOR

PREFACE

There are two reasons for this writing. First, for too many years, years before and almost two thousand years, since the advent of Christianity, the vile hatred expressions and actions of anti-Semitism have been allowed to occur in and among all of the nations of the world with very few exceptions. This religious hatred has resulted in the many pogroms, inquisitions, horrible tortures and injurious assaults, crimes of covetous robbery, rapes, and slaughter. It has culminated, in the Twentieth Century, in the tragic Holocaust consequences that resulted in the murder of over six million innocent men, women and children who were killed because they were Jewish.

While the Holocaust was happening, while millions of innocent Jewish men, women and children were taken from their homes and transported to death camps, like cattle being taken to slaughter houses, the peoples of all the nations, with very few exceptions, knew what was happening, idly stood by, watched, and did nothing to halt this tragic murderous bloody stain on the history of mankind.

The citizens of the United States have always held open the door to those who were leaving the lands of their oppression. The Statute of Liberty was in view of all signaling the freedom and welcome awaiting all of the tragic humans who looked to the United States for salvation and freedom from tyranny. But the door, for the Jews of Europe, was closed and sealed very tightly. At the pre-World War II Evian Conference, discussing the pending tragedy to befall the Jewish people in Europe (especially in Nazi Germany), none of the nations of the world had room for any of the Jews.

The German ship, the St. Louis, sailed from Germany to Cuba with over 900 Jewish passengers, men, women, and children, taking them from the hell of Nazi Germany to freedom. They had entrance visas to permit them to land and live in safety in Cuba. However, when they arrived at Havana, they were not allowed to disembark and have entrance into Cuba. The German ship's Captain tried unsuccessfully to bring them to safety and refuge in the nearby United States.

The Jews were not allowed to land and enter into the United States. The St. Louis was escorted and guarded by the ships of the U.S. Coast Guard to assure that the passengers would not be taken to any dock in the United States. There was no room for the 900 Jewish passengers to permit their entrance into the United States. They tragically had to be taken back to Europe and ultimately sent back to the Nazi Hell.

The English government also shut the doors of the freedom that could have been available to the Jews in the lands of the Palestine Mandate. The English committed crimes in the illegal violation of the Mandate given to them by the League of Nations.

Instead of creation of a Jewish homeland in the Palestine Mandate land, England violated their Mandate giving 82 % of the Mandate Lands to the Sheikh of Mecca and Medina who was fleeing the Arabian Peninsula from the attacking Saudi family. For the Sheikh and his Bedouin tribe they created the new Jewless Kingdom of Arab Transjordan.

The previous English Mandate violation actions continued. As the persecutions of the Jews were underway in Europe, at the start of the Holocaust, the English released their infamous White Paper. This action very criminally and intentionally resulted in closing and sealing the doors of survival and not allowing the Jews to escape with their lives to the safety of the Mandated Jewish Homeland of Palestine. But the English did not shut the doors of Palestine for the Arabs. They very warmly welcomed hoards of many Arabs, from the many Arab lands, into the remaining small portion of the Palestine Mandate Lands. The multitudes of Arabs, that they welcomed, fled from the very good lives of poverty they lead in garbage slums of their many Arab homelands, to the then remaining 18 % of the original Palestine Mandate lands.

The English allowed the Arabs arriving to slaughter Jews. The City of Hebron became an "Arab City" when the 532 Jewish inhabitants were attacked and 133 were massacred by the Arabs. And while the slaughter and massacres were taking place through-out the minuscule 18 % remnant of the Mandated Lands, the English stood by, looked the other way, and did not stop the Arabs' murderous slaughter and did not rescue the Jews.

And now, once again, there has been a strong resurgence of anti-Semitism in Europe and the middle east. This new wave of anti-Semitism now festering in Europe has brought forth, out in the open, the latent hatred of Jews by all too many European Christians. Most of this is now reoccurring and caused by the Jewish hatred ingrained in the large number of Arab Fundamentalist Muslims, now residing in the European countries, who murder in the name of their Allah God. The message of hate and anti-Semitism is also spreading to those European Christians who still and always have had latent anti-Semitic fervor.

Most of this violence, that has caused great injury, pain, suffering, and resulted in murder, has been perpetrated by individuals who had absolutely very little or no knowledge as to why they were committing these violent hateful actions. It is very easy to hate when you do not know any valid reason as to why you are hating. It is very easy to hate when one is taught and directed to hatred and murder by those preaching and promulgating evil hatred to ignorant masses. Tragically this is happening to masses of religious Muslim Arabs now being taught hatred of Jews and the necessity to murder them.

The message of hatred is spread to the Arab Muslims living in European countries as well as those living in the existing Twenty-One Arab League Nations. The masses blindly follow the teachings and instructions of their evil villainous leaders. These include the Arab youth today taught to hate in the Madrashes (Muslim Schools) by Imams, Mullahs, Shiekhs, and Ayatollahs who stress anti-Jewish expressions found in their Koran.

Many European politicians and political leaders know that their millions of new Arab Muslim citizens are under the influence of their religious leaders and teachers and taught and instructed to hate and commit murder and anti-Semitic acts against their Jewish citizens. Still, knowing this, they fail to prevent Arab Muslim anti-Semitism and some even give it endorsement and encouragement.

If one is to hate those who believe in the Jewish religion, the hater should at least study and know the religion to be hated. Most haters, Christians and Muslims, know very little or do not know anything about the Jewish religion that they hate. They also, in too many cases, do not know enough about their own religion.

This is written with the main purpose to present the basic essence of the Jewish religion to those who are the haters of the Jews and their Jewish religion. It is important that they understand and learn what it is that they hate. Perhaps, then, the haters will cease their hatred.

Secondly, there are many who can trace their ancestral roots and their heritage to those who were once believers in the Jewish religion. However, today, some of these descendants do not know anything or little about this, their own religion, and why their ancestors often sacrificed themselves in martyrdom rather than yield their Jewish belief and religion. Some have given up on their religion and belief in GOD because of the Holocaust murder of over six million Jewish men, women, children and they ask, "Where was GOD when all of this murdering was happening?"

Perhaps if they knew more of their religious inheritance, then, they would be more able to understand why their ancestors kept their Jewish religious faith during all of the past two thousand years of the murderous oppressions of the Jews. Indeed, today, among those who declare that they are Jews there is much acrimonious debate as to the definition of Judaism and as to defining "Who is a Jew?"

The purpose here is to explain, in simple understandable terms, what the Jewish religion is all about. Thus those who are prone to hatred of Jews and the Jewish religion will at least know what it is that they hate and they may then seek to understand why they are mislead to the obsession of this hatred. It is also the purpose here to define the basic and fundamental beliefs of the Jewish religion and in that way to define "Who is a Jew?"

To accomplish this definition, it is necessary to review the Ten Commandments given to all of mankind through the Children of Israel by the ONE SINGLE GOD. Further, an understanding review of the Thirteen Principles of Faith, as stated by Maimonides, is an absolute necessity. These, the Ten Commandments of God and the Thirteen Principles of Faith are both presented herein to and for the reader.

IN THE BEGINNING

Western civilized mankind, under the Jewish, Christian and Islamic religions, have professed belief in a creator God. This belief can be traced to the Jewish belief in a ONE SINGLE GOD who Created the world we know, all of the universe that we can see and understand to exist, all of the existing matter that we can not see, and then even beyond this world to the endless reaches, in every direction, of an infinite infinity that we cannot see, understand, and comprehend.

This original Jewish belief finds some common expression in the three primary religions of the western civilized world. The CREATOR GOD is the central figure of those who are faithful believers and adherents in the Jewish, Christian and Islamic religions.

The Jewish religion is the Mother Religion. The Christian and Islamic religions are the daughter religions. The latter, the daughter religions, are both branch religions stemming from the root and trunk of the Jewish religion. To study and understand the two daughter religions, it is an absolute necessity that one must first begin with a comprehensive study of the Mother Religion. ***To be ignorant of the Mother Religion is to also be ignorant of the two daughter religions.***

Common to all of the three religions is an acknowledgment that the individual known as Abraham first recognized that there was only one ONE SINGLE DEITY. He was brought up amidst people, including his own family, who worshipped pagan idols, icons and statues of many god deities. But Abraham firmly concluded that these pagan gods were all, each of them, false gods. He concluded that there was but ONE SINGLE GOD who had created the entire earth, complete with all its terrain and oceans, and all of the creatures and vegetation of the world. He believed that this ONE SINGLE GOD had created all mankind, and him, and the earth, sun, moon and stars and all that Abraham could see and even beyond what he could see. Abraham lived over 4,000 years ago.

The Jewish religion thus began with Abraham. The main theme of the Jewish faith has always encompassed this total believe in the ONE SINGLE GOD. The Jews worship only their ONE SINGLE GOD. They observe, as the day of rest and worship, the Sabbath, the Seventh Day, in accordance with the Sabbath words stated by the ONE SINGLE GOD in HIS Ten Commandments that Abraham's descendants, the Children of Israel, received, on behalf of and for all mankind, from the ONE SINGLE GOD at Mount Sinai.

About 3700 years ago, the descendants of Abraham, who then dwelled in the land of Egypt were placed in bondage, servitude and slavery by the Egyptian Pharaoh. The Torah (bible) states that the leader of Abraham's descendants, Moses, who led them out of the slavery in Egypt, conversed with the ONE SINGLE GOD. He ascended Mount Sinai to receive the ONE SINGLE GOD's Torah and Ten Commandments.

At that time, alone with the ONE SINGLE GOD on Mount Sinai, Moses requested to see the ONE SINGLE GOD. He was then told by the ONE SINGLE GOD that no man could ever see HIM and live. This is very clearly written in the Torah and easy to be understood by all. It was known and fully understood by Jesus and each of his apostles and early followers.

Since no man can ever see the ONE SINGLE GOD and then still be alive, how can so many have said they have seen god or the son of god or the mother of god and still remain alive if these are truly gods?

Two thousand years ago, the first daughter religion, Christianity, was founded by followers of Jesus who was born a Jew named Yeshua Ben

Yosef. Jesus was a student and teacher. He fully knew, understood, and faithfully adhered to the complete Torah and knew all of each and every one of the Ten Commandments and laws stated in the Torah. Jesus knew and believed in these words written in the Torah, **"The LORD our GOD is ONE SINGLE GOD."**

Moses received this Message from the ONE SINGLE GOD. He conveyed this Message to the Israelites, the Jewish people. This Message has since then remained foremost and central to the Jewish faith and is recited by Jews several times in daily prayer is: *"Hear O Israel that the LORD our GOD is ONE SINGLE GOD."*

The ONE SINGLE GOD's Message, established monotheism in a world observing pagan beliefs and the worshipping of many gods, including mother gods and sons of gods, and was worshipped with the bowing down, and veneration of many figures, icons, idols and statues of their father, mother, and son gods.

More than 2500 years ago, nations came into being that were militarily powerful. These nations conquered many peoples and brought with them their pagan religious beliefs, with their icons, idols, statues of their pagan gods. The Greeks and later the Romans came on the scene conquering much of the known western world. The Greeks and Romans believed in many gods. They had father gods, mother gods, and sons of gods.

The Greeks and Romans conquered the Israelites. Both attempted to force the Israelites to abandon their Jewish religion and belief in their ONE SINGLE GOD. They tried to force the Israelites to accept and worship their many pagan gods and venerate their idols and statues. They tried to force the belief in their religions and pagan ways of life upon the Israelites who worshipped only the ONE SINGLE GOD and were not allowed to have idols and statues.

The Greeks and Romans brought the statues and idols of their father gods and sons of god into the Temple of the Israelites. They failed in their efforts to convert the Israelites away from their belief in the ONE SINGLE GOD into an acceptance and belief in their pagan father of gods and sons of gods.

However, they left behind a culture acceptable to some Israelites who were not strong in their Jewish faith and belief. During the Greco-Syrian occupation, some of these Israelites, known as Hellenists, turned away from their Jewish religion. The Hellenists instead accepted Greek philosophy, culture, and aspects of the Greek pagan religion.

The Israelites then revolted against the Greco-Syrians and Hellenists and regained their freedom. As a result of their victory over the pagan forces, they instituted the celebration of Chanuka, a holiday of freedom and of the rededication of their Holy Temple in Jerusalem to the service of the ONE SINGLE GOD.

This Chanuka holiday was understood and known to the founders of Christianity. The reason for the rebellion was to defeat the attempt to paganize the Israelites by having them worship the pagan idol gods of the Greco-Syrians and to sacrifice swine to these pagan gods in the Israelites' Holy Temple that was dedicated to the ONE SINGLE GOD.

About 2000 years ago, during the Roman occupation, a group of these Hellenistic Israelites joined together, initially as a Hebraic cult, and modified their belief in the ONE SINGLE GOD. They included the Greek and Roman belief in more than one god by adding a son god. Thus from the Judaic roots of the monotheistic Israelites, arose the new western religion of Christianity with the Jew Yeshua, Jesus, being recognized and worshipped as a deity as the son of god.

The religion of Christianity accepted the deities of a trinity and the new religion expanded away from the lands of the Israelites. Instead of worshipping the ONE SINGLE GOD, the Christians worshipped the trinity of god, son of god, and a holy spirit or ghost.

Proselytism of pagan peoples spread Christianity throughout the then Roman Empire with various and numerous pagan beliefs, practices, holidays, and cultures being absorbed, adopted, and included within the new Christian faith.

These new absorptions and adoptions of pagan practices, combined with alterations and adulterations of the ONE SINGLE GOD's Commandments, helped to popularize the new religion and make it acceptable to the converted pagans who could not accept the Jewish religion of ONE SINGLE GOD and the ONE SINGLE GOD's Torah and all of HIS Ten Commandments and strict Laws and other Commands.

At first, the early adherents to Christianity, mostly Hellenistic minded Israelites, believed that the new Christian religion was a continuation of the Jewish religion. As early adherents to Christianity, they still kept and observed the same Seventh Day Sabbath and all of the Holy Days and most Commandments as stated in the Torah. With exception of some paganistic modifications, they continued to observe most of the basic laws and most of the Ten Commandments and Torah. As time passed, they accepted more inclusions of pagan beliefs and less adherence to their prior Torah beliefs.

As more years passed, the new religion of Christianity was totally separated from the Judaic beliefs. The words of the Ten Commandments were changed to align the words to meet the necessity and requirements of the new religion.

A new Bible was written. The original Torah was scornfully abandoned as an Old Testament (OT) that was no longer to be adhered to or maintained as being of any significance or importance. The new Bible became the New Testament (NT). But for most Christians, the Torah was then cast aside and the "OT" became the Obsolete Testament.

In the fourth century of the new religion, the Seventh Day, the Jewish Sabbath Day, and other Holy Days stated as commanded in the Torah, were denounced in favor of the first day, Sunday, being the Christian Sabbath day. It did not matter that the ONE SINGLE GOD had chosen, sanctified, declared Holy and Blessed the Seventh Day as HIS Sabbath and commanded its observance. Similarly, all the Holydays cited in the Torah were abandoned and new Christian Holidays, often former Pagan Holidays, were established.

The new religion gained more adherents and expanded as more pagan nations and peoples adopted the new faith that permitted the pagan people to retain and encompass their ancestral pagan practices and beliefs within their new faith of Christianity.

These pagan nations and peoples could not accept the Jewish religion because the practice of this faith required adherence to the ONE SINGLE GOD's Laws and Commandments that opposed their pagan practices, cultures and ways of life. The new faith of Christianity, however, not only allowed inclusion of many of their pagan beliefs and practices but also allowed an expanded propagation of these pagan beliefs and practices.

As Christianity greatly spread among the previous pagan peoples, it could not tolerate the fact that the stubborn Israelites, despised as Jews, and wrongly condemned as killers of the lord god Jesus, steadfastly adhered to their faith and belief in the ONE SINGLE GOD, HIS Commandments, and HIS Torah. They did not accept Christianity. The Jews did not accept the belief that only acceptance of the Christian religion could save their souls for a life in the heavenly paradise.

Christians believed that their religion was a religion of love while the Jewish religion was intolerant, despicable and hateful. Some Christians further believed that they had a supreme, divine, and heavenly mission to convert all of the Jews to Christianity to save their eternal souls even if it meant torturing and killing them. Injustice, persecution, inquisition, torture, pogroms, and murder of Jews followed for two millenniums

The new religion of Christianity, the daughter religion of the Jewish religion, claimed to be a religion of love and a means of eternal heavenly salvation and grace for all mankind.

However, the horrors of injustice, torture, rape, persecution, pogroms and murder were carried out, again and again, in every generation, against the Jews by Christian oppressors throughout all the years of the many centuries of the past two thousand years. This was the ironic love message expressed by the leaders of the new religion.

Some Christians were very obsessed with the belief that they would have to help the Jews to salvation and eternal life though Jewish conversion to Christianity. This belief also lead to a second belief that it was all right to murder and persecute the Jews who were too stubborn to convert. They would thus kill Jews to help assure that the Jews would convert to Christianity and thus be saved.

About 600 years after the advent of Christianity, there arose, from among the pagan idol worshipping peoples of the Middle East and North Africa, a man named Mohammed, who lived in Arabia.

Mohammed knew of the Jewish religion and of the daughter Christian religion. He proclaimed himself the greatest religious Prophet of the One Single God. He established the new religion of Islam with features that at first attempted to encompass and unite both the Jewish and Christian religions into his religion of Islam.

Mohammed sought to bring the Jews and Christians into religious unity under his new religion of Islam. The Prophet of this new religion of Islam gave his adherents, Muslims, a new Bible, the Koran. Then, both the Torah and New Testament were proclaimed untrue and obsolete.

Mohammed recognized the monotheistic principles of the Jewish religion and assigned the role of prophet and teacher to the Christian's son of god, Jesus. At first he appealed to the Jews to abandon their religion and accept his religion and his role as the supreme prophet of all time. His Muslim followers would pray facing Jerusalem, just as the Jews did, and would worship on the same Sabbath, the Seventh Day, as the Jews.

However, the Jews again stubbornly refused to accept this new religion adhering to their ONE SINGLE GOD and HIS Torah and Commandments. They did not recognize Mohammed as a supreme prophet with a new message from the ONE SINGLE GOD. The new Islam prophet then turned away from the stubborn Jews and he and his followers faced away from Jerusalem towards Mecca in prayer. The Christians also did not accept his new religion of Islam.

A new Moslem Sabbath day, the sixth day, Friday, was therefore adopted in defiance to the Jews who worshipped on the Seventh Day as their Sabbath and in defiance to the Christians who worshipped on the first day, Sunday. As the Christians had unjustly dealt with and persecuted the Jews, the Moslems also offered Jews the choice of conversion salvation or the sword. Again, injustice, persecution and slaughter of Jews followed. The Jewish tribes living in Mecca and Medina were massacred.

Today, the Mother Religion, the Jewish religion, is despised and hated by many of the adherents of both of the Christian and Islamic daughter religions. The Jews still stubbornly have maintained their belief in the ONE SINGLE GOD, HIS original Ten Commandments and the original Bible, HIS Torah, with all of GOD's Laws as stated in the Torah. The Jews have still not accepted or converted to either the Christian or Islamic daughter religions.

To this day, too many of the believers in the Christian and Islamic religions have not and do not study, learn, and understand the Jewish foundation and basis of the roots of their own faiths and religions. They do not know and comprehend the religion of the Jews based on their belief in the ONE SINGLE GOD, HIS Torah and HIS Commandments. Still with this lack of knowledge and understanding, too many strongly and wrongly detest, despise and hate Jews and the Jewish religion.

This may have been somewhat understandable during the centuries when most of all of mankind was basically very ignorantly illiterate. It may be rationalized that this ignorance existed prior to the invention of printing and publication of books. Libraries did not exist for study and research reading. Universities and colleges were not in existence.

These were the dark ages of information and times when men and women were dominated by rulers, religious leaders, priests, and Monks who purposely wanted and kept the masses illiterate, ignorant, and subservient. They kept the masses in this state of stupidity purposely with the preachings of many fictions, fables, and untruths.

Christian and Muslim rulers and religious leaders plied their followers with messages and sermons of diatribes, falsehoods, and preached hatreds for the Jewish non-believers in their faiths and religions. They stirred up the masses of their followers with vindictive incitements causing them to persecute and murder innocent men, women, children, and infants because they were Jews and believed in the ONE SINGLE GOD, HIS Commandments, and HIS Torah.

In our modern enlightened age, the very cultured and educated Germans ruthlessly murdered more than six million Jews. One and one half million of those murdered were children and infants. In the main, Christian Churches, with but a very very few exception, were silent as to the torture and slaughter of the Jews.

The Chief Arab Imam of Jerusalem, the Mufti Husseini, as a very distinguished guest of the Nazis, enjoyed touring the Nazi concentration death camps to happily and joyfully observe, approve, applaud, and encourage the Holocaust mass murder of the Jews.

Today, in this age of knowledge, information, mass communication, and widespread education and literacy, there is absolutely no reason for men not to read, study and understand the Jewish roots of their own Christian or Islamic religious faith and beliefs that arose from the Jewish Mother Religion.

In order to comprehend the tenacity of the Jewish people to their continued adherence with all of the principles and practices of the Jewish religion, despite the last two millenniums of murderous persecution, it is necessary and very important that one review, study, and understand the basis and foundation of the Jewish religion. This also provides the understanding for the foundation and roots of their own religion be it Jewish, Christian, or Islam.

This can be accomplished by the study of the Jewish Mother Religion's Ten Commandments, the Torah (the Original First Five Books of the Bible). This should also include the teachings of a Jewish philosopher, Maimonides. He lived almost eight hundred fifty years ago and he organized and expounded the Thirteen Principals of the Jewish Faith and Belief.

To assist in commencing this study, the ONE SINGLE GOD's Ten Commandments, and Maimonides Thirteen Principles of Jewish Faith and Belief, and some basic psalms and prayers will follow with description and explanation.

The definition as to who is a Jew starts with the person accepting and believing in the monotheistic existence of the ONE SINGLE GOD. The Jew believes that everything without any exception, all of matter and substance, all that can be seen and all that cannot be seen, everything, was created by the ONE SINGLE GOD who for all times was, is and will be the ALMIGHTY CREATOR and ONE SINGLE GOD.

The Jew believes totally in the Ten Commandments of the ONE SINGLE GOD and believes in the exact words expressed and given by the ONE SINGLE GOD as HIS Commandments as stated in HIS Torah (Bible). A Jew is a person who believes in these words and understands and knows that all must obey the Ten Commandments of the ONE SINGLE GOD. A Jew is therefore a person that adheres to the beliefs of Judaism.

An atheist, professed "Humanist", or secular non-believer in the ONE SINGLE GOD is not a Jew adhering to Judaism, the Jewish religion. By denying the existence of the ONE SINGLE GOD, that person denies that he or she is a Jew and is therefore not a Jew. A person who accepts the belief that there are gods, plural, or believes in a deity that exists as a trinity does not believe in the ONE SINGLE GOD or Monotheism and is not a Jew.

Judaism is more than a culture. It is more than having the DNA and bodily inheritance from ancestors who may have once been Jewish and believed in the ONE SINGLE GOD. Any person born and given life by the ALMIGHTY CREATOR, the ONE SINGLE GOD, has the ability to recognize that there exists an ALMIGHTY CREATOR being the ONE SINGLE GOD. All of mankind has the free will and ability to rationalize that life is the gift to all of mankind given only by the ONE SINGLE GOD. Any person can utilize free will and become a Jewish believer in the ONE SINGLE GOD.

THE THUNDERING HERD

Ravaging human mobs have all too often behaved and acted like ferocious brainless idiotic stupid beasts. The men and women who were behind the sinfully savage and brutal murders of the millions of men, women, and children who were murdered during the Holocaust years, were certainly inhuman monsters. Their actions, as murderous monster sinners are often concealed and not confessed to their families, friends and community. But all their actions are totally and fully known by the ONE SINGLE GOD who looks down upon all of us and wonders why mankind behaved like a senseless herd of wild animals. And why did so many participate or support these actions and why did the rest of the world's inhabitants maintain knowledgeable silence?

> **Down the slopes into the valley**
> **charged the maddened herd.**
> **Their noise was so ferocious**
> **it drowned out every word.**
>
> **Unrestrained and unconstrained,**
> **a furious angry crashing mass,**
> **they thundered forward uncontrolled**
> **and met death at the pass.**

Stumbling, falling, crushing,
onward, onward surged the tide.
Crushing, trampling, mangling underfoot
destroying blood, bone, flesh and hide.

And when the fury ceased
only pain remained.
And that was for the living
who with the dead were now restrained.

When irrationality subsides
and ravaging mobs deterred
no longer will they perish
amidst the thundering of the herd.

MAN'S DUTY

It is duty of all of mankind to praise the MASTER OF ALL, to believe in, worship and exalt only the ALMIGHTY CREATOR of the entire infinite universe. The ONE SINGLE GOD CREATOR who has not made all men and us to be like all of the pagan ignorant nations of the world. To be like those who do not know or want to know of HIM. HE has not placed us like the families of the earth who do not want to know and cannot understand and comprehend HIM. In Creation, the ONE SINGLE GOD has not designed and set forth our destiny to be like all of those who do not know or want to know and acknowledge HIM. Therefore, it is not our lot to be like all of those who deny the ONE SINGLE GOD.

We bend our knees bowing only to acknowledge the ONE SINGLE GOD's existence as we pray before the supreme KING OF Kings, the Holy ONE. Blessed be HE. For HE is the ONE SINGLE GOD who created for all eternal distances the heavens and is HE who created and founded the earth. The Seat of Glory of the ONE SINGLE GOD and HIS Majestic Throne is in the heavens above. HIS Abode of Majesty is in very high and lofty heavenly heights above. HE is our ONE SINGLE GOD. There is none else and truly the ONE SINGLE GOD is our Eternal KING. There is none besides HIM and this is as it is written in HIS Torah:

"You shall know this day, and reflect in your heart, that it is the LORD who is the ONE SINGLE GOD in the heavens above and on the earth beneath, there is none else."

We hope and pray therefore, our LORD our ONE SINGLE GOD, soon to behold YOUR Majestic Glory, when all of the sinful abominations shall be totally removed from the earth, and all of the false gods exterminated. That is when the world shall be perfected under the reign of YOU the ALMIGHTY CREATOR. At that time all mankind will call upon YOUR Name, and all the wicked of the earth will be turned to YOU. May all of the inhabitants of the world realize and acknowledge and know that to only to YOU must all knees bend, and must every tongue truly vow total allegiance.

May they all bend their knees and bow in prayer only before YOU, LORD our ONE SINGLE GOD, and give honor to YOUR Glorious Name. May they all accept the rule of YOUR Kingdom, and may YOU speedily reign over them eternally forever and ever. For the Kingdom is YOURS alone, and for all eternity YOU will reign in YOUR Majestic Glory, as it is written in YOUR Torah:

"The LORD shall be KING for ever and ever."

And it is said: "The LORD shall be KING over all the earth: on that day, the LORD shall be ONE, and his Name shall be ONE."

THE TEN COMMANDMENTS

These Ten Commandments, as stated in the Jewish Torah (Bible), were written and carved into stone tablets by the **ONE SINGLE GOD.**

ONE: **I am the LORD your ONE SINGLE GOD** who brought you out of the land of Egypt out of the house of bondage.

TWO: **You shall have no gods before ME.** You shall not make unto yourself a graven image nor any manner of likeness of any thing that is in heaven above or that is in the earth beneath, or that is in the water under the earth. You shall not bow down unto them, nor serve them, for I am the LORD your ONE SINGLE GOD, am a jealous GOD, visiting the iniquity of the fathers upon the third and fourth generation of them that hate ME.

THREE: **You shall not take the Name of the LORD your ONE SINGLE GOD in vain** for the LORD will not hold him guiltless that takes HIS Name in vain.

FOUR: **Remember the Seventh Day, to keep it always Holy** Six days shall you labor, and do your work; but the Seventh Day is a Sabbath unto the LORD your ONE SINGLE GOD. On that day you shall not do any manner of work, you, nor your son, nor your daughter, nor your man-servant, nor your maid-servant, nor your cattle, nor the stranger that is within your gate; **for in six days**

the LORD made heaven and earth, the sea , and all that in them is, and rested on the Seventh Day, wherefore the LORD Blessed the Sabbath Day and Hallowed it.

FIVE: **Honor your father and your mother** that your days may be long upon the land which the LORD your ONE SINGLE GOD gives you.

SIX: You shall not murder.

SEVEN: You shall not commit adultery.

EIGHT: You shall not steal.

NINE: **You shall not bear false witness** against your neighbor.

TEN: **You shall not covet** your neighbor's house, his wife, his man or maid servant, his Ox, his Ass, nor anything that is your neighbors.

THE WEATHER OF THE ONE SINGLE GOD: DROUGHT

The ABC TV news anchorman, Peter Jennings, had reported on the drought effecting farmers in the south, southwest, and central United States. A farmer was shown in his field of corn. The corn that should have been four feet high was only inches high. The farmer touched a plant and the plant fell out of the dirt. He kicked the soil and there was only dry sand. Another farmer told the viewers that he had to sell his herd of cattle because there was nothing growing to feed them. Another cattle farmer showed his water pond that he had used to provide drink for his herd and to hose down the cattle in extreme heat temperatures. The pond was rapidly disappearing.

This is not the first time that men have suffered in drought and not the first time that farmers could not raise crops and feed and water their cattle.

The Torah (Bible) tells us that when men do not heed the Laws of the ONE SINGLE GOD or when they lead immoral lives, there would then not be the ONE SINGLE GOD's Blessings of the waters of rain.

It is written in Hebrew in the original Torah (Bible) as follows:

> "It shall come to pass,
>
> that if you hearken diligently to MY Commandments
>
> that I command you this day,
>
> that you shall love your LORD
>
> your ONE SINGLE GOD
>
> and you shall serve HIM with all your heart,
>
> and with all your soul,
>
> that I will give you the rain for your land in its season,
>
> both the former rain and also the later rain,
>
> that you may gather in your corn,
>
> and your grapes for wine, and your oil.
>
> And with the rain that I give
>
> there will be grass in your fields
>
> for your cattle and you also shall eat and be satisfied.
>
> You shall take heed to these words.
>
> Let not your heart be deceived so that you turn aside
>
> and then serve other gods and worship them;
>
> and the displeasure of the LORD, the ONE SINGLE GOD,
>
> will be aroused against you,

and HE will shut up the heaven,

so that there shall be no rain, there will be drought,

and the ground shall not yield her fruit;

and you shall perish quickly from the good land which the

LORD,

your ONE SINGLE GOD, has given you.

Therefore shall you keep these words in your heart and in your soul; and you shall bind them for a sign and remembrance upon your hand, and as frontlets between your eyes. You shall teach them to your children, talking of them, when you sit in your house, and when you walk by the way, and when you lay down, and when you rise up.

You shall write the words of remembrance upon the doorposts of your house, and upon your gates; that your days may be multiplied, and the days of your children upon the land which the LORD, your ONE SINGLE GOD, promised your fathers to give them, as the days of the heavens above the earth.

Man is not the creator of rain. The ONE SINGLE GOD is the ALMIGHTY CREATOR of rain. HIS rain provides the waters for man and beast. HIS water nourishes the soil and causes plants to grow and animals to live. HIS waters enables man to live and to grow corn and to raise cattle. If there is now a drought, then it is man, by his actions and deeds, that is causing the ONE SINGLE GOD to withhold all of the rains of the heavens.

Today, man lives in an immoral society and has abandoned and does not heed the ONE SINGLE GOD's Ten Commandments. Until man returns to the moral ways of life and fully heeds and fully obeys the ONE SINGLE GOD's Ten Commandments and keeps HIS words in his heart and soul, the ONE SINGLE GOD may withhold the rains; there may be drought; corn may not grow from any water nourished soil; and there may not be grass to feed the cattle.

Likewise, man's disobedience of the ONE SINGLE GOD's Commandments may bring the Burning Anger, Wrath, Fury and Indignation of the LORD upon man and may cause and bring about the storms that damage and flood the earth. Can this be the reason that man suffers from Volcanic eruptions, Earthen mudslides, Earthquakes, Floods, Avalanches, Tornadoes, Hurricanes, and Tsunamis?

WEATHER DISASTERS

All events, happenings, and disastrous devastations such as volcanic eruptions, earthen mudslides, earthquakes, floods, avalanches, tornadoes, hurricanes, and the recent tsunami, do not happen by chance or accident. Some of these disastrous events are caused by the actions or inactions of man. However, the ultimate decision as to whether to unleash these disasters is made by the ONE SINGLE GOD who controls mankind's destiny.

At times, man brings future disaster upon himself. He can cut down all of the trees and completely destroy living forests created and given life by the ONE SINGLE GOD. This can lead to the future disasters of mudslides. Man can determine lands where future earthquakes may happen and still construct weakly built housing right over the earth's fault lines. Man can deviate the flow of streams and rivers placing weak dams to impede the flow and these dams may ultimately self destruct and not be capable of holding back the waters. Man can unwisely construct buildings where it is known that past over flows of streams and rivers have flooded the land and can do so again.

Recently, the tsunami struck with mighty waters sweeping over lands destroying man made buildings and causing a very great loss of life. From this terrible tragedy, man has perhaps learned, that it is not safe constructing buildings too close to shores susceptible to the mighty ravaging waters of tsunamis. But what did man do to deserve the tsunami?

Ultimately these disasters do not happen without the Judgmental Consent of the ONE SINGLE GOD. The Torah (Bible) states that the ONE SINGLE GOD looked upon the sinful paganistic activities of the humans living in the Cities of Sodom and Gomorra and decided to destroy these cities. What message then is the ONE SINGLE GOD sending to man when HE unleashes the recent killing and destructive disasters of the tsunami, mudslides, earthquakes, avalanches, floods, tornadoes and hurricanes?

It is for all of mankind to remember that they are not gods and goddesses. They receive all the necessities for life only from the ONE SINGLE GOD. The GIVER can also be the WITHHOLDER. Thus it behooves each individual to recognize that the ONE SINGLE GOD is the ALMIGHTY CREATOR and requires that all heed and obey all of HIS Commandments.

As to the farmer who suffered the loss of his crops because of the drought, was it because of something he had done or his community had done? Or, possibly, was it something the farmer or his community had not done? This requires the farmer and his community to ponder about all their actions and deeds or their non-actions and non-deeds. Did they do or cause anything to give reason for the ONE SINGLE GOD to hold back the rains and cause the drought?

Since no man can ever know any of the reasons for the actions of the ONE SINGLE GOD, all that man must always acknowledge and understand is that the ALMIGHTY CREATOR has reasons for each and every one and all of HIS actions both for creation and also for destructions.

Man must always, at all times, obey all of the Commandments of the ONE SINGLE GOD without sinfully changing, amending or disregarding any of them, and thus not bring upon himself the anger of the LORD.

PSALM 104

My soul, give Blessing to the ONE SINGLE GOD. My ONE SINGLE GOD, YOU are very great. YOU are cloaked in majestic splendor in the light as with a garment that stretches forth out and covers the heavens like a curtain. YOU are the ONE SINGLE GOD who covers HIS upper heavenly sky dwelling with water. YOU are HE who makes the clouds to be HIS chariot. YOU are HE who walks on the wings of wind YOU are HE who makes the winds HIS messengers and the flaming lightening fire HIS attendants.

YOU are HE who established the earth upon its foundations, that it shall forever last. YOU covered it, with the deep water, as with a blanket, and upon the mountains waters would stand. They flee from YOUR rebuke and from the sound of YOUR thunder they rush away. They ascend the mountains and they descend to the valleys to the special places YOU created for them. YOU established a boundary they cannot overstep and they cannot return to cover the earth.

YOU send the springs of waters into the streams and then between the mountains. They provide water for every beast of the field and quench the thirst of all wild creatures. Near YOUR waters live the birds of all of YOUR heavens and from the branches of trees they give forth their song. YOU water the mountains from your upper heavenly dwelling The earth is sated with waters from the results of YOUR Work. YOU cause vegetation to grow and sprout for the cattle, and to provide man plants that, by man's labor, will allow him to bring forth bread from the earth and the wine that pleases man's heart, and also the oil that makes man's face to glow, and also the bread that nourishes and sustains the heart of man

The trees of the ONE SINGLE GOD are sated and also the cedars of Lebanon that HE has planted; there where the birds nest; the stork stays among the cypresses; and the high mountains are for the wild goats; and the rocks are refuges for the gophers.

PSALM 29

Render and give to the ONE SINGLE GOD the great and total Honor due HIS Name. Bow only to the ONE SINGLE GOD in HIS intensely Holy Temple. The Voice of the ONE SINGLE GOD is upon all the waters. The GOD OF GLORY thunders out upon the vast waters. The

Voice of the ONE SINGLE GOD comes in power and in majesty! The Voice of the ONE SINGLE GOD breaks and shatters the cedars of Lebanon! The Voice of the ONE SINGLE GOD springs forth with shafts of fire and convulses the wilderness. The Voice of the ONE SINGLE GOD frightens the animals and strips the forests bare. While all in His Temple proclaim Glory to the ONE SINGLE GOD who sits enthroned at the Deluge as the KING forever.

And the ONE SINGLE GOD spoke all these words, saying:

COMMANDMENT NUMBER ONE

1. **I am the LORD your ONE SINGLE GOD,**

    who brought you out of the land of Egypt,

    out of the house of bondage.

These are the words of the ONE SINGLE GOD worshipped by believers in the Judaic faith and religion. These are the words permanently and eternally carved into stone for all time by the writing of the ONE SINGLE GOD at Mount Sinai. They were written and revealed to mankind by the ONE SINGLE GOD on the stone tablets prepared by Moses almost 3,700 years ago.

When asked what HIS Name was, the ONE SINGLE GOD replied that ***HE IS WHO WAS, WHO IS, and WHO WILL BE.*** By HIS answer, the ONE SINGLE GOD made known HIS eternal infinite existence. This ONE SINGLE GOD knows all of the past; the present; and the future.

The ONE SINGLE GOD never declared to mankind that he was not a UNITY. If the ONE SINGLE GOD had intended to reveal to man that HE was not a UNITY, not ONE and SINGULAR, but was of the nature of more than one entity, such as a father to a son god, or a trinity, the very first word of this, HIS First Commandment, would not have started with the beginning word "I"

This First and most very important Commandment does not state "we" are the god or gods. Nor does the ONE SINGLE GOD state that in future time the "I" would have to be changed to the "we". There are no words to give recognition that the ONE SINGLE GOD was ever to be joined by a deity son or replaced by a trinity.

These trinity beliefs are solely man made and originated by men without any authorization or approval by the ONE SINGLE GOD. They reflect the ancient pagan Greek and Roman beliefs and religions with their multitude of gods, sons of god, goddesses, and families of gods. The pagan Greeks and Romans did not believe in a one single god.

The First Commandment was not written for the moment and was not written to be subject to any change in the future by the ONE SINGLE GOD.

It was written by the ONE SINGLE GOD to last eternally forever as HIS words to all mankind. Nor was it meant to be a Commandment that could or would be allowed to be altered or changed by man in the future.

The First Commandment was carved by the ONE SINGLE GOD into the two stone tablets prepared by Moses on Mount Sinai. It is permanent for all time, and is very explicit and very clear. There is but ONE SINGLE GOD. By HIS Words, there is no son of god or trinity.

The First Commandment was stated as first by the ONE SINGLE GOD because of its very foremost significant importance.

It was to cause mankind to think, understand, and recognize that HE existed, that HE alone was The ONE SUPREME BEING, the SINGLE ALMIGHTY CREATOR of all of heaven and earth and all living things and beings, and that there was and is no other god or gods and that HE was and is and will always be the only ONE SINGLE GOD.

The First Commandment also requires a remembrance that it was the ONE SINGLE GOD who redeemed and freed the Children of Israel from their servitude, slavery, and bondage in the pagan land of Egypt. This

Commandment recognizes the ONE SINGLE GOD as being the GOD OF FREEDOM opposed to slavery. This Commandment and the other Commandments were given, at Mount Sinai, by the ONE SINGLE GOD, through the Children of Israel, to all mankind and that includes me and you and also to and for all of today's Christians and Muslims.

This giving is remembered by followers of the Jewish religion. Annually, the Holydays of Passover are celebrated as Commanded in the Torah (the Bible). At the Passover Holyday Seder services, these words of the First Commandment are restated and remembered. During the Seder it is said that if the ONE SINGLE LORD GOD of the Israelites had not redeemed the Children of Israel then each of their descendants would also still be enslaved in Egypt even to this day.

There is another reason and meaning in why the message to mankind, was given by the ONE SINGLE GOD to the Children of Israel when they were escaping from their slavery in Egypt. Why had the ONE SINGLE GOD waited until the Children of Israel had been slaves and now were wandering freely in the Sinai desert? The actions they took provide the answer. Alone, with their leader Moses disappearing for forty days on Mount Sinai, they lost faith in Moses and his ONE SINGLE GOD and began worship of the golden calf god of their Egyptian slave masters. Now freed they began to worship the god of their slave masters.

The lesson for all who have been enslaved is ***do not worship or accept as your gods the gods of your slave masters.***

The Apostles and the early Christians observed and celebrated the Holydays of Passover. They conducted the Passover Seder. They did this because the founder of Christianity, Yeshua Ben Yosef, known as Jesus, was born a Jew and he and his apostles and followers all observed and celebrated all of the Holydays as stated, described and Commanded in the Torah by the ONE SINGLE GOD.

These Holydays included the Passover Holydays and are celebrated and remembered during the annual Passover Seder. Jesus also celebrated the Passover Seder because of the ONE SINGLE GOD's Instruction and Commandment in the Torah that the Passover celebration was to forever be an annual event. The "last supper", depicted in the famous painting by DaVinci, was conducted by Jesus and was a Passover Seder.

Several hundred years later, the Christian church leaders took it upon themselves to denounce and discontinue the practice of observing all of the Holydays of the ONE SINGLE GOD as stated in the Torah. This included the elimination of the observance of the Passover Holydays. Instead, the Christians were ordered to celebrate the Easter, a holiday named in honor of the pagan goddess Eastre. Easter is the name of the pagan vernal festival.

The very first and early Christians believed that they were not changing the Jewish religion. They believed that their new Christian belief was a continuation of the Jewish religion of the Children of Israel. They knew and fully understood that they were not to bring any pagan thoughts, practices and customs into their religious practices, or worship in a pagan manner, or pray to idols, icons, and statues. Still the ruling elders of Christianity eliminated the observance of the Passover to establish instead the Easter holiday.

The Christian church leaders also, besides Passover, eliminated the Seventh Day Jewish Sabbath, and all of the other Holydays established by the ONE SINGLE GOD in HIS Torah (Bible). These were all denounced and all discontinued to be adhered to and instead changes and pagan thoughts, practices and customs were brought into the Christian religion.

Jewish religious practices, that had been maintained for several thousand years, and are still being maintained and observed as stated in the Torah, and as given by the ONE SINGLE GOD to the Children of Israel at Mount Sinai, are no longer maintained and observed by the Christians. Even though these religious practices had been observed and celebrated by Jesus and his early followers, they were and are now scornfully rejected and discontinued. The later Islam religion also did not recognize the Holydays of the ONE SINGLE GOD.

Observing and obeying the Covenant Command of the ONE SINGLE GOD, Abraham, the founder and father of the monotheism and belief in the ONE SINGLE GOD, was himself and with his sons and descendants circumcised.

Following this Covenant Command of the ONE SINGLE GOD, Jesus, the lord of the Christians, had also been circumcised when he was eight days old. His birthday is celebrated on December 25th and eight days later, on January 1st, he was circumcised fulfilling the Covenant between the ONE SINGLE GOD and man as stated as a Command requirement in the Torah. His Jewish Apostles were also circumcised.

But, this Covenant requirement for the circumcision ritual was not acceptable to the pagan nations converting to the new religion of Christianity. Thus the Church elders once again, without authority of the ONE SINGLE GOD, took it upon themselves to eliminate the circumcision requirement and thus Christians were then and now not required to circumcise their male offspring.

In full observance of the Command of the ONE SINGLE GOD, Jesus fully adhered to the dietary laws as stated in the ONE SINGLE GOD's Torah. Jesus never ate any bacon, pork, ham, shrimp or any other food specifically stated in the Torah as not permitted to be eaten.

This dietary restriction was also not acceptable to the pagans being converted to Christianity. Thus the pagans converting and accepting the new Christian religion were excused from following the ONE SINGLE GOD's laws concerning foods that could not be eaten and they were not required to observe the dietary laws of the ONE SINGLE GOD. They continued to eat all of the foods they had previously eaten when they were non-Christian pagans including the very foods very specifically and expressly forbidden to be eaten by Command of the ONE SINGLE GOD.

The Christian leaders also modified and altered the First Commandment to accommodate their belief in a trinity and to add to the Deity of the ONE SINGLE GOD the belief in the deification of the Jew Yehsua, Jesus, the founder of Christianity, as the son of god. Christians accepted the belief in the trinity of the father, son and holy ghost. In recent years, there has been a group favoring the added deification of Mary the Jewish mother of Yeshua, Jesus, the founder of

Christianity. The "logic' being, that since Mary is the mother of Yeshua, Jesus, who is a god, she also should be recognized and elevated as a goddess to godhood since she was the mother of god.
Several times each day, Jewish worshipers repeat the message contained in the Torah's Book of Exodus.

"Hear O Israel,

The LORD your GOD,

the LORD is ONE SINGLE GOD.

You shall love the LORD,

your ONE SINGLE GOD,

with all your soul and with all your might."

These words were never accepted by the followers of the Greek and Roman pagan religions because they believed in a family of gods. Thus these pagan peoples could not accept the Jewish concept of ONE SINGLE GOD unless it was also predicated to include acceptance of their belief in a mother of god and a son of god similar to their pagan pre-Christian religious beliefs.

However, these words, that the LORD GOD was ONE SINGLE GOD, were known and recited by the Jew known as Jesus and his Jewish apostle followers.

The believers in the Jewish religion do not pray to saints or other beings or to icons, idols or statues. All of their prayers are directed only to the ONE SINGLE GOD. Christians are allowed to pray to a multitude of saints who can act for them as intermediaries with the trinity god. Christians can stand before and venerate or pray to icons, portraits, and statues. Jews have to speak for themselves to the ONE SINGLE GOD.

The advent of the Moslem religion also centered upon the belief in a One Single God. Like the believers in the Judaic religion, the followers of the Moslem religion recognize and pray to only a One Single God and do not pray to a multitude of man proclaimed "saints".

The First Commandment is understandably very clear. There is but ONE SINGLE GOD. The First Commandment does not mention a father god, a son god, and holy spirit or ghost god; it does not mention a trinity. The First Commandment given for all mankind for all time by the ONE SINGLE GOD is not subject to amendments, modifications, changes, updates, or alterations by any man including Church Popes, priests, theologians, elders and leaders.

In accordance with the First Commandment, and recognition and understanding that there is but ONE SINGLE GOD, the prayers of mankind can only be addressed to HIM. There are no intermediaries to whom one should or must pray.

Prayers are not to be addressed to "saints", "prophets", or other "beings", or to a son of god or to a mother of god (goddess). Prayers are to be directed only to the ONE SINGLE GOD who gave to all of mankind, without exception, this very important very first message that HE stated as HIS First Commandment.

The First Commandment was stated as HIS First Commandment, by the ONE SINGLE GOD over 3700 years ago. It was then, when first stated by HIM, and still today remains, the most important of all of HIS Ten Commandments. That is why it remains for all times the unchangeable First Commandment

With the advent of Christianity, the First Commandment, without consent or approval by the ONE SINGLE GOD, was altered and changed to address the deification of a son of god and became the basis for Christian belief in a trinity of gods. The trinity is not the ONE SINGLE GOD.

The subsequent religion of Islam, almost 700 years after establishment of Christianity, brought the belief in a One Single God to the many pagan peoples of the non-Jewish and non-Christian world. This could have been a great message and blessing bestowed and given to the pagans. However, again the First Commandment was altered and changed to eliminate the recognition that the Commandment was first given to the Children of Israel and to totally eliminate all memory and recollections that the ONE SINGLE GOD's First Commandment contained the additional reminding words: **"who brought you out of the land of Egypt, out of the house of bondage."**

The descendants of the believers and adherents of Christianity or Islam were not brought out of the slavery and bondage from the land of Egypt. Thus the above words written and declared by the ONE SINGLE GOD, recognizing the Jewish Covenant relationship between the ONE SINGLE GOD and the Children of Israel, have been cast aside and eliminated and are not a part of the Christian or Islamic First Commandment.

The followers of Islam, while worshipping a One Single God, accept the First Commandment with deletion of the words concerning the Exodus of the Children of Israel from their bondage and servitude in Egypt. Their First Commandment would be:

I am the Lord your God. My name is Allah.

While I have stated in my other command that you are not to murder, it is acceptable to murder innocent men, women and children if they are Christian or Jewish infidels.

The followers of Christianity are compelled, and must of necessity, restate the First Commandment to include their belief in the trinity. Their First Commandment would be:

   We are the Lord your Gods having an existence as your Father God, son of God, and Holy Ghost God, and having a son whom I will disclose to you later and who is also to be your God.

It is the firm Jewish belief however that no man can amend, alter or change the explicit First Commandment of the ONE SINGLE GOD that clearly and completely states:

I am the LORD your ONE SINGLE GOD, who brought you out of the land of Egypt, out of the house of bondage.

While the First Commandment is stated to be a Commandment, it is understood to be more of a statement of true Fact. That true Fact is that there is only ONE SINGLE GOD who created this world and all it contains, and the very infinite universe, and you and me.

Evidence of the ONE SINGLE GOD is contained within each person, within each of us. No man, no matter how brilliant, can ever create, from the dust or any of the substances or contents of the earth, a living being. No scientist or engineer can ever design and create a living human being from either any living substance or from absolutely nothing.

Take a moment to look upon your hand. It is indeed a most amazing creation. Man can engineer and manufacture a robot or mechanical hand but no man can create a complete complex living human or a complex living hand. The recognition that there is a SUPREME ALMIGHTY CREATOR can be seen and understood when one looks about his or her surroundings, this world, and the universe. Look at all of the beauty, complexity, and magnitude of nature and take a moment to reflect that all was resulted from the Creations of the ONE SINGLE ALMIGHTY CREATOR, the ONE SINGLE GOD. Think about it, all of this was created without the help of any human scientist.

The Media advertisement states:

"We are Father and Son.

No job too big or small.

We can do it all."

The ONE SINGLE GOD does not need to bring a son into HIS creation business for the continuity of earthly or universal creative existence.

The ONE SINGLE GOD does not need a son to carry on and continue the business of being GOD.

The ONE SINGLE GOD has not aged, retired, and has not turned over the business of creation and the business of stating, altering or changing HIS Commandments to a son.

The ONE SINGLE GOD who has created everything does not need a son to take over His Creation Business because HE is old of age and therefor must retire.

The First Commandment stands for all time as a declaration that there is but a ONE SINGLE GOD who alone has created everything and continues to create everything, including all of mankind. It is only to HIM and to HIM alone that all of mankind must direct their worship and prayers. Only HE is, for all of us, our HEAVENLY FATHER. There is none else.

The recognition that there is but ONE SINGLE GOD who is the CREATOR of mankind, the earth and all its contents, the infinite universe and all of its galaxies, is the foundation belief of the Jewish religion. It is that which has given the strength and insured the survival of the Jewish faith and has become the substance that has maintained Jewish religious existence throughout all of the periods of persecutions and murders aflicted upon the Jewish people. It has been the test upon the ability of the Jewish people to keep their Jewish faith and belief in the ONE SINGLE GOD even during the period of the madness during which the murderers carried out the sinful actions of the Holocaust against the Jewish people.

Being Jewish is not a matter of race, color, or national origin. Judaism is a religion based upon the main acceptance of the truth that there is but ONE SINGLE GOD who has given mankind an ever lasting, unchangeable TEN COMMANDMENTS.

One can be a member of any race, of any color, or nation of people and be Jewish by religion if one believes in the ONE SINGLE GOD as expressed in HIS First Commandment. One need not have Jewish

DNA or Jewish ancestors to be Jewish. Some believe that if one has a Jewish mother, then that person is automatically Jewish. But, if that same person denies the existence of the ONE SINGLE GOD, then that person is not Jewish.

Being Jewish is being a believer in the ONE SINGLE GOD, HIS Unchangeable Commandments, and HIS Torah (Bible).

It is understood that one may be a Christian or Muslim and be of an entirely different race, color, or ethnic and national origin. Religion does not have anything to do with the color of ones eyes, hair, or skin. One can be a child of parents who believe in any religion and thus also be indoctrinated to accept that religion. But any child need not remain in the same religious belief of his parents and ancestors.

The ONE SINGLE GOD has given each human person the complete ability to exercise free thought, will, and action. Thus each of us is free to choose the belief in any religion. What is required is to have each of us abandon pre-conceived and inherited religious thought and then freely, with full thought, decide which religion to follow

We must all use our ONE SINGLE GOD's given thinking process and decide for ourselves.

One is not Jewish if one does not believe in the ONE SINGLE GOD as completely expressed in HIS First Commandment. Thus Muslims, although expressing a belief in a One Single God but not believing in HIS Unchangeable Commandments and HIS Torah, are not Jewish.

One person may have been a descendant of Jewish ancestors and have Jewish parents but that person is not Jewish if that person does not believe in the ONE SINGLE GOD and in HIS Commandments and HIS Torah or, if, with free will acts to accept another god or religion.

Yeshua, Jesus, and his disciples were born descendants of Jewish parents and ancestors but by any of them, if any, denying the existence of the ONE SINGLE GOD, and denying HIS Commandments, and denying HIS Torah, they were no longer Jewish.

Perhaps the recognition of the existence of ONE SINGLE GOD was best and very simply stated by an American, stated to be non-Jewish, a Poet, Joyce Kilmer, when he expressed his Jewish belief in the ONE SINGLE GOD and wrote the following:

> **"I think that I shall never see**
> **a Poem as lovely as a tree**
> **for Poems are made by fools like me**
> **but only GOD can make a tree."**

Every time I see a tree, I remember the wonderful and thoughtful words of Joyce Kilmer and I know that only the ONE SINGLE GOD made that tree and every other tree, and also everything else that exists including both you and me.

Kilmer did not state that someone other than the ONE SINGLE GOD Created the tree. He did not state, nor has anyone stated that any man, even if believed to be the son of god, has ever created a tree or any living thing.

It is the ONE SINGLE GOD that has given man the ability to think, to rationalize, to deliberate, to reason and to know. The ONE SINGLE GOD has given man a free will to act and accept truths and with his GOD given free will, all are able to understand and recognize that there is but one eternal ONE SINGLE GOD who is the ALMIGHTY CREATOR.

THE IMAGE OF THE ONE SINGLE GOD

In the beginnings of creation of heaven and earth, the Torah (Bible) tells us that man was made in the image of the ONE SINGLE GOD.

All too often however, man defines this creation in a manner that restates this creation. This results in believing that the ONE SINGLE GOD is created in the image of man. The ONE SINGLE GOD is all present, exists for all times, knows all events, and does not need subgods or assistants.

The ONE SINGLE GOD does not need two eyes to see all. HIS vision is not limited to seeing only that which is before HIS eyes. HE does not need two ears to hear all. HIS hearing is not limited to hearing only that which enters HIS ears. HE does not need food and water to sustain and nourish HIMSELF. HE does not need two legs to travel through the infinite universe that HE has created. HE does not need two arms and hands to fashion and create the multitudes of everything in the infinite universes.

All of the universes, from and beyond infinity to infinity, is the creation of the ONE SINGLE GOD. No human mind can understand and be able to comprehend the form, shape, or majesty of the ONE SINGLE GOD. HE has never revealed HIMSELF to be seen by human eyes.

HE has clearly stated that at all times, forever, no living human will ever be able to see HIM and still remain alive.

Man is created in the image of the ONE SINGLE GOD. But this image is not the shape or form of the human being. The body of man is not the image of the ONE SINGLE GOD.

It is the soul of man, shape and form unknown to man, that is created in the image of the ONE SINGLE GOD.

The human body depends upon the material world to remain alive and exist. It must be fed food, provided water to drink, air to breath, and shelter and protection from natures weather and elements. The ONE SINGLE GOD exists forever for all eternal time. Man lives his life but for a very short period of time. The body of man, created from the dust of the earth, dies and his body returns to the dust of the earth.

It is the soul of man, never seen by man, that is in the image of the ONE SINGLE GOD. This image cannot be described and is unknown to man. The soul of man can live on beyond the death of the human body of man. This gift of having an eternal living soul is dependent upon the decision and Judgment of the ONE SINGLE GOD. Those who live their lives in defiance of the ONE SINGLE GOD, HIS Ten Commandments, and HIS TORAH (Bible) destroy their souls. But the soul of man, that may be judged to live and exist and be in the image of the ONE SINGLE GOD, does not make man a god.

THE SOUL OF MAN LIVES AND THE SOUL OF MAN CAN DIE

There is no automatic life beyond death for the human soul. The soul can only live to exist beyond death if man is deserving of this afterlife. Just as the ONE SINGLE GOD can terminate and cut off the body life of man, so too, the ONE SINGLE GOD can terminate and cut off the life of the soul. The soul of a sinner who murders shall die.

When men violate the ONE SINGLE GOD's Commandments, when a man murders another man violating the Commandment *"You shall not murder"*, the murderer's soul ceases then and there to exist and immediately dies. The human form may for a while continue to live on, but no soul of a murderer ever survives. Those that teach and inspire others to commit the sinful crime of murder also have killed their own souls.

There is no blessed afterlife for those who preach and teach, instigate, cause, and partake in murderous actions such as ravaging killing crusades, inquisitions, pogroms, genocides, holocausts, or suicide murderous bombings. The men that advocate or do these evils, deny the existence of the ONE SINGLE GOD, and do not heed HIS Commandments. They are not blessed by the ONE SINGLE GOD to have an eternal living soul. Their bodies may be alive but their souls are dead.

Man possesses a free will to do good or evil. Each person is free to live a life that sustains the living essence of his soul. Those who choose not to obey the ONE SINGLE GOD's Ten Commandments and Laws, during their human term of life, destroy the life of their soul.

There is no heavenly forgiveness for those who, with their own free will, sin and do evil deeds and disobey the Ten Commandments and the Laws of the ONE SINGLE GOD. No human can commit murder and then be forgiven and retain a living soul by expressing a belief in a saint or savior or a son of god. There is no intercession when it comes to the Judgment of the Court of the ONE SINGLE GOD.

There is but ONE SINGLE GOD who is the ALMIGHTY CREATOR who has created, made and established all of the Universe with all of the stars, planets, and heavenly objects that are in the heavens above. The ALMIGHTY CREATOR has created all and everything that we can see and comprehend and even all of the things and objects that man cannot ever see or cannot ever comprehend.

Therefore the Ten Commandments, established and given to all of mankind by the ONE SINGLE GOD, must be always fully obeyed and remain unchangeable in any way or fashion by man. The ONE SINGLE GOD has decreed that, for all times, all men should live justly with all of their fellow men and not commit violations of HIS Ten Commandments and especially not commit murder.

The deeds of the human, disobeying HIS Commandments, can cause the soul, given to the human by the ONE SINGLE GOD, to be punished, for murder, by the death of the soul.

It is utter nonsense and a complete falsehood to believe that a murderer, who has been sentenced to death for his crime of murder, can have his soul saved for all eternity and dwell in the paradise of the heaven of the ONE SINGLE GOD merely by saying to a priest, 'Yes, I do believe in Jesus." Whereby the priest then can say, "My son, you are now totally forgiven and your soul is saved, but to be on the safe side and sure, please say five Hail Marys."

Nonsense. There will not be any forgiveness for the wanton willful murder of a human created by the ONE SINGLE GOD.

The evils of man bring down eternal Judgment of damnation and punishment by the ONE SINGLE GOD and no human person, whether a priest of any religion, can override or veto this Judgment. Forgiveness can come only from the ONE SINGLE GOD and not from any so-called priest, imam, sheikh, or pope. For murder, and especially for murder accomplished in the name of any religion or in the name of any god, there is never any forgiveness.

The ALMIGHTY CREATOR, the ONE SINGLE GOD, created man in body and in soul and did this without the assistance of any man, god, or other being. HIS Creations were accomplished without an assistant and without a son. However, there are many who believe that the ALMIGHTY CREATOR is old or tired (or even expired) and needs a son to carry on the business of creation of the human body and soul.

For all of the eternal endless time that was, is and will be forever, there is but ONE SINGLE GOD who was, is, and will be the ALMIGHTY CREATOR and HE does not need a deputy, assistant, or son. It is only from HIM that mankind receives a living body and soul for which mankind must pray and thank the ONE SINGLE GOD for all the Blessings bestowed by HIM.

No man has ever seen the ONE SINGLE GOD. No man can describe the form, shape, or appearance of the ONE SINGLE GOD. No man has ever seen a human's soul that is created in the image of the ONE SINGLE GOD. This soul is born and given the opportunity for life beyond the death of the human body. But this everlasting life of the soul is predicated upon obeying all of the Commandments of the ONE SINGLE GOD.

Recognition of the existence of the ONE SINGLE GOD is fully and completely expressed and stated in the Prayer, to the ONE SINGLE GOD, that is present in the original "Bible", the Torah. This Prayer was said and repeated daily by the Jewish Yeshua, renamed Jesus, and all his followers, and is still repeated several times daily by Jewish adherents to the Commandments of the ONE SINGLE GOD and HIS Torah.

The recognition and existence of the ONE SINGLE GOD is repeated and enforced in the First Commandment of the ONE SINGLE GOD. This First Commandment, also fully and completely expressed and stated in the Torah, explicitly states, without any later revisions by the ONE SINGLE GOD, that HE alone, and no one else or no god other then HIM, is the ONE SINGLE GOD eternally for ever. HE alone Creates and provides the human body and, in HIS Image, the soul.

The First Commandment of the ONE SINGLE GOD states:

I AM THE LORD YOUR GOD!!!!

and the ONE SINGLE GOD continues HIS Commandment

with these words saying that HE acted to free the Children of Israel

from the cruelty, bitterness, and harshness of slavery

and from the Evil Egyptian Pharaoh's evil and murderous

decree that all male infants born to the Children of Israel

were to be thrown into and drowned in the Nile River.

Who Brought You Out of the Land of Egypt,

Out of the House of Bondage.

Again, this First Commandment, has been, and is being, maintained in obedience by the Children of Israel since the time they received the Ten Commandments at Mount Sinai.

This First Commandment was fully known and adhered to by the Jewish Yeshua, Jesus, and also by his Jewish disciples who never with truth declared that the ALMIGHTY CREATOR was no longer a ONE

SINGLE GOD but was being converted to a trinity of gods similar to the multitude of the pagan gods of Greece and Rome.

The ONE SINGLE GOD never abdicated and never retracted HIS First Commandment. HE never named the Jewish Yeshua, Jesus, as his son and as a god. The ONE SINGLE GOD has continued to be the CREATOR of all living human bodies and the souls of all human beings.

The Image of the ONE SINGLE GOD cannot be seen by looking at any human being. The human body is not in the Image of the ONE SINGLE GOD. The Image of the ALMIGHTY CREATOR, the ONE SINGLE GOD is the soul of mankind and cannot be seen by any living human being. There is absolutely no truth when someone says that he or she has seen a son of god or his virgin goddess mother. Since no one can ever see the ONE SINGLE GOD and remain alive, those who see god son or his mother are dead and cannot then tell us what they have seen.

Each of us as human beings, having free will and control of our after life destiny, must obey the Commandments of the ONE SINGLE GOD. Those of us who do so, live lives maintaining full justice, honesty, mercy, peace, and charity in dealing with others. Thus we can each preserve the life of our soul that is in the Image of the ONE SINGLE GOD and can live on after our bodily death if we act as required to save the lives of our souls.

PRAYER TO THE ONE SINGLE GOD

**Hear O Israel: the LORD our GOD,
the LORD is ONE SINGLE GOD**

**Blessed is HIS Name and Glorious Sovereignty
for ever and ever.**

**You shall love the LORD your ONE SINGLE GOD
with all your heart, with all your soul,
and with all your might.**

And these words which I have commanded you on this day shall be forever always in your heart. You shall very diligently teach them to your children. You shall speak of them when ever you are in your house and when ever you walk on your path, and when ever you lay down to rest, and when ever you awaken.

As recognition and as a for you reminder sign, you shall bind all of these words upon your hand, and they shall also be as a reminder sign that you place between your eyes. You shall write these words and place them upon your house's doorposts and also your gates.

It is for all of us to always and forever praise the LORD, the ONE SINGLE GOD of all, and to proclaim the greatness of the ALMIGHTY CREATOR of the entire Universe for HE has not made us think, believe, behave, and be like all of the pagans of all the other lands. The ONE SINGLE GOD has not placed us to dwell and live and to be with and to act and to think like all of the heathen tribes of the earth. The ONE SINGLE GOD has not arranged and made our lives and destiny to be the same as theirs or arranged that we are to be thinking mentally the same as the numerous heathen nations and pagan peoples. We are able to think clearly with a free will and thought.

We bend our knees in worship and prayer giving thanks only to the KING of kings, the Holy ONE ALMIGHTY CREATOR, the ONE SINGLE GOD, our ONE SINGLE GOD, and we say in prayer "Blessed be HE who is our ONE SINGLE GOD".

The ONE SINGLE GOD has created all that is the infinite heaven and all of the earth's foundations. The Glory of the ONE SINGLE GOD is revealed in all of the heaven above, and the Might of the ONE SINGLE GOD is manifested in the greatest of heights. HE is our ONE SINGLE God; there is none other. The ONE SINGLE GOD is our KING. There is none besides HIM. It is written in HIS Torah that HE has given to us: *"Know this day, and always maintain in your heart, that your LORD is the ONE SINGLE GOD in the heaven above and on the earth beneath. There is none else."*

We therefore believe only in YOU, our LORD, our ONE SINGLE GOD, and wait that we may soon behold the Glory of YOUR Strength and Might, when YOU will remove every one and all of the abominations from the earth and cause all sinful idolatry to cease. We patiently wait and pray for the day when all of the nations of the entire world will become united under the Kingdom of YOU, the ALMIGHTY CREATOR, and all of mankind will acknowledge and recognize and pray only to YOU.

May all understand, acknowledge and know that only to YOU, the ONE SINGLE GOD, alone, all knees of mankind must bend and every tongue must say, vow and must declare loyalty. Before YOU, our LORD, our ONE SINGLE GOD, may all of mankind worship and in prayer and give honor to YOUR Glorious Name. May they all accept the rule of YOUR Kingdom and may YOU be for all their ONE SINGLE GOD.

For the KINGDOM is YOURS, and for all eternal time, YOU, our ONE SINGLE GOD, will reign in Majestic Glory; as this is stated and as written in YOUR Torah:

The LORD, the ONE SINGLE GOD, shall reign for ever and ever.

And it has been foretold;
The LORD, your ONE SINGLE GOD, shall be known by all of mankind as the eternal KING over all the earth; on that day the LORD shall be ONE, and His Name shall be ONE.

It is true and certain that there is only ONE SINGLE GOD, there is no other gods, and there is none that are like unto HIM.

It is the ONE SINGLE GOD who redeems us from the might of evil tyrants, and HE executes HIS Judgment upon all of our evil oppressors.

Great are HIS accomplishments and all things that the ONE SINGLE GOD does and has done and HIS Wonders are infinite and without number.

The ONE SINGLE GOD causes us to triumph over our evil enemies, and raises up our survival, glory, and victory over and above our evil enemies.

The ONE SINGLE GOD brought down upon the evil Egyptian Pharaoh HIS Judgment of punishing plagues, performing signs and wonders in Egypt.

The ONE SINGLE GOD rescued and saved the Children of Israel from harsh slavery, bitter servitude, and bondage, and delivered them from slavery to freedom.

Forever, in every age and generation the ONE SINGLE GOD, our LORD, has been our hope and HE rescued and saved us from evil enemies who sought to destroy us.

May it be that the ONE SINGLE GOD forever continue HIS protective care of all Israel. May HE forever guard HIS children from evil cruelty and disaster.

The ONE SINGLE GOD established the Sabbath Day marking the end of HIS Creation of heaven and earth and all the creatures thereon. HE Blessed only this Seventh Day as HIS Sabbath Day Hallowing it above all other days and seasons as it is clearly written in HIS Torah and stated in HIS Ten Commandments.

GENESIS 2.1-3

On the Seventh Day, the ONE SINGLE GOD finished HIS Creation of all of the heaven and earth and all that HE created to exist thereon including man. And on the Seventh Day HE rested from all HIS Creative Work which HE had Created and made. Then the ONE SINGLE GOD Blessed forever the Seventh Day and HE Hallowed it, and HE gave it to all of mankind forever to be the one Holy Sabbath Day because HE rested thereon from all of HIS Creative Work and HIS Creations which HE, the ONE SINGLE GOD, Created and Made.

The ONE SINGLE GOD rested from all HIS Creative Work, and on the Seventh Day raised HIMSELF and HE ascended to the HIS Majestic Throne of HIS Glory ornamented in HIS Majesty for HIS one chosen and selected day of rest

The ONE SINGLE GOD proclaimed and established the Seventh Day as a Sabbath Day and as a delight. This is the known magnificence and grandeur for the Seventh Day, the Sabbath Day, the day on which the ONE SINGLE GOD rested from all HIS Creative Work. This then was the one day, on the Seventh Day, that was the day HE declared to be HIS Sabbath Day. This was the one day upon which HE HIMSELF stated and rendered magnificent praise for it was the one day and only day that HE selected as HIS Sabbath Day. Therefore it has always been said:

A Psalm, a song, to be for the seventh day, the Sabbath Day selected by the ONE SINGLE GOD. It is therefore good to, at all times, give our thanks unto the LORD, our ONE SINGLE GOD.

Therefore, let all of the ONE SINGLE GOD's creatures acknowledge HIM and glorify and bless HIM. Let every one recognize HIS greatness and render to HIM praise and respectful distinction unto the ONE SINGLE GOD, the KING and ALMIGHTY CREATOR of all, who in HIS Holiness gives the blessed rest for HIS people, Israel, and to all mankind, on HIS Sacred Sabbath Day

> **May we respect YOUR Name, not known to us, LORD, our ONE SINGLE GOD,**
> **that IT shall be forever sanctified by all mankind,**
>
> **and YOUR eternal existence, our KING,**
> **in the heaven above and on the earth beneath**
> **shall be recognized always and glorified, by us.**

Not for our sake and account, our ONE SINGLE GOD, but for YOUR Name's sake, we give glory and thanks, for YOUR Kindness and for YOUR Truth! Why should all of the other nations say, "Where is their ONE SINGLE GOD now?" We know Our ONE SINGLE GOD is in the heavens above and whatever HE pleases, He can do and HE does!

Israel, always trust in the ONE SINGLE GOD. HE is your help and your shield! Priestly House of Aaron, always maintain and keep trust in the ONE SINGLE GOD who is your help and shield! You must always trust in the ONE SINGLE GOD who is your help and shield!

The breath of every living thing shall forever give blessings to YOUR Name, LORD, our ONE SINGLE GOD, and all of the spirit and mind of all flesh shall glorify and extol YOU, our KING. From the everlasting eternity of time, YOU alone are the ONE SINGLE GOD. But for YOU we would have no HEAVENLY FATHER and

KING, DELIVERER, and SAVIOR to rescue, redeem, save and give us sustenance and to show us mercy in and at all times of trouble and distress. Yes, we have no SOVEREIGN but YOU our ONE SINGLE GOD!

YOU were the ONE SINGLE GOD from the beginning. YOU will always be the ONE SINGLE GOD even throughout all of the eternal time that will never end YOU alone are the ONE SINGLE GOD of all that has ever lived and ever will live. YOU are the LORD of all generations. Only YOU, our ONE SINGLE GOD, are to be forever worshipped and extolled in all of the voices of our many praises.

YOU established YOUR world with loving care and kindness and YOUR creatures with loving tender compassion. YOU do not slumber nor sleep. YOU awaken all those that sleep and those that slumber. YOU cause the silent muted dumb to speak, loosen all who are tied and bound, support all of the fallen and raise up all of those that are bent and bowed down.

To YOU alone, our ONE SINGLE GOD, do we give thanks.

EXODUS 31.16-17

The Children of Israel shall forever keep the Seventh Day as the Sabbath observing it throughout their generations **as an everlasting Covenant and** Sign between ME and the Children of Israel forever always that it was on six days that YOUR LORD, the ONE SINGLE GOD, created and made heaven and earth, and all that is existing therein and thereon, and on the Seventh Day, ceased from HIS creative Work and rested.

This precious blessing of the Sabbath Day, O LORD, our ONE SINGLE GOD, YOU did not give and grant to all the pagan and heathen nations of the earth. Nor did YOU, our KING, our ONE SINGLE GOD, give and bestow the Sabbath Day as a Blessing upon all of idolaters. Nor can the unrighteous and evil ones every know and enjoy its rest. But YOU did give it as Blessing in affection to the Children of Israel, YOUR People, the seed of Jacob whom you named Israel and whom YOU did love.

May all the world's people come to recognize and sanctify the Seventh Day as and for YOUR Sabbath Day and may they receive YOUR Blessing and be delighted with YOUR Seventh Day Sabbath Day Gift. For YOU found pleasure in the Seventh Day, and YOU sanctified it, calling it the desirable Special Day to be always maintained forever in remembrance of YOUR CREATIONS.

THE GENESIS OF THE DEFINITION:
THE FIRST DEFINING ELEMENT

Every definition has to have a starting point, an origination, a beginning. So it is also with the construction of the definition that answers the question and defines who is a Jew.

First we have to determine if being a Jew means that one is a member of a distinct human classification such as people, race, color, political party, nationality or citizenship, or does it have to do with being a member of a human religious group?

Some would state the belief that a Jew is a member of a distinct people or nation. But then membership would only be open to those who were of that distinct people or nation. But today, there are many Jews, who are not the same as others and are different as to peoplehood or nationality and who may still be classified as Jews. Jews are then not all members of any separate or distinct people or nation.

Since there are many who claim to be Jews, and are actually recognized as being Jewish and who are not of the same human race, being Jewish does not depend upon race for definition. Likewise, there are those recognized as Jews that are of different skin color. Thus being Jewish does not depend upon racial origin or skin color for definition.

Similarly, various Jews are subjects and citizens of a multitude of diverse countries. They have different recognized citizenships and nationalities. This verifies the understood and recognized understanding that being Jewish is not dependent upon politics, citizenship, or nationality.

By elimination, the first element of the determination of who is a Jew is found to be only based upon religion.

The Jew is a member of a distinct religion that has a certain distinct religious belief and creed. Then what is the religion of the Jews? What makes that religion unique?

The Jew is a member of the Jewish Religion that requires the Jew to recognize and worship only the ONE SINGLE GOD. This is the first element of determination and statement of the answer to the question, "Who Is A Jew?" The definition of who is a Jew starts with "A Jew is a person who believes in the ONE SINGLE GOD". He does not believe in any other god or gods.

The Jew believes that the ONE SINGLE GOD Created this world and everything as described in Genesis (the Beginning) in the Torah that HE gave to all of mankind through the Children of Israel by way of HIS Giving the Torah and Ten Commandments to Moses. One who does not believe in this ONE SINGLE GOD of the Torah and Ten Commandments is a not a Jew. Being the descendent of Jews or having Jewish parents is not alone sufficient. An atheist, secular or non believer, even if born to Jewish parents is not a Jew.

And the ONE SINGLE GOD spoke all these words, saying:

COMMANDMENT NUMBER TWO

2. **You shall have no gods before ME.**

    You shall not make for yourself a graven image,

nor any manner of likeness, of any thing that is in heaven above,

or that is in the earth beneath, or that is in the water under the earth.

You shall not bow down to them, nor serve them;

for I the LORD your ONE SINGLE GOD am a jealous GOD,

visiting the iniquity of the fathers upon the children

even to the third and fourth generation of them that hate ME.

This Second Commandment is very explicit, clear, and understandable. Mankind is not to make any images of any kind whatsoever that represents the ONE SINGLE GOD or that are idols, icons, or statues for worship, adoration, or veneration. Prayers are not be addressed to idols, icons, or statues. No images of any manner or kind are to be made for worship. This includes all idols, icons, statues, and also paintings venerated as representing the ONE SINGLE GOD or other god worshipped.

Thus idols, statues, and icons are not to be used for representing and describing the ONE SINGLE GOD, a son of god, a mother of god, or to depict venerated angels and "saints" and none of them are to be made. Man is not to bow down or bend his knee in genuflective adoration of any images, idols, statues, or idols.

Those who believe and practice the Jewish religion adhere to the ONE SINGLE GOD's Second Commandment. Those who believe and practice the Moslem religion adhere to a belief in a One Single God. Synagogues and Mosques do not contain idols, statues, images, icons or portraits of deities and saints to be worshipped, adored, or venerated.

Jesus never utilized or worshipped, adored, or venerated idols, statues, icons, and images. These, according to the Jewish beliefs of Jesus and those of his Jewish apostles were not ever to be made or used.

The very first early Jewish followers of Jesus, not recognizing that they were the first and early members of a new religion to be called Christianity, did not make idols, statues, images, paintings or icons for worship, adoration, or veneration.

These early followers of Jesus, did not bow, genuflect, and pray to idols, statues, images, icons or portraits. They knew the Second Commandment of the ONE SINGLE GOD did not allow making or using them. They did not need these forbidden items to enable them to comprehend an unseen deity that was not ever to be seen and displayed as an image, painting, icon, statue or idol. They knew it was wrong to make and accept these images, icons, paintings statues or idols as gods to worship. They were to pray only to the unseen ONE SINGLE GOD. In the first and early churches of the Christian faith, there were no idols, statues, images, icons, or paintings representing the ONE SINGLE GOD or Jesus or Mother Mary.

Centuries later, voting against and vetoing the Second Commandment of the ONE SINGLE GOD, Christian church leadership decided to change, alter and amend the ONE SINGLE GOD's Second Commandment. They permitted the making of these statues, paintings, images, icons, and idols and also allowed these items, forbidden to be used and displayed by the ONE SINGLE GOD, to be placed in Churches and also to be used for religious purpose, worship, and veneration. Today these items, Commanded by the ONE SINGLE GOD to be absolutely forbidden, are maintained, used and treasured as holy items by the Vatican and some of Christianity.

In a classroom of a Jesuit operated University, in 1948, a Southern Baptist student asked a Catholic Jesuit Priest, who was then teaching the course of sociology, why the statues, images, and icons were allowed to exist on the Campus and inside the classrooms. He questioned the existence of a statue of Mary and baby Jesus outside on the lawn near the classroom building. He said he had seen students bow down and pray to the statue. The student stated that in his Christian belief, the Second Commandment did not allow statues or icons. He asked why the crucifix, with Jesus shown nailed thereon, was displayed in every classroom? Did these images violate the Commandment of the ONE SINGLE GOD?

ONE: HIS NAME SHALL BE ONE • 55

The Jesuit Priest answered by stating that when the early Christian missionaries came to a pagan village and preached the Christian gospel to the pagan natives, the natives pointed to their statues and said that these were their gods. They then asked the missionaries, "Where are your gods?"

The Jesuit Priest answered that the missionaries responded by showing the pagans the statues of their Christian gods. These statues, images and icons of Jesus and Mary and saints were a vital "necessity" to aid and assist the pagans in "seeing the truth" and then recognizing the Christian gods and saints in order to convince and cause the heathen pagans to then accept the conversion to the religion of Christianity.

The Baptist student replied, "I can understand that you used statues of Jesus and Mary during the times when people were ignorant pagans. But today, when the people are more literate and there is a more widespread education of the people, and there are many universities, such as this one, complete with many Libraries containing thousands of books, tell me, why do you still need the statues and images?"

The Jesuit Priest was silent, had no answer that he would give , and did not then respond.

Today, when an individual enters a Jewish Synagogue he or she will not see a single idol, statue, icon or any other art image or object that represents the ONE SINGLE GOD or any "saints" or "angels". The same occurs when an individual enters a Muslim Mosque. These objects can today only be seen in the some Christian (mainly Catholic) churches or other places of other pagan religious worship. These objects, however, are today adoringly treasured, admired, and venerated in the Vatican.

As has happened many times in past years, in our lifetime, many Christians have stated that they have seen visions of the gods by seeing the son of god, or the mother of god. They have seen these miraculous images and visions of the son of god or the mother of god on the sides of filthy rusting oil storage tanks, in fields and grottoes, and as reflections on dirty office building windows. When seen on the filthy rusting oil storage tanks, huge crowds began to visit the sight at the site, and they began to pray and venerate the miracle of the appearance of the son of god who revealed himself on the surface of the filthy rusting oil storage tanks.

They have seen images of Jesus in such places as in a tortilla in a women's frying pan, in New Mexico, who was frying the tortilla for her husband. Very recently, a ten year old grilled-cheese sandwich was said to facial bear the "recognized" face of the Virgin Mary. The grilled-cheese sandwich was sold to the highest bidder on e-Bay for $28,000.

A pretzel was since been found and said to be in a shape representing the Virgin Mary and baby Jesus. The pretzel owner would tell you to venerate the pretzel and not eat it. The grilled cheese sandwich was worth and sold for $ 28,000. How much for the pretzel?

The women, who saw the face of Jesus in the tortilla in her frying pan, took Jesus in the frying pan to her parish Priest. When the Priest did not, at first, accept as true fact that Jesus was in her frying pan, she took the pan home and placed it in a china cabinet. Word soon was spread through her Catholic community that Jesus was in the frying pan. Then crowds gathered near her china cabinet to light candles before the frying pan and to pray to Jesus the son of god in the frying pan. The Priest, after all of this, later did not dismiss the recognition, by the worshipers, and did not continue to deny that this was indeed after all the true face of Jesus the son of god in the tortilla. The attending crowds venerated and worshipped the tortilla.

How did that women and all of her neighbors absolutely for sure know that it was Jesus in her frying pan? Perhaps they were able to recognized him from a recent picture of him that they saw on TV or maybe they saw his photograph or picture framed and mounted on wall somewhere, maybe in a Church? With each of these sightings of Jesus the son of god and his mother Mary, the mother of god, crowds gather in awe to worship the "holy visions". Others have said that they have seen the miracles of statues and icons weeping.

It is very clearly written in the Torah, the Bible, that Moses, at Mount Sinai, asked the ONE SINGLE GOD to show HIMSELF so that

Moses could see HIM. The Response from the ONE SINGLE GOD to Moses was that no man (or woman) could ever see HIM and live.
How then, is it possible that Christians have "seen" visions of god, the son of god and the mother of god and still remained alive? It is, of course, not possible at all.

The Word of the ONE SINGLE GOD to Moses was clear and understandable. No human can ever see the ONE SINGLE GOD and live. If anyone has seen the "son of god" or "the mother of god" and lived than they have not seen GOD. Then what have they really seen? They have not seen anything and it is very sinful deception to say otherwise. Still for many centuries, there have been many who have presented fraudulent claims to have seen "holy" figures. This has resulted in many believing the "visions" and wrongfully gatherings for praying to these "visions".

Jewish worshipers pray directly only to the ONE SINGLE LORD GOD. They do not pray to those they believe have been prophets or saintly persons. They do not pray to any of the prophets and Rabbi teachers including Moses. They do not direct their prayers to "saints" for help or heavenly intervention with the ONE SINGLE GOD.

No person of the Jewish faith has seen or has ever had "visions" of the ONE SINGLE GOD. They cannot describe the ONE SINGLE GOD to whom alone they address their prayers.

Similarly, Muslim worshipers have never seen their One Single God. They do not pray to "saints". They cannot describe their never seen One Single God.

Jewish worshipers recognize that some have, in the past, been described as prophets. But all of the prophets, the same as the Prophet Moses, have never seen the ONE SINGLE GOD. Some Muslims accept a belief that their prophet Mohammed and his horse ascended to heaven and visited with their One Single God.

However, all so-called prophets were all humans and lived and died as humans. Again, not all so-called prophets have been true Prophets of the ONE SINGLE GOD. True Prophets, just like all of mankind, are the Creations of the ONE SINGLE GOD. They were not meant to be HIS replacements to receive the prayers of mankind.

Prayers are not to be made to any of the prophets or to any of the so-called saints. Prayers are not to be directed to them so that they can be then used by prophets or saints as and for intermediary messengers for the delivery of the prayer messages to a believed deity. Some Christians do pray to intermediary "saints" for help and intervention. There are those who have complete belief that their prayers to god must be made and addressed only to and through the son of god or through an intermediary saint.

The ONE SINGLE GOD's Second Commandment is certainly very clear and understandable without any need for the man made corrections, revisions, alterations or amendments that have been made by man. No advanced university degree study is required or necessary to understand, comprehend, and to fully obey the ONE SINGLE GOD's Second Commandment.

King David's Psalm 115 contains the following:

Not for our sake, ONE SINGLE GOD, not for our sake,

but for YOUR Name's sake we give glory,

for YOUR Kindness and for YOUR Truth!

Why should the other nations say "Where is their GOD now?"

Our ONE SINGLE GOD is in the heavens.

Whatever HE pleases, HE does!

Their idols are made of silver and gold,

the handiwork of man.

They have a mouth, but cannot speak.

They have eyes, but cannot see.

They have ears, but cannot hear.

They have a nose, but cannot smell.

They have hands, but they cannot feel.

They have feet, but they cannot walk.

They have a mouth, but cannot utter a sound from their throat.

Those who make them and trusts in them, will become like them.

Man is Commanded by the ONE SINGLE GOD not to make, decorate, or utilize any idols, icons statues, or images for worship, adoration or veneration. This includes the image of man mounted upon the most despicable symbol of man's torturous cruelty to man, the pagan Roman's devilishly cruelly torturous murderous sinful execution device, the cross.

THE FIRST PSALMS

I*t is to the Jewish King David of Israel, that credit is given for the authorship of the Psalms.*

It has also been said and believed by the Children of Israel, the Jews, that a Messiah would come upon this earth and that he would be a descendant of King David. That is why the Jewish Apostles of the Jew Jesus made very certain to "create" and include a genealogical traced descent from the Jewish King David of Israel to Jesus to bolster their claim that Jesus was the Messiah.

Further, the Apostles claimed that the Jew, Jesus, was the "Begotten son of god". Where did these begotten words come from? Read King David's Psalm number Two.

Here, in Psalm Two, King David, the author of Psalm Two, uses these words to describe himself. But, he did not mean that he was a son of a god or that he, himself was a god deity or was to be worshipped as one. King David recognized that he, and all men and women are the creations of the ALMIGHTY CREATOR, the ONE SINGLE GOD, and that all men and women were HIS begotten children, HIS sons and HIS daughters. *You are also a Begotten son or Begotten daughter of the ONE SINGLE GOD*

PSALM ONE

Praiseworthy is the man that does not walk in the path and counsel of the sinful wicked, and who does not stand in the path of the sinful wicked, and who does not sit in the discussions of any of those that in scorn believe not. But his true desire is in the learning and knowledge of the ONE SINGLE GOD's Torah that he thinks about both day and night. He shall be like a deeply rooted tree alongside streams of waters. He shall be as a tree that yields fruit in due season, and whose leafs never wither and fall. He will succeed in everything that he tries and does. It is not so with the sinful wicked; rather they are like anything worthless that the winds blow and drive away. Therefore, the sinful wicked shall not be forgiven, acquitted, and vindicated in the ONE SINGLE GOD's Judgment, nor will the sinful wicked be allowed to be in the assembly of the righteous. For the ONE SINGLE GOD attends to the efforts of the righteous while the efforts of the sinful wicked cause them to perish

PSALM TWO

Why do the peoples gather, and nations all talk in vain? The kings of the earth take their stand and the princes conspire secretly, against the ONE SINGLE GOD and against HIS anointed. "Let us cut off their attachments uniting the tribes of Israel and let us cast off their ropes from ourselves". HE, the ONE SINGLE GOD, sits in heaven and will laugh and will mock all of them. Then in HIS Burning Anger, HE will speak to them and HE will terrify them with HIS Wrath and Fury.

I MYSELF, your ONE SINGLE GOD, have anointed you my King over Zion, MY Holy Mountain. **You are my SON. I have begotten you this day.** Ask of ME and I will make all the people your inheritance, and all of the ends of the earth I have created will be your possession.

You will smash them with a rod of mighty iron and then shatter and break them like an earthen clay vessel. And now, all kings and judges of the earth, be all of you wise and be disciplined. Serve the ONE SINGLE GOD with awe that you may rejoice when there is fear and trembling. Yearn for justice and purity, lest the ONE SINGLE GOD become wrathful and your way shall be doomed, for in a brief moment HIS Burning anger will kindle and blaze. Praiseworthy are all who trust in HIM.

And the ONE SINGLE GOD spoke all these words, saying:

COMMANDMENT NUMBER THREE

3. You shall not take the Name of the LORD

   your ONE SINGLE GOD in vain.

   For the LORD will not hold him guiltless

   who takes HIS Name in vain.

Because of the words of this Commandment, observers of the Jewish religion will not say or use any names that may be or are believed to be associated with their ONE SINGLE GOD lest they say the name in vain. Followers of the Moslem faith refer to, and name, their god as Allah.

Christians use a supposed name of God and also use the name of the one they believe to be the son of god. "Honk if you believe in Jesus", was stated on an automobile bumper sticker. The sticker was splashed with all of the muck and mud from the roadway. In many similar ways, the name of the Christian son of god, believed to be a deity that is to be respected and worshipped, is said almost daily in vain. Christians should understand that "God's" name should not be stuck on the back end of a car upon the bumper and be subjected to the filth of the road.

A Christian denomination today uses a supposed name of God in it's title. Those who are members of this denomination have failed to understand the meaning of this Commandment. They fail to *witness* the fact of their non-compliance with this Commandment by taking a supposed name of god and thus do not obey this Third Commandment of the ONE SINGLE GOD and they take HIS supposed name in vain.

Often the name and reference to God is vainly used by those who preach their own "superiority" while they foment vicious hatred against others who are not of their race, color, or religion. The symbol of pagan Roman torturous murderous atrocity, the cross, is often used during these diatribes conducted in the supposed name of god.

When Moses asked the ONE SINGLE GOD what HIS Name was, the ONE SINGLE GOD replied ***HE IS WHO WAS, WHO IS, and WHO WILL BE!*** The ONE SINGLE GOD did not reply by giving a name. However, various theologians have believed, that through their own very great wisdom, they have ascertained one or more names.

The Jewish adherents refer to the ONE SINGLE GOD without mention of a name. By this way they avoid any mentioning of HIS Name in vain. They refer to the ONE SINGLE GOD in the Hebrew language as "Hashem", which means "The Name".

Muslims have used the word Allah to name their god who they believe is the god of Abraham. Abraham is named in the Jewish Torah (Bible) as being the first man to accept and believe in the ONE SINGLE GOD and, in the Torah, Abraham is named as the father of the Hebrew (Jewish) people, the patriarch of the Children of Israel.

The Torah does not reveal any certain name for the ONE SINGLE GOD. Abraham never knew the name of the ONE SINGLE GOD neither did Moses who first talked to the ONE SINGLE GOD when HE, the ONE SINGLE GOD, was in the flaming burning bush.

In the Muslim Koran, Abraham is stated to have always been a Muslim and Abraham's god is therefore, they believe, the Muslim god Allah. The Muslim Koran (bible) and faith came into existence in and from the pagan world more than 2,500 years after Judaism's Torah.

Without recourse to attempting to name the ONE SINGLE GOD and thus not naming him, one cannot state HIS Name in vain. The Name of the ONE SINGLE GOD while not being disclosed in the Torah could have been easily so disclosed. But the NAME was intentionally concealed and not stated and made known to man by the ONE SINGLE GOD. It is the absolute duty and responsibility for all to obey

HIS Commandment and not try to determine and express HIS Name lest it be said in any sinful manner or in vain.

For many, there is always the manner of swearing and using a mention of some God. There are some Christians who will swear when angry by saying "god damn it" or "Jesus Christ". The Third Commandment directs that no person shall use the Name of the ONE SINGLE GOD in an angry swearing. This Commandment also directs those of the Jewish, Christian or Islamic religious faiths not to ever utter in vain, or in oaths and swearing, any supposed name of the ONE SINGLE GOD.

The ONE SINGLE GOD and HIS Name is Holy. Therefore HIS Name should not be used or said in profanity or to swear and testify to anything that is not or may possibly not be honest and true. Thus stating and giving deceptive and false oath and swearing in the Name of the ONE SINGLE GOD is a very sinful perjury and an unpardonable offense.

The foundation of Judaism is the beliefs in the historic fact that there was a truthful Revelation given and made known by the ONE SINGLE GOD to Moses, for the Children of Israel and all of mankind, at Mount Sinai. Thus it is necessary for all of mankind to adhere and obey all of HIS Commandments.

This is the Third of the ONE SINGLE GOD's Commandments and mankind is not to use the Name of the ONE SINGLE GOD in vain, in a manner having no real truth, value or significance or in a worthless manner or in empty, idle or hollow or senseless manner.
That is the reason and rational as to why those of the Jewish faith do not and will not use any supposed "name" of the ONE SINGLE GOD. That is why when they make or state reference to the ONE SINGLE GOD, they do so in Hebrew as "Hashem", "The Name".

And the ONE SINGLE GOD spoke all these words, saying:

COMMANDMENT NUMBER FOUR

4. Remember the Sabbath Day to keep it always Holy.

Six days shall you labor and do all your work;

but the Seventh Day

is a Sabbath to the LORD your ONE SINGLE GOD.

On that day you shall not do any manner of work,

you, your son, your daughter, your man or your maid servant,

nor your cattle, nor the stranger that is within your gates.

For in six days the LORD, the ONE SINGLE GOD,

made the heaven and earth, the sea, and all that is in them,

and the ONE SINGLE GOD rested on the Seventh Day.

Therefore the Lord, the ONE SINGLE GOD,

Blessed the Seventh Day as the Sabbath day, and Hallowed it.

This Fourth Commandment not only sets and names the specific day of the week to be used for a day of rest and worship but states that this day, the Seventh Day of the week, has been Blessed by the ONE SINGLE GOD and is the day HE Hallowed. The Seventh Day is the only one day the ONE SINGLE GOD Blessed and made Holy as the HIS Sabbath Day of rest and worship.

The Seventh Day, the Sabbath Day, called and known presently by the pagan name of Saturday, is the day of the week Commanded by the ONE SINGLE GOD to be set aside by mankind for worship and prayer. It was never, at any time thereafter, ever changed by the ONE SINGLE GOD to another day for HIS Sabbath Day.
Early Christians celebrated the Sabbath on the Seventh Day in the

same manner that Jesus, the Jewish founder of Christianity, and his Jewish apostles celebrated the Sabbath Day on the Seventh Day. It was later, in the fourth century after the birth of Jesus, that early Christian leaders *elected* to change the ONE SINGLE GOD's Day of Worship. "All in favor, say aye"; and the elders voted to veto and defy the ONE SINGLE GOD and change HIS Blessed and Hallowed Sabbath Day to the first day.

The sabbath day was changed by the Christian elders because the adherents to the Judaic religion were very stubborn and refused to convert to the new Christian religion. Therefore the Christian leaders set aside the Fourth Commandment of the ONE SINGLE GOD. They separated themselves from the practices and beliefs of Yeshua, Jesus, their Jewish founder and then declared Sunday to be the Sabbath. Their sabbath was to be a day stated to be the lord's day.

When the stubborn Jewish worshipers did not accept the Moslem faith that arose seven centuries after Christianity, the Moslem sabbath day was also changed from the Seventh Day to the sixth day commonly called Friday.

To this date, followers of the Judaic religion still recognize the Hebrew names of the days of the week as being Yom Rishon (the First day), Yom Sheni (the Second Day), Yom Shelishi (the Third Day), Yom Revie (the Fourth Day), Yom Hamishi (the Fifth Day), Yom Shishi (the Sixth Day) and Yom Shevei or Yom Shabbat (the Seventh or Sabbath Day).

The Hebrew names of the days are mentioned in the Torah (Bible). The names of the days, as they are now commonly called, Sunday through Saturday, are not mentioned by those names in the Torah or Bible. These names now used for the days, are days named to honor the pagan gods. These names of days were not known to Jewish Jesus and his Jewish Apostles who used only Hebrew names of the days.

Christians have accepted other, the pagan, names for these days. Sunday, the first day of the week, is named in honor of the pagan Sun god (dies solis). Monday, the second day of the week, is named in honor of the pagan Moon god. Tuesday, the third day of the week, is named in honor of the Norse pagan god of war Tyr or Tiu. Wednesday, the fourth day of the week, is named in honor of the pagan god Odin (Wodin). Thursday, the fifth day of the week, is named in honor of the pagan god Thor. Friday, the sixth day of the week, is the day named in honor of the pagan goddess Frigg.

Saturday, the seventh day of the week is named in honor of the pagan god Saturn and is no longer the day to be kept, maintained and celebrated as the Sabbath Day of the ONE SINGLE GOD.

The founder of the Christian faith, believed by Christians to be the son of god never referred to or mentioned the days by these pagan names. His followers also only knew the names of the days stated in Hebrew as (day one) Yom Rishon, (day two) Yom Sheni, (day three) Yom Shelishi, (day four) Yom Revie, (day five) Yom Hamishi, (day six) Yom Shishi, and (day seven or Sabbath day) Yom Shevie or Yom Shabbat.

From the day the Children of Israel stood at Mount Sinai, from the day they received the ONE SINGLE GOD's Fourth Commandment to strictly observe the Seventh Day, Yom Shevei, as the Sabbath day, followers of the Judaic religion have adhered to this Seventh Day as the ONE SINGLE GOD's designated Hallowed and Blessed day of rest and the day of worship. They knew and accepted the understanding and fact that they could never change the ONE SINGLE GOD's Seventh Day Sabbath.

The Sabbath Day begins during the evening, sun down, of the sixth day and continues until the evening, sun down, of the Seventh Day. During the period of the Sabbath Day, no work, of any kind whatsoever, is to be performed.

Observant Jews do not operate or ride in motor vehicles or travel on the Sabbath Day. They do not turn on or off electrical lights, TV sets, and any electric appliances. They do not make telephone calls. They do not write or use computers and printers. They do not attend sporting events or theater productions. On the Sabbath Day, they do not do any kind of manual labor such as mowing of lawns, or repair and maintenance of automobiles, appliances or homes.

The only exception would be if a life saving act must be performed.

No work means just that, no work. One is also not to direct others to violate the Sabbath Day by having them labor and work in their stead or for them.

Not by direction of the Fourth Commandment of the ONE SINGLE GOD, but in defiance to Him, Christian leaders, several centuries after the advent of Christianity, voted to change the ONE SINGLE GOD's Fourth Commandment and HIS designated, Hallowed, and Blessed Seventh Day Sabbath Day to a new sabbath day they selected being the first day and commonly known as Sunday. They also did not teach their adherents that their new sabbath day was not to be a day upon which no work of any kind was to be performed.

Work is performed on the Christian sabbath first day. It is a day that is not a complete day for rest and worship. One may work, attend a sporting event as a football game, or go to play golf on that day, etc.
The pagans of the western world easily accepted the Christian first day, Sunday, as a day of worship. This had been the days, Sundays, of the Roman Circuses and days of the attending and enjoying gladiator combat. The day could require worship of the god, son of god, and holy ghost god but it was not a day that required the full need to be observed as a complete non-work or non-sport day of rest and worship.

Even today, Christians may attend worship services Sunday morning and then later, the same day, work and perform actions and deeds not allowed by this Fourth Commandment. Today, Christians do not worship on the same sabbath day that their founder, Jesus, and his first and early followers worshipped upon. His Sabbath day, the Seventh day, was as stated in this Fourth Commandment of the ONE SINGLE GOD and not as changed later by the vote of the Christian elders overruling and vetoing the ONE SINGLE GOD.

Some, as Christians, do believe that it makes no difference whether one observes a day of sabbath on any day of the week as long as one has one day of sabbath worship. To them there is no difference between a Sabbath observed on the Seventh Day or the first day. They

ONE: HIS NAME SHALL BE ONE • 69

therefore have amended, altered, and changed the Fourth Commandment deleting any mention or necessity to have the Seventh Day, that the ONE SINGLE GOD hallowed and blessed as HIS Sabbath Day, still to be observed and maintained as the Sabbath Day. Their Christian Fourth Commandment, with exception of those of the Christian Seventh Day Adventists, can be read to omit mention of the specific Seventh Day and to read:

> Any Six days shall you labor and do your work but set aside
> any one day, as Sunday, the lord's day, each week
> that you shall observe as a sabbath day
> for some rest, worship, pleasure, play, sports, shopping, and enjoyment.

No mention is included that one must not do any work or perform any labor on the sabbath. Therefore one may do any kind of work, perform business activity, engage in commercial, industrial and farming work, go shopping, and attend sporting and entertainment events.

There is no Christian indication, dedication or thought that the Fourth Commandment very specifically states that the ONE SINGLE GOD specifically chose the Seventh day, now commonly known by the pagan name of Saturday, as the Sabbath day.

There is an absolute absence of mention that the ONE SINGLE GOD Hallowed and Blessed only this Seventh Day and no other day whether it be the day known commonly by the pagan name of Sunday (the first day, as celebrated by Christians) or the day commonly known by the pagan name of Friday (the sixth day, as celebrated by Moslems).

The Sabbath Day is a day that is to be kept Holy. Mankind can work on the other six days, but the Seventh Day, the Sabbath Day is to be maintained as a day devoted to rest, sanctification, reflective religious thought, and prayer to the ONE SINGLE GOD.

The Sabbath day is not meant to be a day for field labor, for commercial enterprise actions of buying and selling, for travel, for household chores and cooking. One is not supposed to perform ploughing, harvesting, reaping, transport and carrying of loads, starting and kindling of fires, working with one's calculator, computer or writing, or mending of clothes or sewing.

All of these actions that are not to be performed on the Sabbath Day can be performed on the other six remaining days of the week. Nor is work to be accomplished by children for the parents on the Sabbath Day. Similarly, one is not to have a servant or employee do work and labor on the Seventh Day Sabbath Day.

It has been said that the Seventh Day Sabbath Day, a day of rest and prayer, a day kept Holy and in respectful obedience to the ONE SINGLE GOD's Fourth Commandment, has resulted, through its observance by the Children of Israel, the Jewish people, in their survival of the very many hateful murderous oppressions, crusades, and many tragic persecutions during times of inquisitions, pogroms and Holocausts. Despite all the tragic persecutions of the past three thousand years, the Jewish people have remained steadfast in their observance of the ONE SINGLE GOD's Fourth Commandment's Sabbath Day.

THE SABBATH DAY OF THE ONE SINGLE GOD:
HIS FOURTH COMMANDMENT – THE SEVENTH DAY

The Children of Israel received, accepted, and kept the Sabbath Day given to them by the ONE SINGLE GOD. The Sabbath Day is an eternal covenant for all times and generations between the ONE SINGLE GOD and the Children of Israel. It is the recognition and Commandment forever that in six days the ALMIGHTY CREATOR, ONE SINGLE GOD, created and made the heaven and earth, and on the Seventh Day HE rested and that HE requires all of mankind to observe that day as HIS Sabbath Day.

These are some of the prayers recited by the Children of Israel on the Seventh Day, the Sabbath Day of the ONE SINGLE GOD:

It was on the sixth day and the heavens and earth were completely made, created, and finished with all of their array. On the Seventh Day, the ONE SINGLE GOD having completed HIS work which HE had accomplished and done, and it was on the Seventh Day that HE rested after HE had completed, stopped, and abstained from all HIS Creation Work. The ONE SINGLE GOD then Blessed the Seventh Day, and HE Hallowed that day, because it was on that Seventh Day that HE completed and stopped all of HIS Creative Work, and HE abstained from all of any other Creative Work which the ONE SINGLE GOD had prior Created and made.

YOU sanctified the Seventh Day forYOUR Name's sake, being the conclusion of the YOUR Creation of all heaven and earth. Of all the days, YOU Chose and Blessed it; the Seventh Day, and of all days and seasons, YOU Sanctified it and so it is written, for all mankind to know, obey, and observe, as it is written in YOUR Torah (Bible).

Thus, the heaven and earth were completely created, made, and finished, with all that is within as their contents and multitudes. On the Seventh Day, the ONE SINGLE GOD completed all of HIS Creative Work which HE had accomplished and HE then abstained, on the Seventh Day, from any other further of HIS Work which HE had prior done. The ONE SINGLE GOD blessed the Seventh Day and HE sanctified it because on it HE had abstained from all HIS further Work which the ONE SINGLE GOD had Created and Made.

Blessed are YOU, OUR ONE SINGLE GOD, KING of the Universe, Who has sanctified us with all of YOUR Commandments including this Fourth Commandment. YOU took pleasure in us and with YOUR love and favor and YOU gave us YOUR Holy Sabbath Day as a heritage, a remembrance of YOUR Creation. For that day is the forever remembered introduction to YOUR Holy Convocations and a memorial of the YOUR Sinai Gift of YOUR Torah and Commandments. For YOU then did choose us and gave us YOUR Holy Sabbath Day as an eternal heritage for us and all makind. Blessed are YOU our ONE SINGLE GOD, Who has sanctified the Seventh Day as the Sabbath Day to be observed .

Our ONE SINGLE GOD and the ONE SINGLE GOD of our forefathers, may YOU be pleased with our rest. Sanctify us with YOUR Commandments and Grant us our share in YOUR Torah. Satisfy us from YOUR Goodness and Gladden us with YOUR Salvation and Purify our heart to serve YOU sincerely. Our ONE SINGLE GOD, with Love and Favor grant us YOUR Holy Sabbath as a heritage and may Israel, the Sanctifiers of YOUR Name, rest on it. Blessed are YOU, the ONE SINGLE GOD Who eternally Sanctifies the Seventh Day Sabbath for all of mankind.

ONE: HIS NAME SHALL BE ONE • 73

Blessed are YOU our ONE SINGLE GOD, KING of the Universe, Who sanctified us with YOUR Commandments, took pleasure in us, and with Love gave us YOUR Holy Sabbath as a heritage, a remembrance of YOUR Creation. For that Sabbath Day forever reminds us and commemorates the Exodus from Egypt. YOU choose that Seventh Day for us and all of mankind and YOU did Sanctify this Sabbath Day to be as YOUR Holy Day.

Moses rejoiced in YOUR gift to him, of his portion; in that YOU called upon him as YOUR faithful servant. A crown of Radiation and Splendor YOU placed on his head when he stood before YOU on Mount Sinai. Moses brought down the two stone tablets in his hand, on which YOU wrote and inscribed the Commandment for the observation of the YOUR Sabbath Day. So it is written in YOUR Torah that YOU gave to Moses and through him gave to all mankind through YOUR Gift to the Children of Israel.

They shall rejoice in YOUR KINGSHIP, those who observe the ONE SINGLE GOD's Sabbath. They will all be satisfied and delighted from YOUR Goodness. For it is the Seventh Day that YOU found favor in and Sanctified it. It is the most Blessed of days. YOU called it a forever eternal remembrance of YOUR Creation.

The Children of Israel shall forever keep and maintain the Eternal Covenant for all of their generations. It is between the ME, Your ONE SINGLE GOD and you, the Children of Israel, as a remembrance sign forever that in six days Your ONE SINGLE GOD made heaven and earth, and on the Seventh Day I, your ONE SINGLE GOD, rested and was refreshed.

YOU did not give the Seventh Day as the Sabbath Day, our ONE SINGLE GOD, to the other pagan nations of the world, nor did YOU make it, as they did not want it and against their will, to be the inheritance, OUR KING, of the worshippers of graven images and idols. The uncircumcised shall not abide in its contentment. For to Israel, the seed of Jacob, whom YOU have selected to be the recipients of YOUR Commandments as YOUR people and YOU have given the Sabbath Day to all mankind through them with YOUR Love. All of mankind that will sanctify the Seventh Day will be all satisfied and delighted from YOUR Goodness and Blessings for it is only the Seventh Day that YOU found it to be, and Sanctified it as, the "Most Blessed of Days". YOU called it, and all must acknowledge it as remembrance of YOUR Act of Creation.

Our ONE SINGLE GOD, the ONE SINGLE GOD of our fathers, may YOU be pleased with our Seventh Day Sabbath worship and rest. Sanctify us with all of YOUR Commandments and grant us our share in YOUR Torah. Satisfy us from YOUR Goodness and gladden us with YOUR Salvation and purify our hearts to appreciatively serve YOU sincerely.

Our ONE SINGLE GOD, with love and favor grant us YOUR Holy Sabbath Day as a heritage. May Israel, the sanctifiers of YOUR Name, rest on the Seventh Day, YOUR Sabbath. Blessed are YOU, our ONE SINGLE GOD, Who sanctifies the Sabbath Day. We will forever pray only to the ONE SINGLE GOD Who rested from all HIS Works and Who ascended on the Seventh Day to sit on HIS Majestic Throne of Glory. With wondrous splendor HE provided the Day of HIS Contentment and declared the Sabbath Day HIS delight. This is the glory and praise of the Sabbath Day that was recognized to be on the Seventh Day that the ONE SINGLE GOD rested from all of HIS Creative Work.

It is also said, that to the Seventh Day, there is given great praise and honor when there is said a psalm that is a song for the Sabbath Day. It is good to give our thanks to the ONE SINGLE GOD. Therefore let all of us that HE has Created and Fashioned praise, glorify and Bless HIM, the ONE SINGLE GOD. All of us must always render praise, honor and thanks to the ONE SINGLE GOD, the KING of kings, who has Created, Made, and Fashioned everything that exists. You, ALMIGHTY CREATOR, our ONE SINGLE GOD, have given a heritage of contentment for all of the people of the world through YOUR people, Israel, and in YOUR Holiness have thus given all of us, all of mankind, the Holy Sabbath Day.

YOU are the shield of our forefathers with YOUR Word and YOU will in time resuscitate the living souls of the righteous dead with YOUR Utterance. YOU are the Holy ONE SINGLE GOD, Who is unequaled. YOU have granted Sabbath rest to all of mankind through YOUR people, the Children of Israel. On YOUR Holy Sabbath Day, for YOU were pleased with them and all mankind to grant them all rest. Before and to YOU alone we will serve and pray with reverence and awe giving thanks to YOUR Name every day continually with our appropriate blessings. To YOU, our ONE SINGLE GOD, we will ever grateful give our praise. Master of Peace, YOU have sanctified the Sabbath and blessed the Seventh Day, and have given rest with holiness to all people saturated with the delight in the continuance of the memory of all of YOUR Work of Creation. YOU are, for all of mankind, our ONE SINGLE GOD of CREATION.

We give thanks for Your Blessing that we may have the Sabbath Day as a day of worship and a day of rest. Nothing compares with the sweetness of the Friday evening when Your Sabbath is welcomed. My wife lights the Sabbath candles. My sons and I have returned from our prayers in the Synagogue. The entire family is now together to greet the Sabbath. There is conversation about the Sabbath and about our daily lives but no talk of work or business. The television and radio is silent. There is a great joy in knowing that we can spend the restful Sabbath time together as a family. We enjoy our Sabbath meal concluding with all saying the thankful prayer of Grace.

After the Sabbath dinner, we can do what we have wanted to do all week long devoting our time to reading and studying. Our cars are parked and will remain undriven until after the conclusion of the Sabbath. We will not perform work of any kind during the Sabbath. We will not answer our phones, take pen in hand to write, or use a computer. Isn't the Sabbath day of total rest from work wonderful? Is it not great to be with ones family after the week of being apart and separated because of more "important work" activity? We thank the ONE SINGLE GOD for HIS Blessed and Hallowed Sabbath Day.

THE FIRST FOUR WORDS

Everything has a beginning. For all that is said or written there are always first words. These are the most important words. There are first words written in the Torah (Bible). They should be known and appreciated by all. But, unfortunately, most do not know about the first four words or the importance and meaning of what they say.

I recall being in Washington, DC attending a series of meetings. After one day's session, I returned to the Motel with another person who had also attended the meeting that day. We sat in the Motel lounge and had a general discussion. Then later, for some reason, my colleague started to discuss religion. I wanted to change the subject since I knew we would never religiously agree. However, he persisted and continued the religious discussion.

During his religious statements, he several times mentioned that he always went to his Church on the Sabbath day. I responded, after his repeated statements, that he went to his Church on Sunday and not on the Sabbath day. He argued back loudly that Sunday was the Sabbath Day. I stated that the Sabbath day was the Seventh Day according to the Bible and that Saturday was the Seventh Day.

He argued and repeatedly said that I was totally wrong and that Sunday was the seventh day and the Sabbath day. To prove this, he called Room Service and asked that a dictionary be brought to him. He had thought and was certain that the dictionary would confirm that

Sunday was the true seventh day Sabbath day. The dictionary he received to show me his proof was the Webster's New World College Dictionary.

He proceeded to look up and check the following words, "Sabbath", "Saturday", and "Sunday". I asked him to read the definitions out loud. This is what he read:

> *"Sabbath". The seventh day of the week (Saturday), set aside by the Fourth Commandment for rest and worship and observed as such by Jews and some Christian sects.*
>
> *"Saturday". The Seventh day of the week.*
>
> *"Sunday". The First day of the week; it is observed by most Christian denominations as the Sabbath.*

My colleague then changed the subject but continued his religious discussion. I knew that we could never agree on that subject and again tried to change the discussion to another topic. But he still persisted and continued in his religious discussion. Finally, I asked him whether he had ever read the Bible and if so then when was the last time he did so? He responded that he knows his "Bible", the New Testament, very well since he reads all of it all of the time. To prove that, he went to his room to obtain and show his proof by means of the Gideon Bible that had been placed in a drawer in his room.

He returned and displayed the Bible. He flipped open the book to a page past the middle of the book and told to me to read that page. It was near page 500. I turned to page one and asked if he had read that page and the pages following page one. He told me that he had not read those pages because those pages were about the "Old Testament", the OT and were obsolete, not important, and were replaced by the "New Testament". I told him that I did not want him to read the "Obsolete Testament" but asked him to just read, not the entire OT or even the OT's` first entire page but to read only the first four words on page one. He looked at me with puzzled eyes and then read aloud the first four words.

"In the Beginning, GOD."

I asked him whether he truly believed that GOD was also obsolete and whether he truly believed that it was not important to read these words and continue to read all of the first book of the Bible, that he called Genesis, as this was presented in the Gideon Bible? I wanted to know if he really knew that Genesis described the efforts of GOD in creating the world and the universe?

From his answers, I knew that he had never read the Five Books of Moses, the Torah, that he referred to as the obsolete testament. For him, the Bible began with the first words of the Christian New Testament.

> **This is the manner in which all too many read and "study" the book of their religion. They do not start with or know the first four words of the Bible, "In the Beginning, GOD".**

But, the Jew Yeshua, or Jesus, completely knew and understood these first four words. Unlike my colleague, Jesus was learned and knew all of the words of the Five Books of Moses, the Torah. He never stated a belief or certainty that these Books of the Torah were to become obsolete. He never stated a belief or certainty that the Ten Commandments of the ONE SINGLE GOD, contained in the Torah were to become obsolete. He never declared that they were to be replaced with new Christian versions of the Commandments.

Jesus never declared that his disciples were fully authorized and empowered to obsolete the Torah or declare that the New Testaments of these disciples were to replace the Five Books of Moses with a new Bible thus eliminating the first four words **"In the Beginning, GOD"**.

It is in this first book called Genesis that it is stated that GOD rested from his work of creations and that the Seventh Day, now called Saturday, was the day GOD declared to be the Sabbath Day. It was man, not the ONE SINGLE GOD, that declared GOD as being obsolete and no longer to be listened to concerning the Sabbath Day. Man could and did change the day from the Seventh day to the First day. This change was in complete defiance of the ONE SINGLE GOD who Blessed and Hallowed the Seventh day as HIS chosen day of rest and prayer. This is stated in the ONE SINGLE GOD's Fourth Commandment:

"Remember the Seventh Day, to keep it Holy"

And the ONE SINGLE GOD spoke all these words, saying:

COMMANDMENT NUMBER FIVE

5. Honor your father and your mother,

    that your days may be long upon the land which the LORD

    your ONE SINGLE GOD gives you.

Each individual is to always give full and complete honor to his or her parents. This includes the responsibility to also not only give complete respect to the parents but also to give them proper parental obedience. The Fifth Commandment also means that everyone must give the same honor and respect to one's grandparents and all of the elderly even those elderly that are not of our family.

Just as we have and must obey the ONE SINGLE GOD's Fifth Commandment to honor and respect our parents, so must we, in accord with this Commandment, give our respect and honor to all who are our elders. This includes not only members of our family such as older aunts, uncles, and grandparents but also includes all older members of our community, older strangers and older neighbors even if they are not of the same nationality, creed, race, or religion as one's parents and family.

During the Holocaust, younger Nazi German soldiers disobeyed this Fifth Commandment of the ONE SINGLE GOD. They sinfully disobeyed the ONE SINGLE GOD's Fifth Commandment and deliberately showed their disrespect for their own parents and elders when they treated elderly Jews and other elderly conquered peoples with hatred, contempt, disrespect, and viciously harmed, tortured, painfully injured, and murdered them.

This Fifth Commandment was given, through the Children of Israel, to all of mankind. The ONE SINGLE GOD's gift, of the soul of man, exists alive only as long as HIS Fifth Commandment is observed and obeyed, and honor and respect is given to parents and to all who are elders. When one does not obey this Commandment and honor and respect his or her parents and also all who are their elders, then his or her soul is eternally punished and doomed.

Many of the today's problems, of the nations and mankind's society, can be traced to the lack of honor and respect children show, have for, and give to parents and to those who are elderly. This is not always the fault of children and the young. Often, parents do not raise their children properly. Parents, educators, and religious leaders and teachers fail in not teaching children the Ten Commandments' Requirements to do only good deeds and to be truthful, honest, and respectful and honor their own parents and all of the elderly. In too many instances, the Fifth Commandment to honor parents and elderly is ignored by children who are not properly raised and taught the ONE SINGLE GOD's Fifth Commandment by their parents. educators and religious leaders.

It should be fully noted and understood that this Fifth Commandment is a very important and very significant requirements and directive from the ONE SINGLE GOD. HE has emphasized the very importance of this Fifth Commandment by placing this Commandment even before HIS other five following Commandments that one shall not murder, commit adultery, steal, bear false witness, or covet.

However, all too many young persons do not ever heed and obey this important Fifth Commandment. They will not have and do not merit the reward of longer lives in their own lands. Today, sadly, all too frequently, one can observe those who do not honor their parents or the elderly and instead wrongfully have shown dishonor, disrespect, and disobedience to their parents, teachers, and the elderly.

If every one had total commitment to the observance of this Fifth

Commandment, many of the problems of mankind in this world today would be cured and vanish. Parents, educators, and religious leaders have a very important and significant duty and obligation to teach this Fifth Commandment to all of their children and pupils.

In doing so, their teachings will also provide parent, educators, and religious leaders with the then earned and deserved respect and honor that they themselves would then merit, expect, and receive from their own children and pupils. If this was accomplished by all parents, educators, and religious leaders, would there still be the amount of crime, including murder and theft committed by the youth and children?

Would nations continually have to engage in disastrous warfare if parents, educators, and religious leaders, of all nations, especially those that might be on opposing national and political sides, properly taught their children, youth and pupils to honor and respect all elderly persons, without any exceptions, even those elderly considered to be their national enemy or religious opponents in belief?

Were children to be taught to honor and respect all of the elderly, even the elderly of any enemy, perhaps the world would be a safer and more peaceful place with less need for tragic warfare between and among nations with the resultant killings and injuries to the youth then sent to the battles?

It has been observed all too many times that a young seated person will remain seated while the elderly person standing besides them is left trying to barely be able to stand and hold on to something to avoid falling down in a moving bus. The proper action, a respectful action, would be for the younger more able person to give his or her seat to the elderly person. But how frequently is this small effort to assist elderly seniors made today?

How many young men and women would hold a door open for an elderly person barely able to walk? How many of our youth would extend a hand to help an elderly person? All too often, young men and women do not aid or assist the elderly. Some even avoid helping their own elderly parents or any person senior in age to them.

Today, in our world of technology and electronic communications, all too often messages are presented to youth that totally teach and illustrate that they do not have to honor or respect their parents and elders. Television, the internet and computer games often provide an opposite message, that it is ignorantly acceptable and tolerated, that the young need not have respect for their parents and the elderly.

There is either poor instruction on this subject or it is completely omitted in teachings and sermons on the various sabbath days observed by most individuals. Preachers, Ministers, Pastors, Priests, Sheiks, Imams, Mullahs. Muftis and Ayatollahs do not provide any teachings , let alone significant teachings, of the original Torah's Ten Commandments and do not make mention, or place the required stress, on this most important original Torah Fifth Commandment of the ONE SINGLE GOD.

That is why the youth of the nations, even today in a somewhat enlightened world, could and would steal, rape, and murder the elderly just as the youth did during all of the crusades, the inquisitions and the pogroms of the past and during the recent Holocaust against the Jews of Europe. It is one of the main reasons today why the hatreds of anti-Semitism are still today flourishing unabated in all of the many Arab and Muslim Nations and also very sadly in the so-called educated and cultured European countries of England, France, Austria, Germany, Poland, and Sweden.

Were the Hitler Youth ever at any time taught this Fifth or any other Commandment? Is that why they were all too willing to humiliate, beat and torture, and murder all Jews and the Jewish elderly? What were they taught of the Ten Commandments in their churches by their German Preachers, Ministers, Pastors and Priests? They were certainly not taught this Fifth Commandment of the ONE SINGLE GOD! Were there then different Commandments that were then taught? It must have been so and maybe these different Commandments are still today being taught to European youth in schools and religious class rooms.

This is also why Arab Imams, Mullahs, and Ayatollahs can today teach, instruct, and instigate Arab children and young men and women to become suicide murder bombers and murder innocent people in total utter defiance of the ONE SINGLE GOD's Fifth Commandment and also the Sixth Commandment not to murder. These murderous attacks do not differentiate against victims according to their age. The Arab Muslim murderers murder men and women, young and old, infants, children and the elderly. They even have without mercy even also murdered fetuses in the bodies of pregnant women they have murdered.

If all of the Muslim Imams, Mullahs, and Ayatollahs had taught and were teaching their Arab students, young and old, to obey this Fifth Commandment and give honor and respect to their parents and to all of the elderly and to also obey the following Sixth Commandment not to murder, they would not teach their students to hate and instigate them to become suicide murdering bombers. By all of their actions, the Muslim Arab youth certainly in the past and now are not taught this Fifth and Sixth Commandment of the ONE SINGLE GOD. Are there different Commandments taught? It would appear so!

It is incumbent upon all of the youth of all races, religions, and nations to always give complete honor and respect to all of their elders who include their parents, grandparents, family members, teachers, and also neighbors and strangers. The young are not to discriminate by giving this honor and respect to only certain older individuals while discriminating against other older individuals. This type of discrimination is certainly not mentioned or allowed in the requirement to fully obey and adhere to this important Fifth Commandment of the ONE SINGLE GOD.

The ONE SINGLE GOD has given to all of the entire human races HIS Fifth Commandment. It was not given only to the Children of Israel. It is incumbent upon all, without any exception, to obey this Fifth Commandment and honor and respect one's parents and the elderly. In fulfilling this Fifth Commandment, the rational for all of man's hatreds and warfares cannot be rationally accepted and religiously upheld.

The duty owed to one's parents is only secondary to the duty owed to the ONE SINGLE GOD. To children, it is the parents who stand visibly before them in place of their ALMIGHTY CREATOR, the unseen ONE SINGLE GOD. Thus, for that important main reason, are children always required to give their full honor and respect to their parents and to all who are their elderly.

Therefore, likewise, it is the duty and obligation for the parents, with full parental responsibility, to teach, educate, and set the required proper example for their children. The parents must direct their children to travel upon the proper path and ways of righteousness, charity and justice and towards the full obedience of all of the Ten Commandments of the ONE SINGLE GOD.

Parents are not to teach their children in any manner to be disobedient of any of the ONE SINGLE GOD's Ten Commandments. They are not to teach their children to treat their elders with disrespect or to murder or to criminally act against the elderly or anyone. For too many generations and even today, there are parents who violate the ONE SINGLE GOD's Ten Commandments by not teaching them to honor and respect their elderly and by instead teaching their children to hate and murder.

Thus Jihad Muslim parents teach their children to murder others. Therefore they do not deserve to be honored as parents since they teach children to violate the ONE SINGLE GOD's Sixth Commandment not to murder.

Even with the passage of all of the time since the ONE SINGLE GOD gave mankind this Fifth Commandment, it remains unchanged and totally applicable for all past, present and future generations and requires the complete obedience, without any exception, by all mankind and members and believers of all religions.

Honor your mother and father and Honor all mothers and fathers and elderly of all Mankind.

And the ONE SINGLE GOD spoke all these words, saying:

COMMANDMENT NUMBER SIX

6. You shall not murder.

This Sixth Commandment is stated very clearly and concisely. In only four words, the ONE SINGLE GOD has declared and stated that we are not to ever commit murder. We are not to criminally take the life of another human. The infinite worth of all of human life is founded and based upon the fact that it is only the ONE SINGLE GOD who creates and gives life and only HE may take it away.

There are circumstances where one human causes the death of another. It is not against the Sixth Commandment to protect one's self or a member of one's family or even a stranger from possible injury or death at the hands of an attacker. Thus it is not murder if the defense results in the death of the one who is the attacker.

It is not murder if one is called to arms to protect his country during a battle or war and this results in the killing of an enemy. However, it is murder to kill an innocent individual or to willfully intend to take the life of a known harmless person who does not present any threat to the killer. Modern day terrorist murder is a sinful violation of the ONE SINGLE GOD's Sixth Commandment **"YOU SHALL NOT MURDER"**.

Man has been given the gift of a soul, by the ONE SINGLE GOD, that has the potential for continued eternal life. But those who violate this Sixth Commandment and commit the crime of murder have also simultaneously murdered their own souls and they will therefore not have an eternal living soul. Nor will their dead souls ever be returned to an eternal life if they murder and then later express a belief in a savior, a priest, or Imam who can save their souls for a living eternity. Only the ONE SINGLE GOD can forgive and there is no forgiveness for the violators of the ONE SINGLE GOD's Sixth Commandment .
During the past two thousand years, anti-Semitic murderers have killed innocent men, women, children, and infants in the name of their Christian religion and their belief in their trinity god. These murders, in violation of the ONE SINGLE GOD's Sixth

Commandment, were made by those who were adherents to the Christian faith.

They took place during the many times when hate was preached from the Vatican, from the church pulpits, during massacres, during the crusades, during the inquisition, and during the multitude of hateful murderous pogroms and more recently during the times and events of the Holocaust when over six million innocent men, women and children, including infants and fetuses, were murdered only because they were Jews.

It should be always remembered that of that six million murdered during the Holocaust, over one and a half million were defenseless innocent Jewish infants and children that were murdered, some with painful torture.

For ages past and even today, the murderers have rampaged through Jewish villages and communities. They have murdered innocent men and children and also raped and murdered women. They have looted and stole all the property that they could and then they went on their merry way. They have murdered whole families and took their housing, possessions, and furnishings. These killers have murdered the innocent and did so with their full understanding and knowledge that they were willfully and criminally violating the Sixth Commandment of the ONE SINGLE GOD. With these murders, the souls of the murderers died and were not and have not been maintained alive for an after life in the eternal World to Come. They would have no forgiveness ever from the ONE SINGLE GOD and certainly none from any so-called savior or messiah.

During the Holocaust, Nazi murderers committed the crime of murder. Then, after murdering innocent men, women and children, some went to churches to pray to their god as if all of their murdering was very acceptable to their god. Some of these Nazi murders took home to their wives and children the clothing, belongings and even children's toys that belonged to their murdered victims. Some of the murderers and their families even wore the clothing of the murdered victims when they went to pray in their churches.

ONE: HIS NAME SHALL BE ONE • 87

Today, many Muslims are incited and instigated to murder Jews and Christians during prayer sessions in their mosques by their religious Imams, Mullahs and Ayatollahs. They are taught in the mosques that it is greatly acceptable to their Allah god to murder innocent men, women and children who are Jewish and Christian and not of the Muslim faith. They are taught that they may murder these "infidels" who are not defined as Moslems but are Jews or Christians. The Sixth Commandment of the ONE SINGLE GOD is thus very willfully and very happily and purposely cast aside, violated, and is therefore not obeyed.

There is no exception to the words of the Sixth Commandment of the ONE SINGLE GOD. No Imam, Mullah, or Ayatollah, or instructor in a Muslim religious school can change this Sixth Commandment that one shall not murder.

Thus, for Christians and Muslims there is no Commandment or Statement by the ONE SINGLE GOD that says to the Christians and Muslims:

You shall not murder unless the crime is committed against a non-believer in the Christian or Muslim faith.

Perhaps there are some who would argue that the Jewish men, women and children are a threat to their religions of Christianity or Islam. Are these Christian and Muslim peoples, both with populations numerously in the billions afraid of the minuscule population of the few millions of Jews who are scattered throughout the lands of the earth? Are they afraid that the Jews will also disobey the Sixth Commandment of the ONE SINGLE GOD and murder all of them? Do they really believe that Jews are capable of doing to them what they have sinfully done and are sinfully still today doing to the Jews?

Are the Arab Muslim murderers, afraid that the Jews would overwhelm and kill all of them? What is their fear? When did the Jews of Spain or Germany pose a threat to their Christian neighbors? When did Jews run savagely wild and ravage countries of Europe of Germany, Poland, Lithuania, Romania, Russia or other nations of Europe or the Twenty-One Arab Nations or over Fifty Five Muslim

Nations of the world murdering their inhabitants in acts of crusades, inquisitions, pogroms, and holocausts or acts of murder by suicide bombers?

When in the past thousands of years, or today, Christians or Muslims have murdered or still murder Jews, in violation of the ONE SINGLE GOD's Sixth Commandment, are they doing so to give honor and obedience to that ONE SINGLE GOD or to honor and give obedience to the gods that they worship that tolerate, encourage, and approve murder?

In these days, we live at a time when certain Muslims can carry out terrorist murders anywhere in the world. They are educated, indoctrinated and encouraged to become murderous terrorists. The Muslim terrorist murderers who carried out the September 11, 2001 carnage attacks that killed many thousands of innocent men, women and children performed their murderous mission because they were very well educated and trained to murder. Did their religious Imams and educators and trainers teach them to obey the ONE SINGLE GOD's Sixth Commandment not to murder?

Why are Muslims now permitted and allowed to murder in England, France, Germany, Belgium, Spain, Netherlands, and Russia? Let us not also forget the genocidal murders of many hundreds of thousands of black African Christians raped, burned alive and slaughtered by Arab Mulim Militias in Darfur.

Terrorist attacks by murderous Muslim Arabs have been carried out in the so-called Holy Land (the Palestine Mandate lands) during the 1920s, 1930s, 1940s and from 1948 until the present days in Israel, for almost ninety years. These murderous attacks took place many decades before the advent, in 1948, of the modern Jewish State of Israel and they still take place almost daily. Todays crimes of murder by Muslims, in spite of the ONE SINGLE GOD's Sixth Commandment, are not new events and these are not sinful crimes that can be excused and blamed as being caused because poor Arabs are suffering from Israeli occupation. These sinful Muslim murder acts of today are continuations of pre-Israel sinful Muslim murder acts. Now additionally, in these present days, these sinful murderous attacks have

ONE: HIS NAME SHALL BE ONE • 89

taken place and are still continually taking place in many lands and countries.

During the mandate years, even before there was a State of Israel for an excuse, with England having the responsibility for the mandate lands, Imams would, during the Friday Muslim sabbath service, stir up the Arabs attending the services directing them to go out into the streets, when they left the Mosques, and murder any and all Jews that they could.

Arabs then madly, wildly, savagely, and angrily stormed out of the Mosques. With whatever weapon they could find, they savagely attacked Jewish men, women and children to injure and murder them. The Imams had preached in the Mosques that it was acceptable to their god to murder Jews and the Arab masses complied with their Imams teachings.

The English who were to maintain law and order in the mandate lands did not attempt to save any of the Jewish victims of the Arabs' murderous violence. They did not stop the Arab murderous attackers. During the years when Jews were being murdered by the Nazi murderers, England purposely did not allow the Jews to escape with their lives to the mandate lands. Instead, they kept the Jews locked out in accordance with their infamous "White Paper", and at the same time, allowed massive migration of Arabs into the mandate lands. In the City of Hebron, where Jews and Arabs resided, the Arabs went crazy, ran amok, and slaughtered 133 Jewish men, women children and infants.

Even today, Arabs claim that Hebron is and always was an Arab city and that Jews never lived there and should not live there today. In places where Jews have returned, as in Hebron, to reclaim their homes and their lands that were criminally stolen from them by the Arab murderers, the Jews are still subject to murderous Arab attacks.

Thousands of murderous Arab missiles and mortar rounds have been fired against Jewish homes. Some have murdered men, women and children. All of these actions are carried out by the Arabs because they listen and believe their Imams who preach Jewish and Christian hatred, violence and the necessity to murder Jews and Christians as being totally required and acceptable by their god. The Arab teachers and Imams certainly do not teach, preach or carry the message to their Arab Muslim followers that all of the Arab Muslims must and should obey the ONE SINGLE GOD's Sixth Commandment:

You Shall Not Murder.

There is no excuse or justification for all of the Islam Arab terrorists who indiscriminately murder other human beings. All men, women, and children, be they Jewish, Christian or Muslim were all created and endowed with life by the ALMIGHTY CREATOR, the ONE SINGLE GOD. Only HE can give life and only HE should be the taker of life. HE has given to all a human life form and, in HIS Image, HE has given to all a soul. Those who violate HIS Sixth Commandment not to murder, and willfully do murder, cause their souls to die. The choice of life or death, for one's soul, is left to each individual human.

There is absolutely no forgiveness of any kind, by the ONE SINGLE GOD, for those who violate HIS Sixth Commandment and, in specific intentional spite of the ONE SINGLE GOD and HIS Sixth Commandment, willfully commit murder. The Arab suicide murderer bombers not only murder themselves bodily in their human form but they also murder their souls. For them there can never ever be forgiveness by the ONE SINGLE GOD.

Those who preach hate and educate and encourage others to perform acts of murder, as some Imams, Mullahs, and Ayatollahs do, also immediately lose their souls. Even though they may not perform the actual act of murder, once they give voice to educate and encourage others to murder, their souls die. For them, there is no eternal life or reward.

There is no eternal life either for those who carry out the act of murder or those who teach, train and instigate others to commit murder. The soul death penalty Judgment of the ONE SINGLE GOD is not directed only against the murderer. It is also directed against the murderer's teacher.

ON TWO MEN AND THREE CHILDREN IN WHEELCHAIRS

A local Imam in the United States, in a message that was supposed to motivate local newspaper readers to have thoughts and feelings of ecumenical peace and brotherly love, compared two men who were handicapped. Both elderly men had been of senior age and had been living their lives with the continuing constant required use of wheelchairs.

The Imams comparison message was generated because of the assassination of one wheelchair user, the Hamas Leader, the Arab Sheikh Ahmed Yassin who had been imprisoned by Israel because of his murderous terrorist activity that had resulted in deaths of Israeli citizens. The Sheikh had been released and given his freedom by the Israelis and he had lived in the Gaza strip territory. As the leader and a founder of the terrorist organization of Hamas the Sheikh continued to send his Hamas murderers to murder Israeli men, women and children. However, the Imam, in his article, emphasized that Sheikh Ahmed Yassin was a very religious spiritual man who was very humane and was doing much good for mankind and certainly did not deserve to be assassinated.

The Imam compared the assassination of the Hamas Sheikh Yassin to the killing of another man in a wheelchair named Leon Klinghoffer. Mr. Klinghoffer was innocently vacationing on board an ocean liner taking a Mediterranean cruise with his wife. He had never harmed or injured anyone. He was taken in his wheelchair to the deck of the liner by several of the Hamas Sheikh's Arab terrorists. The leading Arab Hamas terrorist shot Mr. Klinghoffer. Then the wounded man, together with his wheelchair was thrown overboard into the Mediterranean Sea to drown and die. Mr. Klinghoffer, an American Citizen, was guilty of only one thing, he was Jewish, or maybe a second thing, he was an American.

Mr. Klinghoffer's killer Arab Hamas terrorist had very well understood the many hate messages preached and taught by the assassinated very religious spiritual Hamas Arab Sheikh Yassin. As a good student and well indoctrinated by the Hamas hate messages of Sheikh Yassin, he defied the ONE SINGLE GOD's Commandment and, in obedience to the very spiritual religious Sheikh Yassin, murdered the innocent man in the wheelchair, Leon Klinghoffer.

Sheikh Yassin, as the founder and leader of the murdering terrorist organization, Hamas, preached and stressed the need for all Muslim Arabs to become suicide bomber martyrs and murders of Jewish Israeli men, women and children. He encouraged parents to be thankful and grateful that they were privileged to have children who would willingly blow themselves up in order to murder Jewish Israeli men, women, infants, and young children.

Thus it was that among the very many suicide murderous bombers he sent to murder Jewish Israelis, the Sheikh once sent a suicide bomber to Tel Aviv where the Sheikh's blessed suicide bomber boarded a bus and then blew himself up murdering many men, women and children. Even many more victims were very severely injured. Some were crippled for life.

On that bus, blown up and destroyed by Sheikh Yassin's murderous Hamas Martyr, besides men and women, there were many children who would be bodily blown apart and murdered. Three of the Hamas suicide bomber's innocent victim children, of one family, all had portions of their legs blown off. These three victim children cannot now ever walk as normal human beings with legs. They will now live their entire lives in wheelchairs thanks to Sheikh Yassin.

Ironically, the three children now in wheelchairs live in a village only a very short distance, minutes away, from where the Hamas Sheikh Yassin had lived, preached his sinful and hateful messages against the ONE SINGLE GOD and humanity, and sanctioned and blessed terrorist Hamas terrorist murderers. Thus the Sheikh that was assassinated bore the responsibility for a great many murders and for the very many victims who tragically suffered serious injuries. The Sheikh was responsible for condemning and placing the three innocent children in wheelchairs for the rest of their lives.

The Sheikh forgot that there is a ONE SINGLE GOD that does not condone terrorist murder. HIS, the ONE SINGLE GOD's Sixth Commandment is **"You shall not murder"**. The Hamas Arab Sheikh and Arabs call their One Single God Allah and, by their murderous actions, they must believe that their Allah requires, approves, and condones sinful murder.

The Hamas Sheikh Yassin, having violated the ONE SINGLE GOD's Sixth Commandment, destroyed his soul and is now not having an eternal blessed good life in the Muslim "Heavenly Paradise" filled with virgins. The same destruction and death of their souls awaits all of the other Muslim Arab parents who heeded the evil and villainous words of the Hamas Sheikh and very gladly and proudly allowed their children to sacrificially become murderous suicide bomber murdering martyrs.
The local United States Imam who compared the innocent Leon Klinghoffer to the murderer Hamas Sheikh Yassin was very greatly wrong in his attempted comparison of the two men in wheelchairs. By the comparison the local Imam has shown and revealed that he too would be happy to encourage his Muslim followers and others to become terrorist murderers. Indeed, it may be suspected, by his written message supporting the villainous Hamas Sheikh, that the local Imam is and has been a supporter of the murderous Hamas Muslim Arabs and very likely probably has been a fund raiser and/or contributor to the Arab Hamas Muslim terrorist gang. By his very wrongful and sinful comparison of the two men in the wheelchairs, the Imam has

given proof that he, just as the Hamas Sheikh Yassin, never learned or knew of the Commandment of the ONE SINGLE GOD or his Allah **"You shall not murder"**.

By his very wrongful comparison of the two men in the wheelchairs, the Imam has shown his approval for the Arab Hamas murderously evil men to continue to carry out their suicide bombing murders that cause innocent children to be murdered or very severely injured by having their limbs blown off of their bodies. The local Imam, by his comparison, tells us all and shows that he agrees with the Sheikh's hateful terrorist murder messages and sermons that resulted in the three children having portions of their legs blown off and their having to spend all of the rest of their lives painfully in wheelchairs.

ON HUMAN SACRIFICE:
THE MURDER OF CHILDREN

Everyday, in the prayer book, one can read of the "Sacrifice of Isaac". Abraham, the father of the Mother Jewish religion, and the supposed "father" of the Daughter Christian, and Moslem religions, was the first to establish the thoughts and principals of monotheism. Abraham established the recognition and belief in the ONE SINGLE GOD. We are told in the Jewish Torah (Bible) that Abraham is ordered by his only ONE SINGLE GOD to sacrificially murder his son Isaac.

This is the son that, according to the Jewish Torah, Abraham and his wife Sarah have long prayed for because they were childless. Now, at their very old ages, and with Abraham and Sarah finally having a child, Abraham is commanded by his ONE SINGLE GOD to murder his son Isaac as a sacrifice to his ONE SINGLE GOD.

Abraham believed with full faith in the Words and Command of the ONE SINGLE GOD. He commenced to comply. Abraham took his son Isaac to the place, now located on the Temple Mount in the old walled City of Jerusalem, where he was to murder and sacrifice his son to the ONE SINGLE GOD. He raised his knife to obey the ONE SINGLE GOD to murder and sacrifice his son Isaac. But then Abraham was told by the ONE SINGLE GOD that he was not to murder and sacrifice his son.

Why was it necessary for the ONE SINGLE GOD to command Abraham to murder his son and then why did the ONE SINGLE GOD command him not to murder and sacrifice his son? What important message was the ONE SINGLE GOD sending to all of his human creatures? What are we to learn from the message contained in "the sacrifice of Isaac?"

At the time Abraham was commanded by the ONE SINGLE GOD to murder and sacrifice his son, the entire world of mankind was basically very ignorant and illiterate and worshipped many pagan gods and idols. Human sacrifice murdering, of children by their parents, was practiced by these pagans peoples of many tribes and nations.

For many pagans, the belief was that by murdering and sacrificing a child to their pagan gods, these same gods would be very pleased with the sacrifice and the parents would therefore be greatly blessed by the pagan gods with a good life and they would also be rewarded by having many more replacement children.

The lesson Abraham learned, the lesson that is written in the Torah for all mankind for all time is that it is a very wrongful sin against the ONE SINGLE GOD to murder and sacrifice one's own child or children or engage in any human sacrifice or any human murder. The Commandment of the ONE SINGLE GOD that **"You Shall Not Murder"** pertains greatly and strongly also to the murderous sacrificing of one's own child. Thus the ONE SINGLE GOD taught this lesson to all of mankind through the lesson HE taught to Abraham.

Today, it is believed by all too many that it is not wrong or sinful to murder and kill any human beings even if it involves the sacrifice murder of one's own child. Arab Muslim parents believe it is very totally and wonderfully acceptable to their Allah God, and is a great blessing and an event of shear joyous happiness, for one to murder and sacrifice one's own child or children in the name of their religion and Allah god. It is therefore most acceptable to strap a suicide bomb belt on the child and send the child forward to commit the crime of murder.It is religiously highly commendable and acceptable to have the child then kill himself or herself and also kill and murder as many other humans as possible. Then the child, as a divine and holy martyr, will go to the wonderful Muslim "heavenly paradise" and be able there to be rewarded and allowed to sexually feast on a multitude of virgins. If the suicide child murderer is a girl does she also enjoy 72 virgins?

It is strange that the Muslims deny the Torah version of the disallowed murder sacrifice of Isaac by Abraham. This was a deed recorded thousands of years before any thought, record or the advent Islam and the Koran, the Muslim Bible. According to the much later dated Koran, Abraham was really a Muslim all the time and not a Hebrew and Abraham, according to the Koran, was commanded by Allah to murder and sacrifice his son Ishmael, the son of Sarah's handmaiden, Hagar and not the Hebrew child, Isaac.

Abraham "the Muslim" proceeded to fulfill the command to murder and sacrifice Ishmael but was stopped by Allah's command not to murder and sacrifice his son Ishmael. But, apparently, by the Muslim version, the message not to murder and kill one's own child was not meant to stop or prevent todays Muslim parents from sending their child to a known suicidal death in order to assure the murdering and killing of other human beings, who had been created and given life by the ONE SINGLE GOD, since they were, by Muslim standards, not humans and were infidels to be murdered.

The ONE SINGLE GOD's unchangeable Sixth Command **"You shall not Murder"** was not given to all mankind except those of the Muslim faith who would thereafter be allowed to murder infidels. However, there is no such an exception for Muslims to this Sixth Commandment. The lesson given by the ONE SINGLE GOD, that one is not to murder and sacrifice one's own children, was not given to all mankind but with an exception that was made for all of those observing the Muslim faith who would be allowed to murder and sacrifice their children.

That being so, then why have there been so many Muslims who have been involved in the murder and sacrifice of their children today? Has Allah changed and now become desirous for human murder sacrifice? Is that what the Imams now teach as being stated in the Koran by their

One Single God? Is that what the Imams now preach as being the real religious Allah message and commandment that is to be obeyed by all Muslims ?

The reason today for the sacrificial suicide murder of children is that Imams now preach that it is totally acceptable to sacrifice murder children as long as the children kill and murder others who may believe in the ONE SINGLE GOD but not be Muslims. Thus the parents, followers of these Imams, send their children forth to commit self sacrificing suicide murder in order to murder many other humans. They believe the sinful preaching of murder from Imams who have strayed away from the Commandment of the ONE SINGLE GOD not to murder and sacrifice one's own child and the ONE SINGLE GOD's Sixth Commandment that **"You Shall Not Murder"**.

Today, in an enlightened world of the increased knowledge of mankind, a world of numerous universities and institutions of higher knowledge, at a time when mankind has greater literacy, scientific, and technical intelligence than in previous generations, why is it that so very many are willing to accept the idea that human sacrifice murder of one's own child is permissible and desirable by the ONE SINGLE GOD?

By today's actions of Muslim parents, as encouraged by Muslim Imam priests, their Allah God has changed the commandments. It is now a very great blessing that is bestowed upon the parents if they allow and condone the human sacrificial murdering of their children. And the blessing becomes even greater if the child becomes a suicide bomber martyr and successfully murders and seriously cripples and maims a great number of any other human beings. They also now have a new revised commandment from their One Single God Allah that it is most acceptable, good, and a blessed event, to murder since one is, by their revised commandment, allowed and ordered to murder all Christian and Jewish "infidels".

Those Muslim Imams who preach and encourage child murder sacrifices, as suicide bombers and killers, have condemned their own souls and the souls of their child murder sacrificed suicide bombers to death and not to any blessed good life in the Muslim "heavenly paradise". The same immediate death of their souls awaits the parents who very proudly and very happily allow their children to sacrificially become murderous suicide bomber killers and then very joyfully and happily celebrate their child's wonderful act of murderous suicide.

Those who teach and preach murder may be bodily alive but their souls are dead. Their souls instantly died when they uttered the first words of their murderous teachings and preaching. In their disobedience and defiance, of the ONE SINGLE GOD's Sixth Commandment not to Murder, they are even more guilty than the murderers they send forth to murder.

It is the very utmost inexcusable sinful crime,

to defy and take action in opposition and against

the significantly clearly stated and expressed

Sixth Commandment of the ONE SINGLE GOD,

and murderously sacrifice one's own child

in order to have and cause the child to become a sinful murderer.

All must read, reread and again reread, study, restudy and again restudy the Torah concerning the ONE SINGLE GOD's Message and Commandment given to and for all of mankind as related to the events of the "Binding and Sacrifice of Isaac" stated in the Book of Genesis in the original bible, the Torah. Also, read, reread and study, restudy and again restudy the ONE SINGLE GOD's Sixth Commandment **"You Shall Not Murder"** stated in the Book of Exodus.

THE PARABLE OF THE FOUR SOULS

Four men were called away from their lives on earth and their souls were brought to the Gates of the World Beyond. At the entrance to the First Gate, there stood an Angel waiting for them and blocking the entrance. The four souls approached the Gate and the Angel stood in their path and blocked their entrance.

The Angel greeting them and said, "I was waiting for your arrival. Each of you will identify yourselves and answer one question that I will ask. Then, you may possibly pass through this First Gate and then go to the Second Gate that opens for the entrance into the Paradise of the World Beyond." If you fail to pass through the two Gates your soul will die and there will be no eternal life for you. The first soul identified himself. "I am Abdul Muhammad."

"Abdul Muhammad", asked the Angel, "do you believe in God? Do you worship and pray only to the ALMIGHTY CREATOR?"

"I am a religious Muslim and accordingly I only believe in the One Single God, whom I respectfully call Allah. As a Muslim, it is only to Him that I worship and pray. I also firmly believe in his supreme prophet Mohammed. I do not of course worship the prophet and I only worship and direct my prayers only to none other than the One Single God Allah."

"Abdul Muhammad, you may pass me and enter through this First Gate and then go to the Second Gate of entrance to the World Beyond", said the Angel.

The second soul identified himself. "I am Julius Kohen."

"Julius Kohen", asked the Angel. "do you believe in GOD? Do you worship and pray only to the ALMIGHTY CREATOR?"

"I believe in the ONE SINGLE GOD. HIS name I do not know and will I not state a name lest I say the name in vain. Only to HIM do I worship and pray. Though I believe in the great teacher Moses, I do not worship the great teacher and I worship and pray only to the ONE SINGLE GOD, the ALMIGHTY CREATOR."

"Julius Kohen, you may pass me and enter through the First Gate and then go to the Second Gate of entrance to the World Beyond", said the Angel.

The third soul identified himself. "I am John Doe." "John Doe", asked the Angel, "do you believe in God? Do you worship and pray only to the ALMIGHTY CREATOR?"

"I believe in the Almighty Creator and I also believe in his son Jesus as a good Christian should. I worship and pray to the Almighty Creator and I worship and pray to his son. I also direct my prayers to holy saints and to the mother of god."

"John Doe," replied the Angel, "the Gates to the World Beyond are closed to you."

"But", the surprised and shocked John Doe questioned, "why is this Gate open to Abdul and Julius but not for me? I am a good Christian and they are not."

"They", answered the Angel, "know that the ALMIGHTY CREATOR is ONE SINGLE GOD who needs no assistants. GOD knows all and does all and does not need other beings to intercede for HIM with HIS creations and creatures.

Do you, John Doe, really believe that the ALMIGHTY CREATOR needs help from other beings that HE created? You have stated your belief and it denounces and is contrary to the essence of the ONE SINGLE ALMIGHTY CREATOR There is therefore no place for you in the World Beyond."

"Does that mean", asked John Doe, "that no good Christian can ever enter into heaven?"

The Angel answered, "All good men of all religions can enter if they are deserving. Those who have been good Christians can enter. They enter not as Christians but as those whose lives have been conducted on the basis of their love and friendship for all other of mankind even if these others were not also Christian. The righteous of all mankind, even Christians, shall always be allowed entrance. Then they will be here reeducated into recognition that there is only ONE SINGLE GOD."

"But", continued the Angel., "you, John Doe, have too many times expressed your despicable hatreds of various diverse people. You have violently expressed hatred of Jews and those you called Blacks. Not your religious belief, but rather, your own actions, thoughts and expressions have resulted in the closing of this Gate for you. There will be no eternal life for your soul in the World Beyond."

The Angel further continued, "On the contrary side, your own brother, George Doe, passed through this First Gate when he arrived here. He was a good Christian man and never thought or held any hatred towards any man. In his own way, he constantly tried to obey what he believed to be every one of the ONE SINGLE GOD's Commandments. He was deemed to be very righteous and deserving of entrance and given the opportunity of heavenly reeducation into recognizing and acknowledging the true belief in the ONE SINGLE GOD, the ALMIGHTY CREATOR. The soul of your brother will live on in the World Beyond. Your brother George lived a life of kindness and justice and he was a very good and honest man and a very righteous Christian and so he can pass through the gates with his living eternal soul."
"But," said John Doe, "my brother George believes as I do in the holy god and his son Jesus."

"Yes," replied the Angel, "however your brother by his own free will acts was a very righteous Christian and was, as a result, allowed to pass through these gates and enter the World Beyond and have his soul live eternally on."

"But because of your evil conduct all of your life, with all of your violently expressed hatreds, you, John Doe, cannot pass through this First Gate and enter and your soul will die."

The Angel allowed the souls of Abdul Muhammad and Julius Kohen to then proceed through the First Gate and he directed them towards the Second Gate There a second Angel stood waiting and greeted them.

The second Angel said, "this is the Second Gate to the Paradise of the World Beyond. I will ask you one question. Your answer, if true, will allow you to pass through this Gate. Tell me that you have understood and always lived your lives completely in accordance with the ALMIGHTY CREATOR's Ten Commandments."

Abdul Muhammad was first to answer. "I have always lived a righteous life and obeyed the laws and commandments of my One Single God, Allah. I have been virtuous in my life and charitable. I have always followed the entire beliefs and its truths as stated in the holy Koran. I should therefore be allowed to enter through this Gate and live my eternal life in the Paradise with my justly earned rewards including all of the 72 Virgins for love and pleasure."

"I have kept the Muslim faith. I have fought for all of the principals of Allah. I have battled to destroy and kill the infidels who are his enemies. I am here standing before you because I was a martyr and killed the infidels by sacrificing myself as a suicide bomber. Glory be to Allah and I am glad I died acting in his behalf."

The Angel listened to Abdul and then replied, " Abdul, the Gate is forever closed to you. You will not be allowed entrance into the Paradise of the World Beyond. Yes, you followed the instigations, instructions and teachings you received from all of those who taught you not only the Koran but also taught and instructed you on how to become a suicide murderer bomber. Because of your willful act of murder and your disobedience of the ONE SINGLE GOD's Sixth Commandment, YOU SHALL NOT MURDER, this Gate is closed to you."

"Accordingly", continued the Angel. "you are not a righteous Muslim person. You have hated and murdered. You are here before me because of your death that you yourself willfully caused when you detonated the suicide bomb belt you were wearing. By your action, you committed murder and killed eight men and women and fourteen infants and children who were on the bus. Twenty One men, women and children were very seriously injured with most suffering the loss of a limb, or hearing or sight. You murdered and injured innocent people because they were Jewish and you were taught to hate Jews. You were not in any manner a righteous man deserving to enter the World Beyond you call Paradise. You cannot enter. Your soul will die."

The Angel continued, "It is the ONE SINGLE GOD's Commandment that YOU SHALL NOT MURDER. But you did murder. You also previously coveted and engaged in theft stealing land and possessions belonging to Jews. You also have thus disobeyed two other Commandments of the ONE SINGLE GOD that YOU SHALL NOT STEAL and YOU SHALL NOT COVET WHAT IS YOUR NEIGHBORS. Abdul, your soul is now dying."

The Second Angel then directed his attention to Julius Kohen and asked, "Did you obey all of the Commandments of the ONE SINGLE GOD?"

Julius Kohen then answered the Angel. "I have tried all my life to follow and obey the exact words of each of the Ten Commandments."

"Unlike Abdul, I have never acted in any manner to injure a neighbor even if the neighbor was not only unfriendly but was also not of my family, friends, or faith. I have not coveted and wanted anything that was not mine. It was not always easy and I some times faced hatreds and discriminations directed at me, but I have worked very hard to earn the daily food and provide for the needs and shelter that my family required."

ONE: HIS NAME SHALL BE ONE • 107

"I am here only because I happened to sit on the bus next to Abdul. When a Young women with an infant in her arms came aboard, I saw the difficulty the woman was having with the infant and I yielded my seat to them and stood in the aisle next to them.

It is now very tragic for me to now hear that she and her infant and so many other people, men, women, children and other infants were tragically murdered as I was by Abdul when he detonated his suicide bomb. I pray to the ONE SINGLE GOD that all of them were already here at these gates ahead of me and that entrance was approved for all of them. I also pray that all who were seriously injured can and will recover without having to live the rest of their lives in agony and pain with forever broken and injured bodies all because of the evil and sinful action of Abdul."

Julius Kohen continued, "All of the ONE SINGLE GOD's Ten Commandments are simple and very easy to comprehend, understand, and follow. I tried my very best to fully obey each Commandment. Unlike the murderer, Abdul, I know and have always believed that there can be no rational reason whatsoever for anyone to murder and cause bodily injury to others or to wrongfully steal from another. I could never understand why poisonous hate had to be taught to instruct, cause and instigate other men to ruthlessly murder others. I could never understand why Arabs like Abdul, who have been blessed by the ONE SINGLE GOD to have more than Twenty Countries and more land than any other of the world's people would still want more land and covet to steal the only One small land promised by the ONE SINGLE GOD to the Children of Israel, the Jewish people. It is this evil wanting and coveting and the resultant very sinful action of murder that has caused my early death that will tragically effect my family, my wife and young children. I would want them to have good long healthy lives obeying the Commandments of the ONE SINGLE GOD."

The Angel listened to all of the words of Julius Kohen and then allowed Julius to pass beyond him and go through the Second Gate and enter the World Beyond. The soul of Abdul perished.

And the ONE SINGLE GOD spoke all these words, saying:
COMMANDMENT NUMBER SEVEN

7. You shall not commit adultery.

This Seventh Commandment of the ONE SINGLE GOD is very direct, clear, and explicit. The Torah (Bible) relates that the ONE SINGLE GOD mandated and directed that an ascertainable sexual morality be observed and maintained by both men and women. The sexual conduct of all mankind is governed and is to be always maintained by the strict moral and ethical law and code of the ONE SINGLE GOD.

The created and stated purpose of having humans in both male or female forms is to procreate children for all of the future generations. Sexual activity is not meant to mainly provide nothing except sexual pleasure. Since sexual activity is the normal recognized means, to procreate children for the next generation, it is necessary and requires that each individual live a sexually moral life. The means to provide children also requires and provides that the parents, the father and mother, should be responsible to lead sexually moral proper lives. This includes proper and moral actions when it is necessary to provide other than normal means of sexual procreation such as by man established artificial infertilization.

In the very beginning, the ONE SINGLE GOD first created only the man, Adam. Then, the ONE SINGLE GOD later created the woman, Eve, as the man's companion and mate. Adam and Eve were the first couple and the first parents of children.

When time and generations passed, and there were more men and women, the aspects of companionship and mating changed. Men often then had more than one female companion and mate. They some times took to themselves several wives and some also in addition had concubines. Today this polygamous practice has been and is almost eliminated in most modern societies.

The now accepted status, practice, and law in most societies is to have lawful marriage only between one man and one women.

Polygamy, the state of multiple marriages, that is marriages to more than one spouse, is not generally accepted any more and is against the law in most societies. However, in some societies, as for example notably within the Muslim society, even today, men may have more than one wife and the polygamy is approved by their society and legally allowed.

In most communities and societies, there have been times when sexual behavior, included brazen and open acts of prostitution and adultery, have been allowed. Today however, in almost all communities and societies, prostitution and adultery are not accepted as proper and lawful sexual behavior.

Those who practice immoral acts have been responsible for the spreading of various sexually transmitted diseases. These diseases have plagued mankind even before and since the destruction of Sodom and Gomorrah by the ONE SINGLE GOD.

Even today, these sexually transmitted diseases, along with the new and recent AIDS and HIV disease, have punished mankind for all of the homosexual immorality and prostitution still practiced and performed in defiance of the admonition of the ONE SINGLE GOD who stated that these sexual deviations and practices are declared by HIM to be abominations.

The Torah records the destruction, by the ONE SINGLE GOD, of the cities and all their inhabitants of Sodom and Gomorrah. These cities were rife with open acts of sexual improprieties, perversions, homosexuality, prostitution and adultery. Sexual activity, in those cities, became a full time game to be played for pleasure without any other recourse to proper marital living and behavior.

There is no morality in engaging in sexual activity that violates the Commandment and the instruction of the ONE SINGLE GOD. In the first book of the Torah, the book called "Genesis", we are informed of the ONE SINGLE GOD's destruction of the cities of Sodom and Gomorrah. In these cities, mankind did not have an ethical and moral life standing. The inhabitants of the cities practiced all sorts of sexual deviations including sodomy, same sex sexual activities, orgies and unions. They also practiced adultery where the adulterous acts were for their sexual pleasure.

The Torah also states that the ONE SINGLE GOD admonished and declared to the Children of Israel, and through them, admonished and declared to all mankind that certain sexual practices were sinful abominations. Thus men were not to have sexual relations with other men and thus women were not to have sexual relations with other women. Modernly, many free thinkers, if we believe they are capable and can clearly and correctly think, accept homosexuality as being a preferred and an accepted way of living. This is definitely in the absolute and complete defiance of the words of the ONE SINGLE GOD who has declared these acts as being very sinful abominations.

The Torah mentions the marriages of men and women. It does not condone or approve of unethical and immoral sexual activity and this includes adultery and homosexuality. The words of the ONE SINGLE GOD, in the Torah, regarding homosexuality are as follows:

I AM THE LORD YOUR ONE SINGLE GOD.

You shall keep My Statutes and Ordinances.

You shall not lie carnally with your neighbor's wife to defile yourself with her.

You shall not lie with mankind as with womankind, for it is an abomination.

You shall not lie with any beast to defile yourself with the beast, it is a sinful perversion.

Do not defile yourself in any of these sinful things.

You shall therefore keep all of My Statutes and Ordinances

and shall not do or Perform any of these abominations.

For whosoever shall do or perform any of these sinful *abominations,* their souls shall be cut off from among their people.

I AM THE LORD YOUR ONE SINGLE GOD.

The Seventh Commandment of the ONE SINGLE GOD reminds and admonishes mankind to lead proper sexual lives and maintain the sacred status of marriage. It requires a prohibition against immoral attitudes, speech, conduct, associations and practices that profane the sacred standing of marriage.

There are not too many words that are used to express this Seventh Commandment. There is not much to misunderstand or to not be capable of complete comprehension or understanding. Those individuals who cannot "understand" or do not want to "understand" are merely setting aside the words and not complying with this Seventh Commandment of the ONE SINGLE GOD. They can offer many excuses for their willful sinful sexual behavior. But the excuses do not correct or result in approval for their adverse sinful sexual actions.

Today, homosexuality is practiced openly. Instead of remaining private in their sinful sexual activities, Homosexuals openly practice their activities labeled in the bibles of religions as being abominations. Homosexuals declare their right to be "married" and have all of the benefits society has recognized and provided for normal married heterosexual couples and their families. They can and very brazenly do declare their way of homosexual life style should be completely recognized and fully accepted. They proudly denounce, act, and make openly known their complete aversion and total willful non-recognition and non-compliance of the ONE SINGLE GOD's Seventh Commandment.

The homosexuals do not pay attention to the Commandment words of the ONE SINGLE GOD that are not heeded. Their sinful sexual actions are continued to be made and performed in defiance of HIS Words that very clearly tell all that it is an abomination for any man to have homosexual relationships with other men or women to have homosexual relationships with other women.

There is not any valid reason that can lead to the total acceptance and to the recognition that these sexual deviations are acceptable actions. They are not approved by the ONE SINGLE GOD for any means that may be given as a reason or an excuse. Without any exception, all are to obey the Seventh Commandment of the ONE SINGLE GOD.

And the ONE SINGLE GOD spoke all these words, saying:

COMMANDMENT NUMBER EIGHT

    8.   **You shall not steal.**

Men and women are allowed to work each day of the week except upon the ONE SINGLE GOD's chosen Seventh Day, the Sabbath Day, and except upon certain Holydays stated in the Torah (Bible). Thus, on six days of the week, for their honest labors and honest efforts and work, they can merit and earn their livings for themselves and for their families.

Through honest labor and means, they can acquire and accumulate various possessions, properties and necessities for life including food, housing, and all of the other required objects, items, and other miscellaneous materials. These items belong to the individuals who have honestly worked and earned them. Property ownership must always be based upon honest acquisition. One must not take or acquire any possessions and property of any kind through other than honest means.

The Eighth Commandment of the ONE SINGLE GOD states that one may not wrongfully or aggressively take possession of another person's property especially without permission. One is not to steal and therefore one is also prohibited from any wrongful taking of possession of some one else's property of any kind by any means including trickery, deception, robbery, theft, embezzlement, fraud, and forgery.

To obtain possession of property, one must always engage in an honest purchase, barter or trade, or by performing honest work in order to acquire another person's material possessions. By this Eighth Commandment of the ONE SINGLE GOD, one cannot take or acquire another's property by taking wrongful possession, cheating, swindling, embezzling, or knowingly and falsely giving insufficient, counterfeit, fake, or fraudulent or false kind or measure of payment, or by robbing and stealing.

Those who are engaged in business transactions should not in any way, form, act, or manner violate this Eighth Commandment of the ONE SINGLE GOD by false and criminal means including theft and stealing. It is also theft and stealing for a seller to knowingly take advantage of another as seller and over charge anyone for an item or to charge usurious interest rates upon any commercial, business, and lending transactions.

Similarly, it is a theft and stealing, for a purchaser to knowingly and falsely make an underpayment for an item when the purchaser takes a knowing advantage of an error of a seller. This can happen when the purchaser knows that the price stated for the item is very wrong and perhaps accidentally marked mistakenly on the item as the selling price or charged erroneously by an employee of the seller. This is not an honest purchase and does not result in an honest acquisition and possession of the item by the purchaser. It is a violation of the Eighth Commandment and is a theft and stealing.

Care must be taken and observed in business practices since some transactions, which may be questionably lawfully allowed under man's laws, may also violate the ONE SINGLE GOD's Eighth Commandment. All those who are engaged in business transactions of any kind or form must always keep their actions completely honest and not ever in violation of the Eighth Commandment.

Thus one cannot in any manner take advantage of another's illness, or lack of knowledge and understanding, or simple mind and poor mental capacity, in order to acquire the possessions of those who are physically or mentally disadvantaged.

Nor should anyone take advantage of the poor, the ill, the handicapped, or those in need, in order to take another persons possessions since this results in actions that are also the exact equivalent to a very sinful stealing and a theft. One should always take special concern and care to always deal completely honestly in all affairs and transactions made with those who are known to be either physically or mentally handicapped or sick and disabled.

An employer must always do justice when dealing with the employee. This mandates the requirement that the employer must fairly make full payment of earned wages to the employee for the work and efforts of the employee. Doing less would be tantamount to a wrongful taking, theft, and stealing from the employee as would providing an unsafe work place.

One's possessions must only be acquired in all methods, manners and ways of complete honesty. This is achieved by honest work performance whether this work is accomplished for an employer who must pay an honest work salary or by the honest labors of those who are self employed. One can also acquire possessions by means of honest and deserving inheritance.

Some can legally and properly acquire possessions and property by mental rather than physical effort and activity. This includes the works of artisans, writers, inventors, designers, and others who earn their livelihoods through study, mental, inventive, and artistic ability and often by providing community enhancing efforts, services and products.

A man that owns a possession, honestly and justly acquired, should be allowed to retain that possession without having it wrongfully being taken away from him by any other individual or by any governmental actions.

However, Governments do have a right and an obligation to acquire assets through proper, necessary, legal and just means, including taxation, where the financial or other asset taken is needed and will be used to provide for the true and just welfare and benefit of all of the people of the community or nation.

But governments do not have the right to unjustly and illegally take individually owned property for this is tantamount to stealing and is against the Eighth Commandment of the ONE SINGLE GOD. Those who rule and govern must do so in a manner that fulfills the entire Eighth Commandment not to steal while they rule.

The Courts of Law must be properly administered to assure that theft is not allowed under the subterfuge of any so-called legal action or process. In many nations, the Courts of Law have been dishonest organizations created by men to not accomplish just and honest means to take or acquire a person's property or possessions. Some Courts of Law have not been lawful and just and have operated only for the benefit of thieving government officials.

These dishonest Courts have wrongfully sentenced a person to prison or even condemned the person to suffer execution in order to seize and take that persons possessions and property. The leaders of the nations that allow their Courts to thus steal and wrongfully and illegally take away the property and possessions of innocent persons are violating the Eighth Commandment of the ONE SINGLE GOD.

Thus the Spanish Inquisition was a very notorious sinfully wrong example of the illegal actions and thefts made by the Spanish Kingdom's ruler's with the total connivance and approval of the Catholic Churches religious leaders. This stealing and theft was performed with the full Papal Orders of approval and also with the approvals of the Spanish Kingdom's Courts of Law. Thus the Spanish inquisition was really an action engaged in the stealing and acquisition of the property of the Jews who then, prior to 1492, had honestly and peacefully resided in Spain with their Spanish neighbors.

The Spanish Inquisition was criminal in every aspect and was a great major very sinful act undertaken in the absolute, and fully known, violation of the Eighth Commandment of the ONE SINGLE GOD. The most sinful part of the Inquisition was that it was supposedly accomplished in the name of and for the benefit of The Spanish Rulers' trinity of gods. This Eighth Commandment violation was also coupled to the important very sinful and criminal violation of the ONE SINGLE GOD's Sixth Commandment that **"You shall not murder"** since all too often the innocent victims of the theft were brutally tortured and then murdered.

Governments and religious organizations have historically silenced the objections and cries of the victims of governmental theft and dishonest takings accomplishing by the murder of the innocent victims. Thus stealing in violation of the ONE SINGLE GOD's Eighth Commandment and Sixth Commandment was continuously accomplished under the approval of the Papal Order of the Inquisition that lasted for almost four hundred years from 1492 until the Nineteenth Century and was tantamount and similar to what later was called the Holocaust of the Twentieth Century. In two aspects, the inquisition was worst than the Holocaust of the twentieth Century since the sinful murders lasted for the longer period of the many centuries and was condoned and approved by the Catholic Church.

The Inquisition, initiated in 1492 by the Spanish Kingdom, followed the refugee Jews from Spain into the Spanish and Portuguese lands and countries established in the newly discovered world of the Americas. Wherever the Spanish and Portuguese flag was planted on the soils of the New World the torturous and murderous Inquisition followed. This enabled the continuation of wrongful theft of property and murder that lasted many times longer in years than the years of the hateful sinful murderous Holocaust.

These inquisition actions were no different than the later multitude of actions of the theft, taken, with the full approval of the German Courts of Law, during the period, from 1932 until 1945, by the Nazi Government. Jewish property and possessions were stolen and taken under the laws promulgated by the Nazis. The laws of "legal theft" were upheld and enforced by their so-called Courts of Law. Again, just as during the Spanish Inquisition, the German Nazis, by murdering and stealing, were guilty of willfully and intentionally disobeying and violating the ONE SINGLE GOD's Sixth and Eighth Commandments.

There are other kinds of very serious stealing and theft. One very notable example is the kidnapping of a young child who was taken away from his parents under the Papal Order and Court Law of the Catholic Church. This is presented herein in the writing about the Papal approved kidnapping of the Jewish child, Edgar Mortara.

It is the most serious and sinful violation of the Eighth Commandment of the ONE SINGLE GOD to steal a person. This is a greater sinful violation of the ONE SINGLE GOD's Commandment than the mere stealing of another's wealth or property or other material possessions. It is the stealing of a life. There is absolutely no forgiveness of any kind by the ONE SINGLE GOD for the sinful stealing away and kidnapping of a person. Today, these actions of stealing and kidnapping are all too often tragically accomplished by those who claim a belief in the Muslim One Single God.

Today, in many Muslim countries, those considered infidels, Christians and Jews, are often stolen away and kidnapped. In all too many times, as happened in the Islamic Arab state of Iraq, the person stolen away and kidnapped may never be heard from again. This is what has been occurring in Iraq as those kidnapped have been beheaded by murderers.

Again, the Two Commandments of the ONE SINGLE GOD, Commandments Six and Eight are sinfully intentionally violated. As for the kidnap murderers, their souls die when they perform their kidnapping and murderous acts. There is no life in the World to Come for their souls after death of their bodies. The ONE SINGLE GOD does not condone, in any way or manor, the intentional violations of HIS Commandments, HIS Eighth Commandment not to steal or kidnap and HIS Sixth Commandment not to murder.

Thus one should never intentionally and knowingly take an item or object that is not one's own. One should always respect your neighbor's property for it belongs to your neighbor and is not yours. Do not take your neighbor's possessions. Just as you shall not ever kidnap and steal away your neighbor, his wife, or children, from his family, loved ones and community, you shall not kidnap and steal away any person. For these actions are very serious sinful and unforgivable violations of the Eighth Commandment of the ONE SINGLE GOD.

Again, the Eighth Commandment is simply and clearly stated and one does not need an explanatory dictionary or great level of intelligence to know that it is very wrong to steal. The few Words of the ONE SINGLE GOD are very easily understood. However, all too often even business Moguls with brilliant minds find it very easy to connive and steal.

THE SINFUL KIDNAPPING OF EDGAR MORTARA

The continuing stubborn insistence of the Jews, with their maintenance of their unique Jewish religious belief in the ONE SINGLE GOD and their religious observances, never failed to arouse fear and distrust among Christians who were still inclined to look upon all of the Jews as deniers of the true faith.

This attitude was reflected sharply and deeply in the Edgar Mortara criminal kidnapping case of 1858. This kidnapping served as a basis and foundation for the very evil and hateful actions later to take place during the Holocaust when over one and a half million Jewish infants and young children were taken from their Jewish parents and brutally tortured and murdered. Recently it has been revealed that by Papal order, the few Jewish children who were sheltered from Nazi murder and hidden in Catholic Churches and convents were not to be returned to their Jewish parents if the parents survived the Nazi death camps and came to claim their children. These children were to be held as the property belonging to the Catholic Church.

In retrospect, the case concerning the Jewish child, Edgar Mortara, born in Bologna, Italy was an action and event that ultimately resulted in the Holocaust actions against Jewish children. The Jewish Mortara family, believers in the existence of the ONE SINGLE GOD, lived in

Bologna which was then under the Papal jurisdiction. At the age of one, the infant, Edgar Mortara, became seriously very ill. His family had hired a Catholic nurse to care for him, and without consulting or obtaining permission from Edgar Mortara's Jewish parents, the nurse had him secretly baptized in her Catholic belief that otherwise he would die a heathen.

For several years, the Catholic nurse kept the unauthorized baptism her quiet secret. Finally, however, during a "confessional" she revealed her secret to a Priest who reported the information to the Catholic Holy Office. When informed of the baptismal, Pope Pius IX stated and maintained, that since the baptismal sacrament had been thus administered, Jewish Edgar Mortara no longer was Jewish and did not belong any longer to his Jewish parents but now was a Catholic and belonged to the Catholic Church.

By a Papal order approved and issued by Pope Pius IX's Holy Office of the Inquisition in Rome, on June 23, 1858, the then six year old Jewish child, Edgar Mortara, taken and torn out of the arms of his Jewish parents by the very brutal criminal and sinful actions of a troop of Papal soldiers. The Jewish child was stolen away, sinfully kidnapped, and placed in a convent, never, never again to be with his Jewish parents and to be brought up as a Catholic

Pope Pius IX's kidnapping actions very shamefully and very disgustedly stained and marked his period of Catholic Church rule.

There was great outrage that made men everywhere throughout the world wonder if the illiterate Dark ages had really ever come to an end. It was the start of what would later, in the next century, become the Holocaust phase of the seizures, kidnapping, and murders of the over one and a half million Jewish infants and children.

The Papal authorities determined that the Jewish Edgar Mortara, no longer, since baptized, a Jew, was to be educated as a Catholic Christian and granted all of the privileges of Christian citizenship. Despite great pressures exerted and placed upon Pope Pius IX by most foreign governments, including Catholic ones, all of the pleas and requests, that the criminally and sinfully kidnapped Jewish child be returned to his Jewish parents and their belief in the ONE SINGLE GOD, were sinfully rejected.

All efforts of Edgar Mortara's saddened Jewish parents to recover their stolen kidnapped son were completely futile. All of multitude of voices and outcries, from all of the shocked and concerned people, Christian and Jewish, everywhere remained purposely deafly unheard and very sadly unanswered. Despite all humanitarian pleadings and efforts, the Pope sinfully and strongly rejected all requests to restore the wrongfully and sinfully kidnapped Jewish child to his grieving Jewish parents.

News of the sinful criminal kidnapping abduction of Edgar Mortara by Pope Pius IX spread throughout the world. The Mortara criminal kidnap case created a great world wide concern and sensation. In every land where Jews resided they voiced appeals to their governments for any and all diplomatic aid, actions, and efforts to obtain the immediate release of the sinfully kidnapped child, Edgar Mortara, and his return to his grieving parents.

Even the Catholic sovereigns, Napoleon III, Emperor of France, and Emperor Francis Joseph of Austria, both personally appealed to Pope Pius IX for the release of Edgar Mortara to his Jewish parents.

They were joined by many Protestant rulers of other nations in the outcry and they expressed their sympathy and also requested that Edgar Mortara be returned to his Jewish parents. Everywhere, concerned and decent humanity were greatly outraged by the sinful kidnapping action. But Pope Pius IX remained very stubbornly without any conscience and without any humanitarian mercy and concern. The Pope was sternly and totally unmoved and without any human mercy or action.

It was reported that Pope Pius IX was without any human compassion. It was reported that the Pope responded to each and every plea and to all who were concerned in very great anger with these words. "I will not ever ever set the saved Catholic child free to return to be a Jew since he is now a saved Catholic, and in contempt, I snap my fingers at the whole world!" The rabbis of Germany sent Pope Pius IX a pleading petition requesting that the kidnapped Jewish Mortara child be returned to his Jewish parents. Their petition to the Pope was never acknowledged and remained unanswered.

Many important persons traveled to Rome to see and meet the Pope. Moses Montefiore journeyed from England to Rome and requested a meeting with Pope Pius IX to discuss the matter and to arrange for the release of the criminally kidnapped Jewish child. The Pope very sternly and indignantly refused to see or meet with him or others who requested to see and meet with him.

Six year old Jewish Edgar Mortara continued to be a kidnapped captive prisoner inside the Catholic Church. He was never again ever allowed to see his parents and his family. He was considered the property of the Catholic Church and was brought up as a Catholic and remained one. Pope Pius IX who was strongly and greatly angered by all of the concern and notoriety which the action of the criminal kidnapping of Edgar Mortara had received, raged and vented his total anti-Semitic hateful resentment upon all the Jews under his jurisdiction.

But the Edgar Mortara criminal kidnapping contributed to the problems of Pope Pius IX in 1870. Once, Pope Pius IX is reported to have declared to Edgar Mortara, the Jewish child he criminally kidnapped from his Jewish parents, "If only you knew how much this matter of saving you as a Catholic has cost me because by saving you from your Jewish parents and the Jewish faith, I have saved you and your soul! "

Despite the then continuing pressures of many appeals to Pope Pius IX by most foreign governments, including even Catholic ones, all pleas, that the Jewish child, Edgar Mortara, be released and returned to his Jewish parents, were very coldly ignored and rejected.

American Jewry, in 1858, though still quite unorganized at the time, found itself noisily and vociferously demanding the release action of Edgar Mortara. This was accomplished with a good deal of support from the American press and the American people. Newspaper articles were written about the criminal and sinful kidnapping of the Jewish child, Edgar Mortara. But, nevertheless, all of the outrage and outcries for humanitarian justice were ignored totally and completely. The sinfully kidnapped Jewish child, Edgar Mortara, was held captive and raised as Catholic. Edgar Mortara died years later as a Catholic missionary priest in Belgium.

What started in 1858 as an action against the ONE SINGLE GOD with the criminal kidnapping of only one Jewish child, Edgar Mortara, became the example for the next century Nazi criminals. Pope Pius IX snapped his fingers and the world did nothing to end the crime committed against one Jewish child and one Jewish family. Hitler and his criminal Nazi gang, following The Popes example, also were snapping their fingers at the whole world as they committed their murderous crimes against millions of Jewish children and millions of Jewish families.

Thus the very sinful criminal kidnapping action of Pope Pius IX denied the existence of the ONE SINGLE GOD and denied HIS Commandments:

1. "YOU SHALL NOT STEAL",
   as Pius IX stole the Jewish child from his Jewish parents.

2. "YOU SHALL NOT MURDER",
   as Pius IX released his anger against all of the Jews and thus encouraged and contributed to further actions that ultimately later resulted in the murder of over six million Jewish men, women, children, and infants.

3. "YOU SHALL NOT COVET",
   as Pius IX coveted the Jewish child, Edgar Mortara, and set the example for future similar actions that took place after World War II when Pope Pius XII was reported to have issued his evil decree and order that the few Jewish children that had been sheltered from Nazis in Churches and convents be retained and not returned to their few Jewish parents who had somehow survived the Holocaust death camps.

The later result of the action of 1858 was that the Nazis later murdered over one and a half million Jewish infants and children who were often painfully tortured, starved, and murdered.

Some of the Jewish infants and children were tortuously used for the Nazi's devil doctor Mengele's medical experiments and then brutally murdered. Some of the children were thrown while still alive into the crematorium ovens. Pregnant women had their pregnancies aborted with fetuses torn from their bodies. All of this can be traced to, and was the result of, the criminal kidnapping of the one Jewish child, Edgar Mortara, by Pope Pius IX.

And the ONE SINGLE GOD spoke all these words, saying:

COMMANDMENT NUMBER NINE

9. **You shall not bear false witness against your neighbor.**

The Ninth Commandment clearly states that one should not falsely testify against anyone. This Commandment goes beyond testifying in Court and giving testimony. It is the statement of this Commandment that should guide the lives of all mankind to always speak, write, and in all means, convey an expression of the truth at all times.

Every one is commanded and directed by the ONE SINGLE GOD to speak and act truthfully. One is not to communicate, at any time, any false information and expressions, or to act falsely, or to knowingly lie and cheat anyone at any time.

This Commandment also extends to, and concerns, each and every manner in which nations communicate, negotiate, and deal with one and another. Because this Commandment of the ONE SINGLE GOD has not been recognized and adhered to, in the past and even today, by the nations, history becomes, all too frequently, mainly a very sad recording that serves only to remind all mankind that nations ultimately can and will too frequently tragically engage in wars that arise and are driven by the untruthful and deceptive self-serving politics that cause nations to settle their differences on the battlefield.

Rulers have lied to their subjects. Nations have lied to each other. Almost everyday, the nations of the world are somewhere at war because their national rulers have lied and cheated in order to attempt to achieve or obtain their questionable, often dishonest. or criminal political objectives, or to subjugate the peoples of other nations and seize their lands and possessions.

One must remember that false propaganda and public relations (PR) information has often been used by nations to advance their dishonest claims and criminal objectives. In today's world, there is not a continuing peace between all nations. Instead there is warfare conducted that results in an ever increasing daily death toll of innocent civilians.

This is the result of all of the false PR and teachings with children provided massive amounts of deliberately false school teachings. They are taught to hate and become murders to kill for their countries and religion. This today is being wrongfully and sinfully conducted by Islam Imams and in the Islam madrasses.

In the just past twentieth century, twice the entire world was engulfed in wars (WW I and WW II) that resulted in the deaths of many millions of men, women, and children. Most of these wars resulted from the criminal actions by national rulers and were commenced because the rulers knowingly and willfully lied to their subjects. When national rulers do not recognize and follow the edict of this Ninth Commandment of the ONE SINGLE GOD, then the people of those nations suffer punishment for the non-compliance.

The evil of non-compliance, with this Ninth Commandment, can be known and seen when the history of Nazi Germany is studied. The rulers, the Nazi party and their leader, Hitler, propagandized with deception and lies to the German people and with lies to the nations of the world. They lied about their objectives and goals. The Nazi leaders lied to the nations of the world about their very desperate need and requirement for more living room land. They lied and said they did not want war. They lied and said they only needed more land and there would be "land for peace".

At first they said that they wanted only the Czechoslovakian Sudetenland where Germans already lived. When they were given the Sudetenland for peace, they then stated that they only wanted the Polish Danzig Corridor. They again lied and stated that they did not want war and there would be peace in exchange for land. This time the Nazi lies did not work and the result was World War II with more than fifty million tragic deaths and millions more suffering war injuries.

The German people accepted and applauded all the lies and falsehoods that their Nazi leaders presented. They believed all of the Nazi Anti-Semitic propaganda, deceptions, distortions and untruths about the Jewish people who were denounced as being responsible for and the cause of all of the troubles, disasters and problems of the German people and their nation. While a few Germans did assist and try to protect their Jewish friends and neighbors, most Germans did absolutely nothing to stop the mass murdering of the Jews.

The Nazi violated the ONE SINGLE GOD's Ninth Commandment. In addition their lies, about the Jews, lead the people of the German nation and people of other European nations, to violate the ONE SINGLE GOD's Sixth Commandment, **"You Shall Not Murder"** and HIS Eighth Commandment, **"You Shall Not Steal."**

More than six million innocent men, women, children and infants were tragically murdered in a Holocaust because they were Jewish. These millions had homes, furniture, bank savings accounts, stores, and businesses. Some were medical doctors, nurses, teachers, professors, engineers, scientists, lawyers, and some were employed in other businesses. All of their properties were stolen by the Nazis and also their many European accomplices

The German people and people of other European nations, under the domination of the Nazis, happily and willfully aided and helped the Nazis to murder Jews and also gladly engaged in the crimes of stealing the possessions of the Jews. Of the over six million Jewish men, women and children that were murdered over one and a half million were children and fetuses still in the womb.

Very tragically and ironically, the Catholic Church and all of its anti-abortionist church members then maintained their utter complete silence about these events. They did not denounce the Nazi abortion of Jewish children torn from their mother's wombs. Indeed some of the Concentration Death Camp personnel and guards, having been very willing to believe all Nazi lies, were also very happy to work at killing the Jews, including children and fetuses, and then later going to pray at their churches.

It is most important that all of mankind understand and recognize that the expression of truth should always be the main and total objective of all discussions, conversations and actions. There would not be any disputes and wars between nations if the truth was always the established and only manner for all communication between all persons and all nations. Yes, however, there could be disputes arising, even with truth, from misunderstandings. But these could be amicably and peacefully resolved by the nations having the objective of accomplishment of truthful diplomatic discussions, truthful negotiations, and truthful determinations and agreements.

Distortions and lies also effect the lives of individuals. Today, too many marriages are often dissolved by divorce only because one or both of the spouses are not truthful. Lies destroy marriages and thus lies destroy families. Often then, the lives of innocent children are impacted and ruined because one or both parents have not spoken and acted in truth. Children also may destroy their future lives because, early in life, they are victims of untruths or they are taught and learn to be deceptive and to lie.

It is very essential that parents and teachers maintain and illustrate to their children and students that truth is the only acceptable standard of conduct and action. Accordingly, it is therefore a most important duty and responsibility, of parents and teachers, to educate their children and students concerning the ONE SINGLE GOD's Ninth Commandment to be truthful.

Historically, early illiterate and uneducated mankind was captive to pagan religious directions and thoughts expressed by their leaders, monks, priests, and teachers who taught and lead their followers in all untruthful manners. This could, in reflection of the past historic dark ages, be understood since the pagan leaders, monks, priests, and teachers were also themselves mostly illiterate and uneducated and unable to comprehend untruth from truth.

As mankind became more literate and knowledgeable, the pagan teachings of their leaders, monks, priests, and teachers no longer prevented their followers from seeking the truth. They no longer had to be silent when they could determine and know that they were receiving messages, sermons and lessons that were complete untruths and that were in violation of the ONE SINGLE GOD's Ninth Commandment.

Still, too many, even today, continue now to blindly accept the untruthful teachings of false leaders, monks, priests, and teachers. However, today, mankind is more educated and has greater open opportunity to be literate and understanding. Thus pagan lies of ancient pagan leaders, monks, and priests can today be recognized and known to be untruths and lies and there is no longer any acceptable excuse whatsoever for mankind not to seek the truth. But what excuse can be made for the astonishing fact that today, in the more educated, literate and knowledgeable present, mankind still does not search and seek the truth and is still willing to listen to and accept the lies and deceptive untruths of lying false leaders, religious ministers, and teachers?

Each person must understand that the Ninth Commandment requires that all must seek, understand, acknowledge, follow and express truth at all times in all conducts and expressions and in the full obedience to the ONE SINGLE GOD's Ninth Commandment.

And the ONE SINGLE GOD spoke all these words, saying:

COMMANDMENT NUMBER TEN

10. **You shall not covet your neighbor's house;**
    you shall not covet your neighbor's wife,
    nor his man-servant, nor his maid-servant,
    nor his ox, nor his mule, or anything that is your neighbor's.

When individuals or nations covet anything that does not belong to them, they have all too often very tragically committed criminal actions against others or initiated tragic wars against other nations in order to obtain the coveted possessions and lands belonging legally to the other individuals or nations.

The Tenth Commandment of the ONE SINGLE GOD addresses the envy that one may have because another has a certain possession that is most greedily desired or wanted by the envious person or nation.

There is no harm in merely having a want or desire for something coupled to having a goal or objective to honestly earn or merit the object of the want and desire. There is a way to work, earn and merit obtaining an item or an object and to honestly satisfy the want or desire without any need for stealing and taking any illegal and criminal action.

However, all too frequently, individuals greedily covet and want another's possession. As an illustration, a child may want another child's toy. It is in itself not wrong to want the toy. If the child can ask for and peaceable temporarily obtain the toy merely to play with it, and then returns the toy, there is no violation of this Tenth Commandment. But, if the desirous child attacks and injures the child owner of the toy to take possession or steals away the toy, then there is a violation of the Tenth Commandment.

Similarly, a grown up individual can desire and want something that another person owns and possesses. There is nothing wrong with having a desire or want as long as this does not lead to greed and to any illegal, dishonest, or criminal action in taking away the other person's rightful possession.

Most wants and desires are normal and can be satisfied by honest means. You want something, so you purchase the item. You do not have the funds to purchase the item, so you can work to earn the funds in order to make the purchase or you may work directly with or for the owner to earn the possession.

To covet is to desire eagerly and is wrong when it is also a greedy want and desire of something that rightfully belongs to another person and that leads to a taking that is not in an honest and legal manner. The Tenth Commandment speaks against the covetous wanting and desiring of another's house, spouse, worker, animal or any object.

In the past, and still today, many marriages and families have been torn apart because of wrongful covetous lust. To covet can result in crimes of theft and murder committed to obtain the home, real estate, and other financial possessions and belongings that are owned by another.

There are some instances today when workers have been coveted and wrongfully recruited away from their jobs by others who do not care about the damage they may do to the worker, his family, or his prior employer. In the historic past this was accomplished to satisfy covetous objectives to obtain slave laborers. Nations either kidnapped the workers or engaged in warfare to obtain them and keep them as slaves.

Modernly, technology has provided mankind with automobiles, electronic equipment and appliances. These items, resulting from scientific and technical advances, have at times become the items that are today the object of greedy desire and coveting by many persons. Although these items can be obtained and purchased, they are often the objects of covetous criminal takings. By stealing and taking these objects, the covetous taker violates the ONE SINGLE GOD's Tenth Commandment.

Nations also can violate the Tenth Commandment when they attack and go to war to obtain the possessions of another nation. Nations can be envious and have greedy wants and desires for that which another nation may possess. This greed can be for the land or resources of the other nation. The result is all too often bloody warfare in which many innocent men, women and children are murdered or seriously injured for life.

Nations may also foment wars to spread their political or other ways of life. This also is the result of an obscene covetous philosophy that indicates that it is right to forcibly take possession of another nation's political or other ways of life and in turn compel the defeated nation to accept the political or other ways of life of the victor.

Today, for reasons that include covetous desires, nations have engaged and undertaken murderous terrorism or warfare actions in order to forcibly steal and take away possessions belonging to the nation of others of a different religious faith. Religions have likewise been the attackers upon others of another religion for covetous reasons.

This has resulted in many harsh and horrible criminal actions conducted in the name(s) of god(s) of the various religions of man. Religion has been used in the past to stir a people into the crime of attacking others not of the same religious belief. Attackers then take covetously possession of all the belongings of the defeated attacked members of another religion. They covetously take the homes, property, and possessions and in past historic years they also took the wives and daughters of the vanquished. In parts of the world, even today, this is common practice.

Today, in the Middle-East, in the Holy Land, Muslim Arabs covet the entire minuscule land territory of the Israelis. They covetously want the entire possession of all of the lands that were once titled as the Palestine Mandate lands and placed under the governorship of the English Government after World War I, by the victorious allies and the League of Nations, to establish a Jewish Homeland. At that time, the Jewish population was greater than the combined Christian and Muslim Arab populations.

The English Government then illegally gave most of the mandated lands to the Muslim Arabs to create the new, never existing before, kingdom of Transjordan for the Arab Sheikh of Mecca and Medina who was driven out of the Arabian Peninsula by the Arab Ibn Saud family. The remaining land then still available for a Jewish Homeland, as stated and manifested in the original mandate, was reduced to approximately 18% of the previous land area of the Palestine Mandate.

When the United Nations, after World War II, decided to divide the little remaining residue of the Mandate Lands into one small portion for the Jews and a much larger portion for the Arabs, the Arabs disapproved. They covetously wanted all of the land and sent the armies of the several surrounding Arab nations to attack the Jews and seize all of the land.

The Arabs especially then covetously wanted and still want all of the little land now possessed by the Israelis. They desired to have all of the land and the Israelis were to have absolutely none of the land. They then coveted and still covet and want possession of the all of the land that historically was given to the Children of Israel by the ONE SINGLE GOD as recorded and revealed in the Torah. The Torah and Mother Jewish Religion preceded the daughter Arab Muslim religion by more than several thousand years.

Today, even though the Arabs have already received approximately 82% of the Palestine Mandated Lands, for the never before historically existing Arab Kingdom of Transjordan, wrongfully and illegally established by the English Government, the Arabs still continue to covet and still want more, all of, the land.

Already having more land territory than any other of the world's peoples, Arab Muslims covetously want all of minuscule Israel's land and they will and have murdered Israelis to take their land. They want it understood that it must be "recognized' that the Arabs "desperately" need more land.

The Arab Muslims now possess more land territory than the entire land territory of all of the combined fifty United States. The vast, largely uninhabited vacant Arab lands now stretch and reach all the way from the Atlantic Ocean to the very distant Gulf of India.

Still the Arabs are not satisfied. They desperately covet and state their absolute essential need of the very tiny portion of the land of Israel that exists on the very small portion of the land that is between the Mediterranean Sea and the Jordan River.

Instead of the Arabs thanking their Allah god for all their very vast areas of the world's land given to them as their possessions and also giving thanks for the great and enormous wealth he has bestowed upon them, the Arab Muslims most greedily covet and want more. The other of world's nations, and the United Nations, are not acting to correct the covetous mindset of the Arab nations. Instead, there is today, an increasing active pressure upon Israel for the Israelis to yield their land to satisfy the Arab's stated covetous needs and desires for even more land.

There is an oversell on the proposal to have peace on earth, between the Arabs and Israel, being accomplished by a "Road Map to Peace" based upon the principle and foundation of "Land for Peace". History reveals that this type of peace is inclined to result in failure. The Road Map to Peace, executed in 1938, in agreement made by and between the Quartet of England (Chamberlain), France (Deladier), Italy (Mussolini) and Germany (Hitler), based upon land (Czechoslovakian) for peace, failed to result in peace. Instead it lead to warfare, World War II, that took the lives of over fifty million people. There is a saying that those who do not comprehend the past history are doomed to repeat the same tragic mistakes.

The United Nations and the new Peace Quartet of the European Union, Russia, United Nations and the United States are totally mistaken in having their full understanding and "honest" belief that there can be peace in the world between the Arabs and Israelis. They believe that this world peace can be accomplished based upon the Road Map to Peace only when Israeli land is given for peace to be achieved between the Arabs and the Israelis.

For this world peace to be effective, Israel must not selfishly withhold their "huge and vast" land from being given to respond to the covetous Arab "desperate" need and desire. What is more important to the nations of the world? Is it the continued existence of the State of Israel or is it the ability to satisfy the covetous lust for land of the Arabs? From the expressions and actions of the United Nations, it is far more important to satisfy the covetous Arab lust for land. Thus, world peace can indeed result, the United Nations "honestly" believe, if only the proponents of a "Greater" Israel would yield all of the land the Arabs need and covet. Israel is today way too large. It has to be "honestly" recognized by all nations that the Arabs have a very "desperate honest" need for more land territory.

To bring about resultant world peace, the Land for Peace Quartet that designed the Road Map to Peace did not apply any pressure on the Arabs and disrupt their terrorists from murdering Israelis. Instead the Quartet complied with the message made by the late deceased Arab Professor Edward Said whose message was "Force Israel". Therefore in compliance, pressure is only to be made upon Israel and then Israel must be made to yield all of its Land for Peace to the coveting Arabs.

This greedy covetous attitude of the Muslim Arabs is a very sinful violation of the ONE SINGLE GOD's Tenth Commandment. It has simultaneously resulted in the Arab Muslims also violating the ONE SINGLE GOD's Sixth, Eighth and Ninth Commandments by continuing intentionally and willfully to murder the Jewish people of Israel in order to satisfy their covetous desires to steal way all of the possessions of the Israelis including their very small and insignificant amount of Israeli land territory.

THE THIRTY COMMANDMENTS

The ONE SINGLE GOD's Ten Commandments are not the same for those who follow and adhere to the Jewish Religion and those who follow and adhere to the Catholic and Protestant versions of the Christian Religion. A comparison is stated below.

*This is the Jewish Version,
the First and Original Version of the Ten Commandments
written into stone tablets,
by the Finger of the ONE SINGLE GOD
as stated and as contained in the Torah.*

1. I am the LORD your ONE SINGLE GOD who brought you out of your bondage in the land of Egypt.
2. You shall have no other gods besides ME, You shall not make for yourself a graven image nor any manner of likeness of any thing that is in heaven above or that is in the earth beneath or that is in the water under the earth. You shall not bow down to them or serve them, for I am the LORD your ONE SINGLE GOD, and I am a jealous GOD visiting the inquity of the fathers upon the third and fourth generation of them that hate ME.

3. You shall not take the Name of the LORD your ONE SINGLE GOD in vain for the LORD will not hold him guiltless that takes HIS Name in vain.
4. Remember the Seventh Day, to keep it Holy, Six days shall you labor and do you work; but the Seventh Day is a Sabbath unto the LORD , in it you shall not do any manner of work, you, nor your son, nor you daughter, nor your man-servant, nor your maid-servant, not your cattle, nor the stranger that is within your gate; for in six days the LORD made heaven and earth, the sea, and all that in them is, and rested on the Seventh Day, wherefore the LORD Blessed the Sabbath Day and Hallowed it.
5. Honor your father and your mother that your days may be long upon the land which the LORD your ONE SINGLE GOD gives you.
6. You shall not murder.
7. You shall not commit adultery.
8. You shall not steal.
9. You shall not bear false witness against your neighbor.
10. You shall not covet your neighbor's house. You shall not covet your neighbor's wife, nor his man-servant, nor his maid-servant, nor his Ox, nor his Ass, nor anything that is your neighbor's.

This is the Christian, Catholic-Lutheran, version of the Ten Commandments.

1. I am the Lord your God and you shall not have other strange gods before me.
2. You shall not take the name of the Lord your God in vain.
3. Remember to keep holy (the First Day,Sunday) the Lord's Day.
4. Honor your father and your mother.
5. You shall not murder.
6. You shall not commit adultery.
7. You shall not steal.
8. You shall not bear false witness against your neighbor.
9. You shall not covet your neighbor's wife.
10. You shall not covet your neighbor's goods.

This is the Christiam, Protestant, version of the Ten Commandments.

1. I am the Lord your God who brought you out of the land of Egypt, out of the house of bondage. You shall have no other gods before me.
2. You shall not make for yourself any graven images.
3. You shall not take the name of the Lord your God in vain.
4. Remember the Sabbath day (the First Day,Sunday) to keep it holy. Six days you shall labor, and do all your work on the other six days.
5. Honor your father and your mother.
6. You shall not murder.
7. You shall not commit adultery.
8. You shall not steal.
9. You shall not bear witness against your neighbor.
10. You shall not covet your neighbor's house; you shall not covet your neighbor's wife or anything that is your neighbor's.

It should be noted by Catholic-Lutheran and Protestant readers who believe in the god deity of Jesus, that Jesus was born, raised, and educated as a Jew. Jesus knew the Hebrew language and could speak, read and write in Hebrew. He knew only the Jewish version of the ONE SINGLE GOD's Ten Commandments. Jesus never knew the modified, altered and changed commandments that was to become the later approved church versions of the Christian faiths, sects and denominations. Nor did Jesus ever make or approve any alterations to the ONE SINGLE GOD's Ten Commandments. These alterations were man made.

While some of the Ten Commandments seem to be the same or very similar for Jews, Catholics- Lutherans, and Protestants, there are several very noted and important significant differences.

The Christian versions of the First Commandment, for Catholic-Lutheran and Protestant, appears the same in expressing the fact that there is ONE SINGLE GOD. There is no mentions of a son of god or a second god or a trinity of gods. The Commandment also combines the statements from both the Original First and Second Commandments.

The Second Commandment appears to be in variance as three different versions. The original version, expressed in Hebrew in the Torah (the original bible sometimes called the "old testament") and very often treated as the Obsolete Testament states the following:

"You shall have no gods before ME."

The commandment continues with these words admonishing all to refrain from idol worship by making any type, kind, or sort of idol or image to be used to represent the ONE SINGLE GOD:

"You shall not make for yourself a graven image nor any likeness of anything that is in heaven or that is in the earth beneath, or that is in the water under the earth. You shall not bow down before them, nor serve them, for I am the LORD your ONE SINGLE GOD, a jealous GOD, visiting the iniquity of the fathers upon the third and fourth generation of them that hate me."

The Catholic-Lutheran version has trouble with this Commandment and resolves the problem by changing the order of the Commandments and skipping over to the Third Commandment and with their second commandment thus discussing that one should not take the Name of the LORD your GOD in vain. This skipping also allows for the appearance of statues, icons and images to be used in churches and in homes.

The Protestant version contains a portion of the original Hebrew version and does not allow the making of images.

The Third Commandment in the original Torah in Hebrew states:

"You shall not take the Name of the LORD your ONE SINGLE GOD in vain for the LORD will not hold him guiltless that takes HIS Name in vain."

The Catholic-Lutheran version skips to the Fourth Commandment and states that one should remember and keep holy the lord's day with the Jew Jesus recognized as being the lord. But this statement concerning a day, the Seventh Day, hallowed and blessed by the ONE SINGLE GOD and dedicated as a chosen day for rest and worship is a completely modified version of the original Fourth Commandment and not the Third Commandment. In selection of a lord's day, it was necessary and important therefore to amend, modify and change the order and wording of the Christian version of the Ten Commandments.

The inserted belief, that the ONE SINGLE GOD of the Jews, the FATHER Who Is In Heaven, was the ALMIGHTY CREATOR of all and everything, was therefore amended. This changed version allowed the importation and incorporation of the various pagan beliefs of the ancient Greeks and Romans who had religions that included the worship of their god family, with their god having a son. This is what necessitated and required the changes to be made for the commandments.

It was the words of the ONE SINGLE GOD that stated, as the Fourth Commandment, that the ONE SINGLE GOD Hallowed and Blessed the Seventh Day, the Sabbath Day, as HIS Day. This was changed by the early Christians (Catholics) to be a lord Jesus day.

The Protestant version of the Third Commandment is similar to the original Hebrew version.

The Fourth Commandment in the original Torah in Hebrew states:

"Remember the Seventh Day, to keep it Holy."

"Six days shall you labor, and do your work; but the Seventh Day is a Sabbath unto the LORD your ONE SINGLE GOD, in it you shall not do any manner of work, you, nor your son, nor your daughter, nor your servants, nor your cattle, nor the stranger that is within your gate, for in Six Days the LORD made heaven and earth, the sea, and all that is in them, and rested on the Seventh Day, wherefore your LORD Blessed the Seventh Day and Hallowed it."

The Catholic-Lutheran version skips and omits the above and instead inserts the original Fifth Commandment to honor one's father and mother. The Fourth Commandment caused many problems and troubled the early founders of Christianity.

About three hundred years after the death of Jesus, the elders, meeting in council in Italy, voted and decided to de-Jewdify their religion and changed the Sabbath Commandment calling for sabbath to be to be held and maintained on the day, Sunday, that they called the lord's day.

They could have chosen any day and they chose the First Day, Sunday, as their sabbath day of worship. These Christian elders believed that they could alter and change the words and directions of the ONE SINGLE GOD. They could act and change the ONE SINGLE GOD's Commandments. They held an election and vetoed the ONE SINGLE GOD and then voted: "all in favor of Sunday say aye."

The Protestant version of the Fourth Commandment mentions the direction of the ONE SINGLE GOD to observe and maintain one day a week as a sabbath day and directs that one should only perform work on the other remaining six days of the week. However, since the Protestant version of the Christian religion followed several centuries after the establishment and existence of the Catholic religion, the early Protestants therefore disregarded the exact direction of the ONE SINGLE GOD to keep the Seventh Day as the Sabbath Day that was Hallowed and Blessed by the ONE SINGLE GOD. The Protestants also held the first day, Sunday, to be the lord's day.

Instead of giving recognition to the words of the ONE SINGLE GOD, the Protestants followed the Catholics and accepted the change of the Sabbath Day of ONE SINGLE GOD to the Catholic's Sunday lord Jesus day. However, even today, Protestant Christians who are Seventh Day Adventists still keep and maintain the Seventh Day as their Sabbath day of rest and worship.

The Fifth Commandment in the original Torah in Hebrew directs one to honor his or her father and mother. This is similar to the Catholic-Lutheran fourth commandment and to the Protestant fifth commandment.

The Sixth Commandment in the original Torah in Hebrew directs that one should not murder. This is similar to the Catholic-Lutheran fifth commandment and the Protestant sixth commandment.

The Seventh Commandment in the original Torah in Hebrew directs that one should not commit adultery. This is similar to the Catholic-Lutheran sixth commandment and the Protestant seventh commandment.

The Eighth Commandment in the original Torah in Hebrew directs that one should not steal. This is similar to the Catholic-Lutheran seventh commandment and the Protestant eighth commandment.

The Ninth Commandment in the original Torah in Hebrew directs that one should not bear false witness against one's neighbor. This is similar to the Catholic-Lutheran eighth commandment and the Protestant ninth commandment.

The Tenth Commandment in the original Torah in Hebrew directs that one should not covet his neighbor's house, wife, servants, animals, or anything that is and belongs to one's neighbor. This is similar to the two separated Catholic-Lutheran ninth and tenth commandments and to the Protestant tenth commandment.

Thus there are three different versions of the ONE SINGLE GOD'S Ten Commandments. The oldest version, the Original one that Moses received at Mount Sinai, and that was written and carved into the stone tablets, for all mankind for all time, by "the Finger of the ONE SINGLE GOD" is stated in the oldest Original Biblical Text, the Torah, and is the Jewish Version.

The versions that followed were authored and written by man and not by the ONE SINGLE GOD. These changed versions were required and necessary in order to justify and serve as the proof, foundation, and basis of the new Christian religion denomination versions that followed the Jewish religion more than fifteen hundred years later. The Christian versions did not exist during the lifetime of the Jew Jesus and were totally unknown to him.

The older Version, the original ONE SINGLE GOD's given Jewish Version, was well known to Jesus and his Disciples. They knew, believed, accepted, and adhered to the original Jewish Ten Commandments and did not know or approve of the later man made changed versions that defied the ONE SINGLE GOD by changing HIS Ten Commandments totally without HIS Approval and HIS Permission.

The later religions of Christianity and Islam also established their own bible versions and not the version of the original Jewish Torah. Again, this was accomplished and accepted by all who recognized the new daughter religions of Christianity and Islam and accepted the bibles of these religions that were written without the ONE SINGLE GOD's Approval and Permission. The New Testament became the new Torah (bible) for Christianity and the Koran became the new Torah (bible) for Islam. These later bibles incorporated all the changes to the Ten Commandments aligning altered commandments with teachings and beliefs of the new religions.

The original Ten Commandments of the ONE SINGLE GOD, carved eternally into stone by the ONE SINGLE GOD, are to be observed and obeyed by all of mankind without exception.

Man is not authorized, in any way, to make any changes, alterations, or deletions to the ONE SINGLE GOD's Ten Commandments.

FAMOUS PSALMS

THE 23RD PSALM

A Psalm of the King of the Children of Israel, King David.

**The LORD, the ONE SINGLE GOD is my shepherd.
I shall not ever want.**

HE always leads me into plush meadows.
HE sets me down besides the quiet still waters.
HE restores my soul.
HE always leads me on the paths of justice for HIS Name's sake.
Though I may walk in the valley of the shadow of death,
I will not fear evil, for YOU are always with me.
YOUR rod and YOUR staff comfort me.
YOU prepare a table before me in the presence of my enemies
YOU anoint my head with oil.
My cup spills over.

**May only goodness and mercy be with me
all of the days of my life,
and I shall dwell in the House of the LORD,
the ONE SINGLE GOD, for ever.**

THE 24TH PSALM

A Psalm of the King of the Children of Israel, King David.

**The earth and all its fullness belong to the ONE SINGLE GOD,
and also all the inhabited land
and all of those who dwell thereon.**

The ONE SINGLE GOD established all the land upon the seas and
upon the rivers.
Who may ascend the mountain of the LORD, the ONE SINGLE GOD.
and who may stand in the place of HIS Holiness ?
One with clean hands and pure heart;
who has not sworn in vain and has not sworn falsely.
He will receive a blessing from the ONE SINGLE GOD
and also just kindness from the ONE SINGLE GOD of his salvation.
This is the generation of those who seek the ONE SINGLE GOD
and of those who strive for HIS presence.
Who then is the KING of GLORY?
The ONE SINGLE GOD, HE is the KING OF GLORY.
Open up Gates so that the King of Glory may enter.

The ONE SINGLE GOD is the KING OF GLORY!!!

OF THE PRIESTHOOD

AND THE PRIESTLY BLESSING

From the dawn of the earliest of man's years of existence on earth, various religions have been formed and established with certain religious leaders and teachers recognized as priests. These individuals were then and are still now believed to be "Holy" and to be capable of, and authorized to speak for and on behalf of the god or gods of that religion. The ancient religions of early pagans and later the Egyptians, Romans and Greeks all had their religious priests.

The Jewish religion did not initially have any priests. When the Children of Israel were saved and rescued from their slavery in

Egypt, the ONE SINGLE GOD saved and rescued them by sending Moses, as his servant rescuer, to take the Children of Israel out of Egypt. At that time of the exodus from the slavery in Egypt, the ONE SINGLE GOD then appointed the brother of Moses, Aaron, to be the first Priest. Aaron was a married man and had children. The Priesthood was at that time first established by the ONE SINGLE GOD and would thereafter consist only of the descendants of Aaron.

Thus the ONE SINGLE GOD informed the Children of Israel that for all of generations, the Priests would be expected to be only the descendants of Aaron. As Aaron, Priests would be married men and have children. The sons of the Priests would also, by birth, be known and recognized as being Priests.

No other male not descendant of Aaron, from among the Children of Israel, could ever become a Priest. There was to be no recognition that any man could hear the voice of the ONE SINGLE GOD or hear any other "voices" telling them that they were to become Priests and calling them to the Priesthood. No person was to "volunteer" to be a Priest

In Hebrew, a Priest is called a Kohen. Priests are called Kohanim (plural). Even to this day, there are families that are known by names as Cohen, Kohen, Kahn, and similar names and are descendants of the Aaron, the first appointed Priest of Israel. These descendants are still recognized as Kohanim even thought they no longer fully perform as Priests.

Those who, at the time of Aaron the first Priest were designated to assist the Kohanim were called Levites. Still to this day their descendants are still known by the names Levi, Levine or even Levin. The rest of the Children of Israel were then and to this day just plainly called as Israelites.

Modernly, the Priests, ever since the destruction of the Second Temple in Jerusalem by the Pagan Roman Army, have not led the religious services of the Jews. This leadership has rather been relegated to those now known and recognized as Rabbis. The Rabbis, who are not

"Holy" Priests, are the recognized teachers of the Jewish religion. But as Rabbis are not "Holy" Priests, they are trained and learned teachers who teach their students and congregations all of the aspects of the Jewish religion. The Rabbis also interpret and determine, as necessary, religious questions and provide the answers found to be in the Torah, Laws and all Commandments of the ONE SINGLE GOD.

It is still however, customary, to have the Kohanim, the members of the Congregation who are descendants of Aaron the first Priest, take part in some of the religious services. Thus only the Kohanim are given the first honors by being the first to be called to the Torah to recite the blessing over the Torah. The Kohanim also, during certain services, are called upon to bless the Congregation in attendance and recite the Priestly Blessing. These are the words of the Priestly Blessing recited by the Kohanim:

Our ONE SINGLE GOD

and the ONE SINGLE GOD of our fatherly patriarchs,

Bless all of us with these Blessings.

The Three Blessing of your Torah

that was written by the hand of your servant Moses

and was then said by Aaron and his sons

as Priests of your Holy People who said:

"May the ONE SINGLE GOD Bless you

and keep you safeguarded.

May the ONE SINGLE GOD

shine his countenance upon you.

May the ONE SINGLE GOD

concentrate his countenance upon you

and give you peace."

THIRTEEN PRINCIPLES OF THE JEWISH FAITH
BY MAIMONIDES

1. I believe with absolute perfect faith that the CREATOR, Blessed be **HIS Name**, is the **AUTHOR** and **GUIDE** of everything that has been created, and that **HE alone has created and made, does make, and will make all things.**

2. I believe with absolute perfect faith that the CREATOR, Blessed be **HIS Name, is a UNITY**, and that there is no unity in any manner like unto **HIM, and that HE alone is our ONE SINGLE GOD, who WAS, IS, and ever always WILL BE.**

3. I believe with absolute perfect faith that the CREATOR, Blessed be **HIS Name, is not a body**, that **HE** is free from all incidence of matter, **and that HE has not any form whatsoever.**

4. I believe with absolute perfect faith that the CREATOR, Blessed be **HIS Name**, is the First and Last.

5. I believe with absolute perfect faith that to the CREATOR, Blessed be **HIS Name**, and to **HIM** alone, it is right to pray, and that it is not right to pray to any being besides **HIM**.

6. I believe with absolute perfect faith that all the words of HIS Prophets are true.

7. I believe with absolute perfect faith that the Prophecy of Moses our Teacher, peace be unto him, **was true, and that he was the Chief of the Prophets, both of those that preceded and of those that followed him.**

8. I believe with absolute perfect faith that the whole LAW, the TORAH, now in our possession, is the same that HE gave to Moses our Teacher, peace be unto him.

9. I believe with absolute perfect faith that this LAW, the TORAH, will not be changed, and that there will never be any other LAW from the CREATOR, Blessed be **HIS Name.**

10. I believe with absolute perfect faith that the CREATOR, Blessed be HIS Name, knows every deed of the children of men, and all their thoughts, as it is said, it is HE that fashions the hearts of all, and HE that gives heed to all their deeds.

11. I believe with absolute perfect faith that the CREATOR, Blessed be HIS Name, rewards those that keep HIS Commandments, and HE punishes those that transgress them.

12. I believe with absolute perfect faith in the sending by the ONE SINGLE GOD of the Messiah, and, though he tarry, I will wait for his coming.

13. I believe with absolute perfect faith that there will be a resurrection of the dead at the time when it shall please the CREATOR, Blessed be **HIS Name,** and the remembrance of **HIM** for ever and ever.

THE FIRST PRINCIPLE OF FAITH

I believe with absolute perfect faith that the CREATOR, Blessed be HIS Name,

is the AUTHOR and GUIDE of everything that has been created, and

that HE alone created and made, does make, and will make all things.

Since the dawn of time, man has pondered about the riddle of his existence. How did he come about to live and exist? What made the heaven above and the earth below? How did all of the waters of the oceans, seas, lakes and rivers come into existence and how were they formed? And from what were they created?

Where did the sea plants, fish and living creatures of the waters come from? How and from what were they created? Who made the oceans and seas and dry land, the earth? What were these made from? Where did the materials come from to make them? How and by whom were all of the land living humans, animals, plants and vegetation created? Why and for what purpose was all of this created?

Some today still believe that Darwin found out all of the secrets and knew all of the "answers". First, according to Darwin's Theory, there was certainly absolutely nothing and later all of the "nothing" formed into pools of muck and mud and then, somehow lightening, coming out of nothing from out of nowhere, struck the muck and mud and created one celled things that became living things. The one cell living whatevers from out of whereever then started to evolved into two cell creatures and then evolution was rapidly changing every thing. and so on until even today.

Ultimately the one celled things became larger and larger and today some have evolved and exist as large elephants and multi-ton weighed whales. Some of the one celled things wound up as blades of grass and weeds, some as diverse kinds of flowers, some as other plants, shrubs and trees, some as insects like ants and roaches and spiders, some as ant eaters, gorillas, dogs and cats, etc., and some as racially diverse men and of course also women. Of course all of this is nothing but simple, pure, and absolute utter nonsense.

One need only look all about oneself to see and appreciate all of the wonders of the created world and the distant universes of stars, planets, moons and suns that exist and we can see and also those that are so distant that we cannot see. Who and what created everything? Darwin? Who and what created man and placed him to live on this fabulously designed land masses of mountains, valleys, hills, canyons, plains, deserts, and provided all of the various natural raw materials and chemicals that exist on land and in the sea?

This that you are now reading is written upon paper produced from trees growing all over the lands of this earth. The reader breaths the provided air into his lungs through unique nostrils and sees with his unique eyes to read this and digest the material here presented and being understood by the brain. Where did the air come from and who designed our ability to breath and to see?

The reader is a very unique being. He lives in a dwelling designed and built by man. But who provided all of the various raw materials used to construct the dwelling walls, floors, ceilings, windows, doors, heating, ventilating, plumbing and electrical devices and systems?

Without any of the raw materials required to make every part of man's dwelling, could man construct the dwelling? To construct the dwelling, man needs and has been given a brain to think, to determine, locate, and process the raw materials and to design and build the necessary tools that are all required to design and build the dwelling. Mans unique body design allows him to work and construct them and things he needs and requires for his existence and for his dwelling.

The same is true of all of the knowledgeable advances man has learned and made in all of the various fields of science, mathematics, transportation, medicine, agriculture, manufacturing, and technology, etc. But how, what, or who has devised and endowed man with the ability to think, become knowledgeable, and advance in all of these fields of endeavors? Would all of this have been possible if man was merely a derivative of lightening coming out of nowhere and striking mud and muck coming out of nowhere which then, by chance, just happened to create a one celled living creature that somehow had the intelligence to evolved and to become man?

Man also has pondered these questions almost since time immemorial. From his early ability to think, man has believed in spirits or gods that must have created him and everything man could see. Early man thus worshipped a vast number of a made up divinity of a multitude of gods. Often his worship of all kinds of gods was based upon ignorant imagination, fear and a lack of the capability of understanding knowledge and clear thought.

The huge tree, early man thought, could it be a god or represent the god? The animals, who could best him in combat and eat him, might they not also be and represent gods? Man came to believe that there were gods who lived high up on mountain tops that he could not reach. Some believed that the gods looked and appeared very manlike, like him. They had bodies similar to man with heads, arms, legs and they had needs and wants just like man but they were gods compared to lowly man.

Some believed in gods that were part man and part animal or beast. They believed that there were male and female gods and they had children, sons and daughters of the gods. Some believed gods controlled the weather and could, if angry or evil, cause droughts and famines or could bring deadly storms. When the gods were pleased by man, and decided, they could be good, they could bring needed rain.

Some gods provided the earth's women with fertility and children or caused women to be barren and not to have children. Some gods gave earth's inhabitants fertile soil and allowed the vegetation to grow and provide food for man. Conversely, the gods could cause the earth's vegetation not to grow and cause man to suffer a lack of food. Some gods could provide man with plentiful animals and fish for food. But the gods could also, in punishment, cause sickness, disease, and illness among man. Gods could be placated by sacrifices. Some gods could protect them from wild beasts and even from other men who were their enemies and were gods for hunting animals or gods of war.

With so many kinds of gods, early man adopted and worshipped in many ways many forms of pagan religions. Prayers, thoughts and especially sacrifices were then made to placate and please all of the gods. Sometimes the sacrifices were animal sacrifices and other times they were even human sacrifices. Some believed that if they sacrificed their first born child to the gods, the gods would be overwhelmingly pleased with them and thus bless them so that they would have many more children. Man, in his pagan ways and ignorant expressions of religions, created idols, statues, icons, symbols and primitive sketches of his gods. His tribal leaders or elders would establish the religion and the existence of the many gods and determine the manners of their religious beliefs, sacrifices, and worship.

Thus man existed with his many pagan gods until one man, named Abram, came to clearly think and rationalize that there was a SUPREME ALMIGHTY CREATOR who alone created the world and the universe and every thing thereon and therein. This CREATOR, that Abram determined to be the only GOD that truly existed, was to him the ONE SINGLE GOD. Thus Abram became the first human to arrive at a religion of monotheism and comprehend and recognize that there was only the ONE SINGLE GOD. This is recorded and documented in the Jewish Torah (Bible) wherein it is written that the ONE SINGLE GOD then conversed with Abram and the ONE SINGLE GOD changed his name to Abraham.

Further, the Torah reveals that the ONE SINGLE GOD asked Abraham to perform a human sacrifice and murder his son Isaac. Abraham and his wife Sarah had been childless and in their older age, finally had a son, Isaac. Now Abraham was directed by the ONE SINGLE GOD to murder and sacrifice Isaac. Abraham firmly believed in the ONE SINGLE GOD and therefore started to comply but Abraham then was told that he was not to murder and not to sacrifice his son Isaac. The ONE SINGLE GOD had first made his request for the sacrifice to test Abraham to see if he would indeed obey HIM and then to also, secondly, to make him understand that man was not to engage in human sacrifice and certainly not to engage in murder and sacrifice of his children.

In this First Principle of Faith, Maimonides set forth the belief of Abraham the first believer of monotheism, founder and patriarch of the Jewish people. Maimonides also reaffirms Jewish belief that there was, is and always will be a ONE SINGLE GOD who was, is and will always be the SUPREME ALMIGHTY CREATOR who has, does, and always will design and create all that has, does, and will ever exist on the earth's lands, in the seas, and the heaven above.

The belief and expressions of monotheism confirms the belief in the ONE SINGLE GOD and totally precludes any belief also in any other supernatural being or god. If one is to maintain a religious belief in a single SUPREME ALMIGHTY CREATOR, then one has to acknowledge and believe only in the ONE SINGLE GOD.

One cannot belief in the existence of other gods or in the son of god or in a trinity of gods. Nor can man be elevated into god like saints that are then accepted as representatives and intermediaries to receive prayers and worship. All prayers have to also acknowledge and be addressed only to the SUPREME ALMIGHTY CREATOR, the ONE SINGLE GOD.

Today, among all of the major western religions, only the Jewish and Islam religions state that they are religions that are based upon the total acceptance of monotheism. The Christian religion states that it is a religion based upon monotheism but then proceeds to recognize a trinity of gods based upon a father god, a son god and a holy ghost or spirit god. Further, Christians are allowed to address their prayers to deceased humans, who were elevated to "Sainthood" upon their death. They can seek the "heavenly intervention" by the "Saints" that in their behalf stand with and before the father and son gods. Likewise, Christians are allowed to address their prayers to the son of god or to name him in prayers addressed to their god. The religious acceptance of the inclusion of the trinity of gods, in their prayers, results in a religion that is pluralistic and not monotheistic.

The Jewish religion pre-dated the much later Islamic religious faith by several thousands of years. Ancestors of the early Muslims, for the thousands of prior years before the existence of the Islamic religion, were pagans who worshipped many pagan gods. They have now, in their Islamic religious belief, their Koran as their bible. The Islamic Koran accepts monotheism but challenges the authorship of monotheism. By their belief, Islam has always existed and is the only one true religion. As Muslims their Islamic belief is that the ONE SINGLE GOD has cast aside the Jewish people and has instead accepted as HIS "new and only people", the Islamic Muslims, the descendants of the former idol worshipping pagans.

This denies and challenges the belief that the ONE SINGLE GOD has known, does know and will know what HE does, why HE does what HE wants, and to whom HE purposely first addressed HIS ever lasting Torah and Commandments and with whom HE made his ever lasting Covenant. Could He not have first made all of HIS existence and truths known to all of the pagan worshipping ancestors of the Muslim people before HE made his Covenant giving HIS Torah and Commandments to the Jewish People? Why did the Jewish people first recognize the existence of the ONE SINGLE GOD and worship HIM only thousands of years before the pagans whose descendants are now Muslims? Why were the Muslims not first in this belief?

The First Principle of Faith and belief, as stated by Maimonides, is based upon the total acceptance that the ONE SINGLE GOD was introduced to all mankind in the Jewish Torah and that HE is the SUPREME ALMIGHTY CREATOR, and the AUTHOR of all the Holy Torah Writings and Commandments.

The ONE SINGLE GOD, by HIS decision for HIS own reason, did not first, before the choosing of the Children of Israel, reveal HIMSELF, or provide or convey to the Muslims, in their religion of Islam, HIS revelation of HIS existence. Thus the pagan ancestors of today's Muslims did not originally know of HIM or believe in HIM, for thousands of years maintaining their paganism.

This First Principle of Faith and belief is not just solely for Jewish worshippers. It is a principle of belief that every person, Jew, Christian, or Muslim must accept. All must understand and acknowledge that there is a SUPREME ALMIGHTY CREATOR who has created them and everything in this world and universe and that HE is the only ONE SINGLE GOD that is to be worshipped by all of mankind.

OF CREATION

Blessed is HE, the ONE SINGLE GOD,

who spoke, and the world and the universe came into being.

Blessed is HE who first Created and maintains Creation.

Blessed is HE who speaks and does.

Blessed is HE who decrees and fulfills.

Blessed is HE who does justice

and has mercy on the earth and it's inhabitants.

The ONE SINGLE GOD has created this world we live in and HE has created all of everything in the infinite universes, the suns, the moons, stars, the planets and worlds, and of course, HE has created you and me.

You and I can gaze in awe at the wonder of our hands. No scientist or engineer can duplicate this miraculous creation of the almighty ONE

SINGLE GOD. Our hands are the result of living cell growth. From the human egg cell and human sperm, the entire creation of the human commences. During the process, hands come into existence.

Even with the most complex and advanced computers and scientific technology, the most educated and learned scientist and engineer cannot create a living egg cell and the living sperm to generate a human being and cause human hands to grow.

The miracle of the creation of the hands and of the entire living human cannot be repeated in any science laboratory. To further complicate the design and fabrication of the human body, there are two versions; a distinct male version and a distinct female version.

The human is a live being of such enormous design and structural complexity that only the ALMIGHTY CREATOR, the ONE SINGLE GOD, can cause the human body to exist, develop and have all aspects of life.

Darwinism is very wrong in the theory of that life just happened by mere chance of spontaneous evolution to come about accidentally through chemical and environmental inter-activity. His theory is that somehow something happened and caused life. Perhaps lighting, from out of a non-existent nothing from out of nowhere, somehow managed to strike muddy muck, from another non-existent nothing and nowhere, that just happened to be located in a non-existent but somehow suitable environment, from nothing and nowhere, of atmosphere, temperature and pressure. This is an invalid theory regarding the creation of life. His theory that human life just happened to come into being and was evolved, and still evolves, by merely some chance or accident is absolutely totally wrong.

One celled creatures did not just happen, by chance happening or accidentally, to exist, coming forth out of the muddy muck from nowhere, and then start a living chain reaction that would lead to more larger and complex life forms that has resulting in all of the trees and vegetation, and in all of the insect, animal, bird and fish life, and certainly not in human life.

Scientists and engineers can intelligently, with modern knowledge and technology, construct robots with mechanical and electronic capability to perform some actions somewhat similar to those that can be performed by humans. But these robots cannot be made to live and have all of the human capabilities. Nor would the robots come to life if we placed them in muddy muck and struck them with lightening.

Today, scientists can determine and map the human genetic code. This code did not come into existence because of a Darwinistic happening, or by accident, or by chance. This complex code was designed and was created only by the ONE SINGLE GOD, the ALMIGHTY CREATOR. Understanding the genetic code may help scientists comprehend the nature of the human body and may be of enormous medical value but it will not ever enable even the most astute and capable scientists and engineers to design and create a complete living human being or create a human soul.

When one looks at the wondrous beauty of nature, one can see that all of creation did not come about merely accidentally or by some chance. When you look upon the magnificent variations of kinds, shapes, and colors of flowers, you can see, understand, and know that no human artist can compete with the ONE SINGLE GOD in Creating and Painting nature.

When you see all of the magnificent buildings and structures that man can build, you can acknowledge that if the ONE SINGLE GOD had not created and provided man with a mental capability, and a body that allows constructive work, and with all of the raw materials used as building and construction materials, man could not build anything. Man can build and construct but he cannot "create" anything. The work of Creation is performed only by the ALMIGHTY CREATOR, the ONE SINGLE GOD.

All around you, as you look, you can never see the ONE SINGLE GOD, but you can know that all you can see about you in a room, the walls, the ceiling, the floor, the door, the windows, the light fixtures, and everything else, is evidence that there is an ALMIGHTY CREATOR, the ONE SINGLE GOD, who exists and who has created every thing that man has used for his buildings and constructions. The same is true when one views all of the creations one can see of all of the world of the outdoor's nature.

We know that electricity exists and flows through the wires but we cannot see the flow. We know that there are radio, television, computer, and wireless phone electrical signals and messages in the airs that surround us but we cannot see or hear these signals and messages without radios, televisions, computers and wireless phones. Even when all of these man made devises are turned off, the air is still full of these unseen signals and messages. Even if we do not have any receiving instruments, the air is still full of these unseen signals and messages.

Similarly, there are many things that exist and cannot ever be seen by the human eye, so too there also exists the ALMIGHTY CREATOR, the ONE SINGLE GOD, who cannot ever be seen by any and all of mankind. But HE does exist and one can see the evidence of HIS Creative Work and HIS Existence everywhere. Look about you, all you see was not created by nothing from nowhere just by a chanced accident.

Look up into the sky and heaven above, and even though unseen, you know that there are countless stars, suns, moons, planets and other heavenly bodies out in space. Some you can see and others are there but beyond your human sight capability. But they are there. They came into existence not because of the foolish wrongful Darwinian theory but because the ONE SINGLE GOD, the ALMIGHTY CREATOR Created all of them.

The three religions, Jewish, Christian, and Islam recognize the existence of a deity. They each have diverse understandings and beliefs. The Mother religion, the Jewish religion, over four thousand years old, maintains the initial belief in an unseen deity, the ALMIGHTY CREATOR, the ONE SINGLE GOD. This belief is addressed and described in the Jewish Torah.

The oldest of the daughter religions, the Christian religion, now two thousand years old, also states a belief in the same deity but adds a son of god and a holy spirit god and thus maintains the worship of a trinity. This belief is addressed and described in the Gospels of the New Testament.

The youngest of the daughter religions, the religion of Islam, thirteen hundred years old, also states a belief in a one single god but with differences declares that the god they believe in is not the same as the Jewish ONE SINGLE GOD. This belief is addressed in the Koran.

While the three religions differ, there is the common recognition and belief in the existence of an ALMIGHTY CREATOR. It is this common ALMIGHTY CREATOR that has fashioned and created all that exists and has given life to some of the creations such as man. While there remains specific differences between the total and entire beliefs that are the basis for each of the religions, there is no significant difference in the essential belief in the existence of a SUPREME ALMIGHTY CREATOR and in HIS Creation of everything of this world and beyond. Those of the Jewish religion express the following:

Blessed are YOU, Our ONE SINGLE GOD, KING

and CREATOR of the entire infinite Universes that exist.

We give thanks and we acknowledge YOUR Creation Work.

Only Our ONE SINGLE GOD

can Create and make all and HE

is the only LIFE-GIVER for all the worlds.

THE SECOND PRINCIPLE OF FAITH

I believe with absolute perfect faith

that the Creator, Blessed be His Name,

is A UNITY and that there is no Unity in any manner like unto HIM,

and that HE alone is our ONE SINGLE GOD,

who Was, Is and ever Will Be.

The Second Principle of Faith strengthens and reaffirms the First Principal. Man has never seen and never will be able to see the SUPREME ALMIGHTY CREATOR. No man knows the shape or figure or appearance of the SUPREME ALMIGHTY CREATOR or knows what he looks like. No Man knows the unrevealed Name of the SUPREME ALMIGHTY CREATOR.

The ONE SINGLE GOD is ONE. HE is a UNITY. This is what Maimonides very simply states and expresses in his Second Principal of Faith.

When Moses saw the burning bush that was greatly aflame but not being consumed by the fire, he approached the burning bush. The

SUPREME ALMIGHTY CREATOR, present in flames of fire that were not consuming the burning bush, made HIS presence known to Moses. At that time Moses asked the ONE SINGLE GOD for HIS Name. The SUPREME ALMIGHTY CREATOR responded and said that "HE WAS Who WAS, Who IS, and Who WILL BE." Since then many have tried to rationalize and determine the Name or Names of the SUPREME ALMIGHTY CREATOR, the ONE SINGLE GOD. Some have even given HIM a name or several names. To this day, no person knows the Name of the ALMIGHTY CREATOR, the ONE SINGLE GOD.

When Moses was with the SUPREME ALMIGHTY CREATOR, on Mount Sinai, he requested to see the SUPREME ALMIGHTY CREATOR and was plainly told that no man could or would ever see HIM and remain alive. Thus no man will ever be able to see the ONE SINGLE GOD and live.

However, many have said that they have seen the ONE SINGLE GOD. Some who claim that god is not a single entity, have claimed to have seen god's son or the mother of god. Somehow those who have said they have seen god, the son of god or the mother of god have possessed such powers that we are to believe they can see "god" and remain alive.

Nonsense!! There has been and is absolutely no truth in the stated and reported many sightings and visions of a god, son of god, mother of god, or any so called saints. Or were these seeing persons mentally and physically really dead?

The Second Principle of Faith states that there is only a ONE SINGLE GOD, a UNITY and that there are no other gods, or other things or beings who are deities or who are the son of god or the mother of god. It is only to this ONE SINGLE GOD that man is to give recognition and acknowledgment as being the GOD and Creator. It is only to the ONE SINGLE GOD that man should and must address his prayers and worship.

As a UNITY, the ONE SINGLE GOD is not a trinity. HE is not composed of divisible parts of any arrangement as necessary to being a father god, a son god, and a holy something god. The basis of the religious belief in a trinity of gods was made, without approval of the ONE SINGLE GOD, after the sinfully wrong decisions of men and not by any divine guidance or message from the ONE SINGLE GOD.

It is not for mankind, to elect to acknowledge any other being or beings to be a god or gods. This is not within the right of creatures, such as man, who have themselves have been designed, created, and given life by the SUPREME ALMIGHTY CREATOR. Man must not and should not exercise a "right" to denounce the ONE SINGLE GOD and then establish or elect instead another god.

Man cannot acknowledge any other being or beings, also created by the ONE SINGLE GOD, as being the person or persons to be recognized as god or gods or the son of god. Nor should any one address prayers of worship to that person or persons. This would be sinful and very similar to idol worship and in complete deliberate defiance of the ONE SINGLE GOD's Ten Commandments. The First Commandment also states, as does the Second Principle of Faith, that the ONE SINGLE GOD exists and is a UNITY.

The Jewish monotheistic belief has always been and still firmly remains that there is a UNITY, a SUPREME ALMIGHTY CREATOR, the ONE SINGLE GOD. This belief is also contained in the religion of Islam that came into being several millenniums later following the Jewish religion. It was not the Jews that obtained and took this monotheistic belief from the later religion of Islam. It was the opposite, as pagan Arab tribes, in adopting the recognition that there existed only a single god, thus started their monotheistic religion of Islam.

It is very truthfully known and acknowledged that it was the later religion of Islam that obtained and took the monotheistic belief of the One Single God, a Unity, from the Jewish religion. This important Koran expressed belief was taken from the Torah of the Jews. This monotheistic belief in the ONE SINGLE GOD is absent in the Christian religion. The belief in a trinity of gods is not a monotheistic belief.

ONE: HIS NAME SHALL BE ONE • 163

Christians, at that time two thousand years ago, first began to start the acceptance in the belief that the ALMIGHTY CREATOR had a partner and assistant, the son of god. Centuries later this was fully accepted and acknowledged as Christian faith with the spreading of the trinity of gods belief across Europe and throughout the Roman Empire. Then and thereafter, Christians accepted belief in the three gods of the trinity, the father, the son, and holy ghost or spirit god.

Early mankind, and even some who today live and dwell on this earth, have believed that there are or were a multitude of gods. The ancient Egyptians believed that their rulers, the Pharaohs, were deities and that there were also other gods. Other peoples and nations have similarly accepted the belief that their rulers were deities.

The Greeks and Romans believed in many gods and at times also believed that their rulers were like gods. More recently, some Japanese believed that their Emperor was, as a descendant of the gods, therefore a god.

The truth is forever always in our own sight. We can look about and see all of the creations of the ONE SINGLE GOD. We can see the blue sky, orange sun, and white and dark clouds in the sky and the stars and moon at night. We can see the green grass, the multi-colored flowers and different large and small trees. We can see all of the many diverse animals and all of nature. We can accept the misguided theory of evolution and believe that creation of everything came about by nothing but chance, or we can more intelligently reason and instead recognize that everything was created by the ALMIGHTY CREATOR, the ONE SINGLE GOD.

The buildings that now house all of mankind were all constructed using all of the many various materials that the ALMIGHTY CREATOR, the ONE SINGLE GOD created and made. Without HIS created materials, man could never make, build or construct anything. Take a moment to think and to look all about you. Inside the building you are in, your home, your place of work, or other type of building, look at the walls, floor, ceiling, doors, windows, electric lights, switches, and outlets.

Ask yourself, could man have ever made all of these building items without all of the materials that the ONE SINGLE GOD created and provided to man? Would we have, for example. helpful tools, appliances, means to grow and harvest agricultural crops, irrigation and water and sewer systems, and vehicles for land, water and air and space travel without all of the materials created by the ONE SINGLE GOD, the UNITY, the ALMIGHTY CREATOR?

When we speak of the ALMIGHTY CREATOR should we believe that we should speak with complete and total recognition that there are a plural multitude of creators? Should we believe that all creation came into being because of the actions of the trinity gods of the father god, the son god, and the holy ghost god?

This Second Principal of Faith recognizes the ALMIGHTY CREATOR as a UNITY and that HE is the ONE SINGLE GOD. It is only to HIM that man can pray and worship and with our prayers give thanks for all that HE has created and provided for man.

THE THIRD PRINCIPLE OF FAITH

I believe with absolute perfect faith that the CREATOR,

Blessed be HIS Name, is not a body, and that HE is free from all the forms and

incidents of matter, and that HE has not any form whatsoever.

Early man tried to reverse the order of creation. Instead of the ONE SINGLE GOD being his ALMIGHTY CREATOR, man became the creator and created his god, and most of the time, he created his multitude of many gods often of various forms and shapes. For each of man's created gods, man also created, as he wildly imagined, an image, form, and shape of each of his gods.

Some of man's created and imagined gods took the shape of items or elements of nature such as trees, mountains, animals, birds, and objects such as the sun, moon, clouds and stars in the sky. Man had quite an imagination, about his god or all of his many gods, ignorant as his imagination was. When he learned to make images of his gods, his imagination allowed him to shape and form many diverse gods.

Today some of this ignorance still exists for some of mankind. God for some of them, has a shape and form similar to man's shape and form.

The ancient Egyptians had their gods with mixtures that were partial animal, birds, and man's forms and shapes. The Greeks and Romans had their human shaped gods. Since man had eyes, ears, nose and mouth, their gods also had these same features.

Their gods, similar to man, walked on two legs and could hold things in their two hands. Their gods also, as they did, ate and consumed food and wine and very often had drunken sexual orgies and festivities. To appease their gods, mankind often practiced animal and human sacrificial murder. They often constructed statues as idols that were made for representing their gods and they worshipped these idols.

The founder of monotheism, Abraham, was born, lived, and raised in this totally pagan environment. All about him, mankind worshipped and prayed and sacrificed to their idol and statues gods. It was Abraham who very independently and intelligently completely thought all things through about the idol and statue gods. He rationalize that there was an ALMIGHTY CREATOR, a ONE SINGLE GOD, who had created everything. He never saw the ONE SINGLE GOD who he determined had no describable form, shape, or body that he could understand and see.

The Jewish religion was thus founded by Abraham in his absolute understanding and belief that the form, shape, figure of the ONE SINGLE GOD was not known to anyone and could not be described or determined by him or any other man. Abraham and later his descendants did not ever see, know, and therefore could not contemplate any form or shape of the unseeable ONE SINGLE GOD.

Later, the Torah (bible) relates that Moses, as a shepherd, while tending a herd of his father-in-law's animals, saw a burning bush that was blazing in fire and burning but was not being consumed by the fiery flames. He approached the burning bush. From the burning flames and from the midst of the blazing fire, he heard the voice of the ONE SINGLE GOD, that he could not see, speaking to him.

It was in this scene of the burning bush that Moses, hearing the voice of the ONE SINGLE GOD, looked to see and could not see the ONE SINGLE GOD and see HIS form or shape. Being in a fire consuming burning bush that was not being consumed, Moses understood that the ONE SINGLE GOD did not have an ordinary existence or any known form or shape like a human. The ONE SINGLE GOD could exist in the fire of the flaming burning bush. He could not understand what kind of form, shape, or existence allowed and permitted this?

Later, once again, alone with the ONE SINGLE GOD on Mount Sinai, Moses expressed his interest and desire to see the ONE SINGLE GOD. He made his request asking to see the ONE SINGLE GOD. He was then told by the ONE SINGLE GOD that no man could or would ever see the HIM and still remain alive.

Still, mankind, even today, has not, with the exception of those that adhere to the Jewish and Islam religions, accepted the fact and understanding that the ONE SINGLE GOD has no form or shape whatsoever that can be seen, known understood, or described by any man. The Jewish religion fully acknowledges and also understands the expressed Words of the ONE SINGLE GOD that no man can ever or would ever see HIM, see HIS form, or see HIS shape, and still remain alive.

Thus it is very questionable, and unbelievable as to how only non-Jews, mainly Christians, have however somehow been able to have seen the ONE SINGLE GOD, and other so called deities and still remained alive.

From time to time, there have been Christians who have proclaimed and stated that they have seen a son of god and a mother of god and after seeing the deity have still survived and lived. They say they can absolutely truly describe the visions they have seen of the son of god and mother of god. Once they have said that they have seen these visions, crowds often gather to the place and site of the where the vision was seen and there, at the site, they pray and worship.

They can even have the seen visions described in drawings. The visions are always seen in the supposed likeness of the human male or female form. The visions resemble the likeness of men and women drawn in "holy" pictures or presented in the shapes drawn by artists in paintings, or made by artists as "holy" statues and idols and shaped in human form. The son of god and his mother of god have often been seen. Some sightings have been in grottos, fields, on filthy rusting oil tanks, on the reflections from dirty office windows, in greasy tortilla frying pans, and most recently on a grilled cheese sandwich and also as shaped on a pretzel stick.

For all of man's wildest imaginations, the words of Maimonides still ring forth loudly with the greatest of all eternal truths. In this, his Third Principal of Faith, Maimonides states this absolute and great truth. Maimonides has stated that the unseen form and shape of the ONE SINGLE GOD is beyond the comprehension, understanding, reasoning, and determinations of all mankind. This includes those who have the very most highly intelligent and most educated of human minds.

The ONE SINGLE GOD's shape and form is unlike anything ever known or to be ever known and ever understandable by any human now and eternally forever. It therefore is absolutely necessary that mankind recognize, confess, and accept this inability to comprehend the form or shape of the ONE SINGLE GOD.

It is for all of mankind to therefore totally accept and realize that as mere creatures of this ALMIGHTY CREATOR, it is not our task, duty, or requirement to create a form or shape for the ONE SINGLE GOD. All must ever and always be completely and totally obedient to HIS Laws and HIS Commandments.

All of mankind must ever and always accept the truth and fact, that as the ONE SINGLE GOD stated to Moses, no human being can ever and will never see HIM and live. Therefore all must acknowledge and understand that never will any living human ever see HIM and none can ever know of and be capable of seeing HIS Form or Shape and then remaining alive.

As Maimonides clearly states, and as all must accept as true, the ONE SINGLE GOD has no known body form or shape that mankind can comprehend. HE is the ALMIGHTY CREATOR of all matter whatsoever and the Creator of all things and of everything that mankind can ever see, ever visualize, or, ever if unseen, and being beyond the sight of man, recognize to exist. All must accept that there are many things that will never be revealed to mankind. There are many things that mankind will never fully comprehend and understand and that will never be, by mankind, seen.

The ONE SINGLE GOD, the ALMIGHTY CREATOR of all of the substances and materials in all of the infinite universes, is not composed of any known or unknown matter that mankind can or will ever determine. The ONE SINGLE GOD is free of all incidents or elements of any matter known to mankind. The ONE SINGLE GOD has no known and understandable, to mankind, form or shape whatsoever.

From all of these truths, mankind must always understand that our prayers and thoughts must be directed only to the ONE SINGLE GOD who is beyond all of mankind's ability to see, understand, or to imagine as to HIS form and shape.

There are matters that the ONE SINGLE GOD can and does not reveal to mankind. That is HIS Prerogative as the ALMIGHTY CREATOR , the ONE SINGLE GOD. It is not for mankind to ever question or challenge any of HIS Decisions or to attempt and try to reason why HE does not reveal HIMSELF to the vision of man's eyesight.

THE FOURTH PRINCIPLE OF FAITH

I believe with absolute perfect faith that the CREATOR, Blessed be HIS Name, is the FIRST and the LAST.

Historically, early man was illiterate and not too well learned and intelligent. He had many fears and wanted and created the protection he needed by his creation of a god or gods. He therefore, in his very simple mind, imagined anything, that he could imagine, as being a protective and needed god. Thus man created his own gods. All of his gods were figments of his unintelligent imagination. He believed these imaginary gods would provide him with all of his needs and protect him.

Man created all of his many gods and saw them as being in any form or shape that he could imagine. Often he tried to make images of these gods and often he made them into idols. Some gods, he believed, were for special purposes such as bringing good weather and rain or providing him and his family with food and protection from tribal enemies or wild ferocious beasts. To have children, he and his wife had gods for fertility.

Man created many of these gods and also later uncreated these gods. He could believe in them and then cast aside his belief in them when accepting and creating new gods. It was therefore man that was the creator of god or the gods. Various tribes and peoples had their own god or gods and after tribal wars, victors often made the conquered accept the god or gods of the victors.

In this Fourth Principal of Faith, Maimonides refutes the idea and does not believe in man as being the creator of god or gods. He states, as this important Principal of Faith, that there is an ALMIGHTY CREATOR who alone was and is, the ONE SINGLE GOD. Further the CREATOR is not ONE SINGLE GOD who will exist for only a period of the eternal time but will forever exist.

The CREATOR has existed, now exists, and will exist eternally for all time. There will never be another CREATOR. The ONE SINGLE GOD is the ONE CREATOR that, as Maimonides states, is the First and the Last. This was not the belief of early man. Even today there are those who do not accept this belief that the CREATOR has always existed and is forever always the First and the Last. There was, is, and will be only ONE ALMIGHTY CREATOR who is the ONE SINGLE GOD.

The many different gods that early man invented and believed to be "the creator" existed only as long as man desired these gods to exist. They existed only as long as he had a need for them to save him from danger and the unknown. At the same time, man believed that he had to sometimes placate his gods so that they would not be angry with him. Man invented and practiced various ways and means to please and placate his gods through animal and human sacrifice including the murderous sacrifice of his own children. He believed that these gods, that he invented and whom he worshipped, were the creators of everything.

If a neighboring tribe conquered him, man could easily and quickly divest himself of all belief in his own creator gods. He then could also very easily acknowledge and accept the conqueror's many creator gods as then being his own new true gods. It was helpful, for his changing belief, if the new gods could be shown to him in the idol or statue forms and shapes. These many imagined gods were also believed by man to be the creators of earth, all things, and man.
The Jewish religion, established by Abraham, became the first to have

thought through and accepted the truth that the ONE SINGLE GOD was the ever existing and eternal true sole, one, and only ALMIGHTY CREATOR of everything man could see of the world and heaven above.

The Children of Israel, the Jews, recognized HIM to be the SUPREME CREATOR of all that is in or on the earth and sea, and also the SUPREME CREATOR of all of the endless eternal universe up to and even beyond man's knowing and visually recognizable infinity.

The very first words in the Jewish Torah (Bible) are the most significant and important words ever written stating
"In the beginning GOD".

The next words declare that this ONE SINGLE GOD was and is the ALMIGHTY CREATOR who created and creates everything, the heaven and earth, and all in or upon the earth or the seas and all therein, and all of the galaxies and universes that exist. The ALMIGHTY CREATOR, the ONE SINGLE GOD, created every thing.

The Torah reader is informed that the ONE SINGLE GOD's creation of all of the entire universe was accomplished in only six days. The reader is then told that the ONE SINGLE GOD, having CREATED everything in the six days, rested on the Seventh Day and that HE Blessed and Hallowed the Seventh Day, as a Special Day, to be kept always Holy for ever without any man made amendment or change.
That Seventh Day was and is still called the Sabbath Day. The ONE SINGLE GOD never recognized or approved any other day to be HIS Sabbath Day. However, man in his superior status decided to change the sabbath day to the first or sixth day.

Today, other religions may recognize and have accepted only a partial portion of the statements presented in the First Book of the Torah (Bible). The First Book is titled by one word in Hebrew that means "In the Beginning" and it is also commonly known as "Genesis" or the origination.

Those who want to study and understand the bible must first start with these very first words on the very first page of the Torah. They cannot cast aside and ignore the First Book or the remaining Books of the Torah. They cannot comprehend and understand their own religions without thus starting their study with Genesis Page One since the Torah is the first and foundation and basis for their own bibles. They cannot ignore the first words on the first page of the Torah. They cannot and should not intelligently skip over and start at page one of the New Testament or Koran

The Christian and Muslim religions contain, express, and teach the belief that while their god created every thing, he did not set aside and very purposely bless and hallow a special day, only the Seventh Day, as the ONE SINGLE GOD's day, the Sabbath Day. Thus the Fourth of the original Ten Commandments are cast aside and not adhered to and obeyed.

Christians and Muslims are taught that they can ignore the statements in the Torah that HE did so state. They are taught that the statements are not to be accepted as conclusive or as indicative of any reason why the sabbath day of their god, for rest and worship, could not be the first day or the sixth day or any other day selected by the votes or decision of mankind

There is a somewhat common Christian and Muslim belief that there was a devine creator. But their creator gods are not the same as the Jewish believed ALMIGHTY CREATOR. The Jewish belief is that the ONE SINGLE GOD is the ALMIGHTY CREATOR who gave all of mankind, through the Children of Israel, HIS Torah (Bible) and also HIS Specific Ten Commandments that HE wrote and therein stated that HE WAS, IS, and forever WILL BE for all the eternity of times, the only ONE SINGLE GOD.

It is the Jewish belief that all humans should and must acknowledge that HE, the ONE SINGLE GOD, is and was the ALMIGHTY CREATOR who alone created every thing including themselves. HE is the only ONE that is the CREATOR and the ONE SINGLE GOD and that never before, or in their lifetime, or at any time thereafter, will there be any other CREATOR. It is also the Jewish belief that the ONE SINGLE GOD has never ever since and will never ever in the future create another Torah (Bible). It is also believed that HE has not made and will not make any changes, amendments, alterations, or revisions whatsoever to HIS Torah, Laws and Commandments.

With this recognition comes the responsibility to truthfully acknowledge that the eternal sole and only ALMIGHTY CREATOR is the ONE SINGLE GOD. Man must also understand and acknowledge that neither he nor any other living human has ever seen or will ever in the future see the ALMIGHTY CREATOR.

Therefore, no living being knows HIS Form or Shape. Further, all mankind must always understand and acknowledge that only to this unseen ALMIGHTY CREATOR, whose, form, shape, and appearance is unknown and cannot even be imagined, is man to address his thoughts and prayers and that man should forever only bless this ALMIGHTY CREATOR as his ONE SINGLE GOD.

It is written that the time will come when all of mankind everywhere shall acknowledge this belief in only the ONE SINGLE GOD as the only ONE ALMIGHTY CREATOR. Then all of mankind shall worship and address all of their prayers only to HIM. Then as all of mankind shall pray only to HIM, they shall also bless only HIM as their only ONE SINGLE GOD. Then, at that time, it is also written that the ONE SINGLE GOD shall be to all of mankind as ONE and HIS Name shall then be ONE. At that time, all of mankind shall acknowledge and have their sole allegiance only to the ONE SINGLE GOD who is the First and the Last.

THE FIFTH PRINCIPLE OF FAITH

I believe with absolute perfect faith that to the CREATOR, Blessed be HIS Name,

and to HIM alone, it right to pray,

and that it is not right to pray to any being besides HIM.

Early man practiced a religion of the ignorant. He did not know or had great difficulty in trying to understand why he was alive. He did not mentally delve into any substantial or difficult and thorough thinking about a creator or a god. For him, as he had many fears concerning, nature, weather, animals, and his necessities of food and water, he gradually developed a need to have someone or something to turn to for protection and shelter and a means of sustenance. So early man invented one god or gods.

Gradually man assumed and believed that there were creators and gods who could protect him. Some heard the thunder and lightening and assumed that these were either gods or the voices or actions of gods. Man pondered about the sun and the moon. Were these gods? Were these the dwellings and homes of gods? Or could it be that the gods dwelled up there in the highest of the mountains that he could see?
As time passed, man turned to the nature that he saw surrounding him

and then assumed the belief that certain objects of nature were really the gods. He began to worship these objects by sacrificing to them. As time advanced he also invented and created many kinds of gods. Then he began to form various shapes of idols to represent and be for him his gods.

Different tribes and nations, at different times, created many different gods. Later, the tribes would engage in warfare and savagely fight each other to show that their invented and created tribal or national gods were the only true gods and were more powerful and protective then the false gods of the other vanquished tribes.

To these gods, man sacrificed animals and sometimes vegetation and food for his gods. These were his attempts to please and placate the gods so they would provide him with the gods' protections and better living conditions. The gods could give him better weather, more fruit and vegetables and herds of animals. They could make him successful in his farming, hunting and fishing and save him for the other enemy tribes.

The gods would also save him and not allow him to be ill, injured, or eaten by the wild animals. Men and women also believed that the gods could make them fertile and enable them to have children. The gods could be friendly or appear to display complete anger and displeasure with man. At times, the gods would have to be appeased by the sacrifices that included human murder sacrifices.

It was during a later period that man first began to think and contemplate about the gods and then established a new belief that the gods were more man like in form and image. Then man began to make images and idols of his gods that were formed, shaped, and looked more like man.

Early man sacrificed to these man like gods and then also began to worship and pray to these gods using the man shaped idols that they made. Into this world, at that time, the Torah of the ONE SINGLE GOD relates, in the First Book of Genesis, that one man, named

Abram and later called Abraham, came to the very thoughtful conclusion and recognition that all of man's created gods and idols were utter nonsense fictions and did not exist. Himself, born into a pagan family, Abraham clearly thought and concluded that there was an ALMIGHTY CREATOR who had created all matters of everything and had also created him. He did not believe in addressing his prayers, worship, or sacrifices to the man like idol images that were supposed to be the gods of mankind.

Abraham realized that there was only one, the ONE SINGLE GOD, who was the ALMIGHTY CREATOR of all that he could see and imagine existing upon the earth and in the heavens above. Abraham never saw the ONE SINGLE GOD but he conversed with HIM. Abraham is recognized as the first man to formulate the monotheistic thought and belief that there exists and is only ONE SINGLE GOD.

Abraham and his descendants, the Children of Israel, believed only in the ONE SINGLE GOD. They worshipped and prayed only to the ONE SINGLE GOD. At that time, mankind was still religiously very ignorant and pagan and still engaged in both human and animal sacrifice. Abraham and his descendants also sacrificed but only to the ONE SINGLE GOD. Their sacrifices included only sacrifices of animals and vegetation.

In Genesis, one can read that the ONE SINGLE GOD commanded and directed Abraham to sacrifice his son Isaac. When Abraham was ready to obey the ONE SINGLE GOD and thus sacrifice his son, he was then told by the Angel of the ONE SINGLE GOD that he must not do this. He must not murder sacrifice his son. The ONE SINGLE GOD was testing Abraham to see if he would obey and do as he was told.
The ONE SINGLE GOD also wanted to teach Abraham and his descendants that it was very sinfully wrong to murder sacrifice one's child or any other human being. Thus, while men of all of the other tribes and nations continued to perform human murder sacrifice, Abraham's descendants, the Children of Israel, obeyed the Words of the ONE SINGLE GOD not to perform murder for any reasons and especially for the ritual of human murder sacrifices.

Sadly, the murder sacrificing of children continues even to this very day as Muslim Imams declare such acts godly and tell and instruct their Muslim followers to send their Arab youth to murder sacrifice themselves, in order to murder other innocent men, women and children, by becoming suicide murder bombers. These preachings and resultant acts of murder are made in very sinful total defiance of the Sixth Commandment of the ONE SINGLE GOD that **"YOU SHALL NOT MURDER"**.

The Fifth Principal of Faith, as presented by Maimonides, states that all of mankind is only to pray to the ONE SINGLE GOD and to no other gods, saints, or beings. Further, that mankind is to not to practice sinful human murderous sacrifice but is only to express his devotion and address his worship and prayers only to the ONE SINGLE GOD and do so without actions of sinful murder.

For four thousand years, the Children of Israel believers in the Jewish faith have adhered to this Fifth Principal of Faith. They have never practiced sinful murderous human sacrifice. They have faithfully always worshipped and prayed only to the ONE SINGLE GOD. They have adhered to the monotheistic belief in the only ONE SINGLE GOD that was first and originally established by their ancestor Abraham.

Pagans who became Christians ceased human sacrifice. But, during the past two thousand years, the murderous advents of the Christian Crusades, Inquisitions, Pogroms and the Holocaust have been sadly historic events wrongfully and sinfully undertaken by some of the Christians. All of these tragically sinful actions by some Christians have been very knowingly sinful contemptuous violations of the Commandments of the ONE SINGLE GOD. Sadly all too often, these actions have been undertaken with the blessings of Christian Church Leaders.

These have been unforgivable actions resulting in murders of millions of innocent men, women and children. The victims were murdered only because they were Jewish and believed in the ONE SINGLE GOD and not the Christian version of the trinity of gods.

Often these murderous Crusader, Inquisition, Pogrom and Holocaust actions were unjustly undertaken only to allow the murderers to seize and steal the possessions of the murdered victims. Perhaps they will have forgiveness granted by the many saints that they pray to and venerate but they will never be forgiven by the ONE SINGLE GOD.

Today, the Muslim world is set upon the wrongful and sinful path of defying the ONE SINGLE GOD. The Arab Imams, Mullahs, Muftis, Sheikhs and Ayatollahs preach, teach, instigate, and send all of their followers to sinfully murder and kill humans, to murder especially Christians and Jews. They do so in total defiance of the Commandment of the ONE SINGLE GOD not to murder. They do not adhere to this Fifth Principal since they have their own one single god to whom they pray and in whose name and for whom they gladly sadly perform human suicide and murder sacrifice.

This Fifth Principal of Faith is based upon the worship of only the one recognized ONE SINGLE GOD. It requires the complete obedience of all of the Commandments and Laws of the ALMIGHTY CREATOR, the ONE SINGLE GOD. It does not make any exceptions to allow the prayers of mankind to be addressed to a trinity of gods. It does not make any exceptions to allow prayers to be addressed to any other one single gods whose followers and believers do not fully and completely obey all of the ONE SINGLE GOD's Ten Commandments. All of mankind must obey HIS Commandments and all of mankind must address their prayers only to the ONE SINGLE GOD.

THE SIXTH PRINCIPLE OF FAITH

I believe with absolute perfect faith

that all the words of the Prophets are true.

Among the Prophets of Israel, there were some that were designated as Major Prophets and some that were designated as Minor Prophets. The Major Prophets were Moses, Jeremiah, Isaiah, Samuel and Ezekiel. Among the Minor Prophets were Amos, Hosea, Micah, Nahum, Nathan, Jonah, Elijah and Deborah.

The Prophets voiced their concerns over the right and wrong actions of the Children of Israel. They directed their statements to the people to encourage them to always at all times remain true and faithful to their ONE SINGLE GOD and to HIS Torah, to all of HIS Laws, and to all of HIS Commandments.

They warned the Children of Israel not to turn away from their true ONE SINGLE GOD and not to follow the practices of their Pagan neighbors. They urged and reminded them to be obedient to all of the Commandments and Laws of the ONE SINGLE GOD and not to live their lives maintaining behaviors and religious practices that were Pagan. They warned the people not to engage in idolatrous practices and worship and that these were sinfully and not in accordance with all of the Commandments and Laws of the ONE SINGLE GOD. The Prophets repeatedly warned all of the Children of Israel of the punishment they would receive for disobeying HIS Commandments and Laws and partaking in any of the idolatrous religious and other practices of their idol worshipping Pagan neighbors.

The Prophets were preachers and teachers and stated their prophecies of the future depending upon the behavior of the Children of Israel. Often, when they determined that the Children of Israel were not adhering to the Words of the ONE SINGLE GOD, they issued their very stern prophetic statements condemning the actions of the sinners and warning about the punishment that would surely descend upon the Children of Israel, if they did not heed all of the Words, Commandments and the Laws of the ONE SINGLE GOD.

The prophet Mica warned;
    It has been told to you, what is good,
    And what the LORD requires of you.
    You are to only do justly, and to love mercy,
    And walk humbly with your ONE SINGLE GOD.

The Prophet Isaiah warned:
    Of Pagans, their land is also full of idols.
    All of the Pagans worship
    the idol work of their own hands.
    They worships that which their own fingers have made.
    You are not to venerate or worship idols.

Isaiah's 's prophetic vision of the end of all days was:
    The mountain of the LORD's House shall be established
 at the top of all of the mountains and shall be exalted above all of the
                                hills;
    and over all of the nations that shall acknowledge unto it.

    For out of Zion shall go forth the Law
    the TORAH,
    And from Jerusalem,
    shall go forth
    the Word of the ONE SINGLE GOD.

The most famous words of the Prophet Isaiah have been repeated many times and these words are now inscribed and posted near the United Nations Building in New York:

> **The wolf shall lie down with the lamb.**
> **The leopard shall sleep with the kid.**
> **And a little child shall lead them.**
> **The suckling shall play**
> **at the den of the Asp.**
>
> **They shall beat their swords into plowshares**
> **And make their spears into pruning hooks.**
> **Nations shall not lift up swords**
> **against other nations.**
> **Neither shall they learn war any more.**

All of these words of the Prophets, as stated in this Sixth Principal of Faith, by Maimonides, have been true. When, at any time, the Children of Israel deviated from the Word, Commandments, and Law of the ONE SINGLE GOD and when they copied and practiced the ways of their Pagan neighbors, they were punished. When it shall be that all of the Children of Israel will cease to do this, then there will be the ONE SINGLE GOD's salvation granted for all of the Children of Israel.

Today, it has been the so-called non-Pagan nations, observing the mainly Christian and Muslim religions, that have cruelly oppressed the Jews, the Children of Israel. Casting aside the Commandment of the ONE SINGLE GOD, they have murdered millions of the Children of Israel, the Jews. Nations still know war and neither the lion nor the wolf lies down in peace with the lamb. There is no true peace any where on earth.

The prophecies have been true. The prophecy of Isaiah that nations shall not lift up swords against each other and that they will no longer learn or conduct war will also some day in the future still come true. But this will only occur when all of mankind totally accepts the Commandments, Torah, and Laws of the ONE SINGLE GOD.

It is wrong and a very significant major error to think and believe that the prophecies were only meant for the Children of Israel, the Jews. All of the prophecies are meant for all of the human creatures who are all the children of the ONE SINGLE GOD. The prophecies of the prophets, just the same as the Torah and Ten Commandments of the ONE SINGLE GOD, were given to all of mankind to impact all of the behaviors of their lives and guide all of mankind to correct living.

The Torah and Ten Commandments that were given by the ONE SINGLE GOD and that were received by the Children of Israel were given to be provided to all of mankind for obedience. The ONE SINGLE GOD at all times knows man's every thought and every deed.

Man's individual deeds, in obedience or non-obedience to the Commandments and Laws, are always thoroughly known and important to the ONE SINGLE GOD. So also are the hopes, thoughts, ambitions, and aspirations of man that drive and compel him in his actions. These actions and accomplishments ultimately determine, for or against him, the ONE SINGLE GOD's Judgments as to the outcome of man's life.

No man acts in a vacuum and no deed ever goes unrewarded or unpunished. The prophets' prophecies include the dictum that one cannot cancel out a bad deed by performance of a good deed. Each action and deed of man is separately judged and treated independently. However, good deeds can perform some repair of bad deeds.

Maimonides carefully compared the prophetic revelations of all of the prophets to the illumination by lightening on a very dark night. He noted that some prophets were granted only one such lightening-flash from the ALMIGHTY CREATOR, the ONE SINGLE GOD. Some prophets had repeated prophecies similar to lightening-flashes that were often repeated. Maimonides believed that, as to Moses, his prophetic capability was continuous the same as an unintermittent light.

The prophets of Israel declared in the words of their prophecies, "Thus said the LORD" with their absolute conviction that the thoughts they expressed arose in their minds and were the Will and Commands and the Exhortations that they were to issue in HIS Name. These, they believed came into their thoughts at HIS prompting and were fully vested with HIS Authority and Direction.

The prophets' revelations were made to the Children of Israel but were equally meant to be for all of mankind. All are to live lives of goodness, justice, mercy, and charity while maintaining true belief and continuous obedience to the ONE SINGLE GOD, and HIS Commandments and HIS Laws

THE SEVENTH PRINCIPLE OF FAITH

I believe with absolute perfect faith

that the prophecy of Moses, our Teacher,

peace be unto him, was true,

and that he was the Chief of the Prophets,

both of those that preceded and of those that followed him.

The first man stated and recognized as being a Prophet of the Children of Israel was Moses. He was born in Egypt at a time when the Hebrews, the Children of Israel, were human slaves in total bondage and in servitude to their evil slavemaster Egyptians. At that time, when Moses was born, the evil Pharaoh who ruled Egypt had evilly decreed that all of the male born infants of the Hebrew slaves, the Children of Israel, were to be murdered by being drowned by being thrown into the Nile River.

Moses, who was to become the First Prophet and teacher to all of the Hebrews, thus started his life by being born a slave child being prepared to be thrown into the Nile River to drown in accordance with the evil decree of the Pharaoh.

The baby Moses was placed, by his mother, in a water proof basket and then taken by his sister Miriam who placed the basket in the Nile River. The Pharaoh's daughter retrieved the basket from the Nile and then raised the Hebrew baby Moses in the Pharaoh's house to be as and for her own royal son.

The entire story of Moses is stated in the Second Book of the Torah, the Book of Exodus. Raised as a royal "prince" and member of the Pharaoh's household, Moses one day saw an Egyptian mercilessly beating a Hebrew Slave. He fought and defended the slave and in doing so he killed the Egyptian.

As a result, he had to flee from Egypt into the desert to save his life. There he met the daughters of the Pagan Medianite Priest, Jethro. He stayed with Jethro, married one of the Pagan Priest's daughters, and tended sheep for his Pagan father-in- law, Jethro.

One day in the desert working as a shepherd, Moses saw a burning bush on fire. It was burning with strong heated fire but not being consumed by the flames. He could not understand why the bush was not being consumed and destroyed by the flames of the fire. When he approached the burning bush, the voice of the ONE SINGLE GOD was heard by Moses coming from the midst of the flames of the burning bush. Moses was directed by the ONE SINGLE GOD to return to Egypt and, as Agent of the ONE SINGLE GOD, take the Hebrews, the Children of Israel, out of Egypt, out of the bitterness of slavery.

Moses appeared before the evil Pharaoh performing signs and miracles exactly as he was told to do by the ONE SINGLE GOD. When the Pharaoh stubbornly would not release the Children of Israel from slavery, the ONE SINGLE GOD came down on the Pharaoh and the Egyptians with HIS Judgment of Justice and the Punishment of Ten Plagues that were, each one of the plagues, accompanied and delivered with the burning anger, the fury, the wrath, and the indignation of the ONE SINGLE GOD.

Before each one of the ONE SINGLE GOD's Ten Plagues that punished the Pharaoh and the Egyptians, Moses delivered the messages and warnings of the ONE SINGLE GOD to the Pharaoh.

Stubbornly with a "hardened heart" the Pharaoh refused to heed and would not listen to words and warnings of Moses. The Pharaoh did not believe that Moses was in communication with the only ONE SINGLE GOD and that Moses was HIS First Prophet and gave him true words and warnings.

The tenth and last plague is still remembered today and every year celebrated as the Jewish Holyday of Passover. It was titled the Passover since the ONE SINGLE GOD passed over the houses of the Children of Israel while entering the houses of the Egyptians where the first born males of both man and beast perished.

The Passover was celebrated by Jesus, the Apostles, and early Christians in complete obedience to the Commandment for observance as stated by the ONE SINGLE GOD. Christians thus continued to celebrated the Passover Holyday until the fourth century when the Nicene Council of Christian elders, without any authority from the ONE SINGLE GOD, decided to deviate and change the ONE SINGLE GOD's Commandment and decided that Christians should not celebrate Passover since it was a Jewish Holyday.

Moses took the Children of Israel out of their bondage and slavery. The evil Pharaoh pursued him and the freed Hebrew slaves. On the way to Mount Sinai, at the Reed Sea with the Pharaoh and his Army in pursuit, Moses raised his staff and the waters of the Reed Sea parted. The Children of Israel escaped, between the waters of the parted sea , walking on dry land.

The evil Pharaoh then ordered his soldiers and charioteers to pursue the Children of Israel on the dry land of the parted Reed Sea. Moses then put down his staff and the parted waters no longer remained parted. The Egyptian soldiers and charioteers all were drowned in the Reed Sea.

Moses took the Children of Israel away from Egypt into the Sinai desert to Mount Sinai where, at the direction of the ONE SINGLE GOD, he climbed the mountain. He was then alone with the ONE SINGLE GOD on Mount Sinai for forty days.

There, on Mount Sinai, Moses received the Torah and also received the Ten Commandments that the ONE SINGLE GOD personally wrote and carved into the two stone tablets that had been prepared by Moses. Moses brought the Torah and two stone tablets of the Ten Commandments down from the mountain and gave them as an ever lasting treasured covenant inheritance to the Children of Israel.

The Torah and the Ten Commandments given by the ONE SINGLE GOD to the Children of Israel, and meant for all mankind, became the eternal strengtheners of the Covenant that the ONE SINGLE GOD had made between HIMSELF and the Patriarch Abraham of the Children of Israel, the Jewish people.

These, the Torah and Ten Commandments, have since always been and have since stayed and will stay eternally forever as part of the eternal Covenant made by the ONE SINGLE GOD with the Children of Israel. All Jewish Synagogues and Temples buildings have a cabinet known as the Holy Ark that contains and safeguards the treasured Holy Torahs and Ten Commandments given, to the Children of Israel, for all of the world's mankind. The Torah and Ten Commandments are used for and during religious services.

During all of the centuries of Christianity and Islam, Synagogues and Temples have been destroyed together with the ONE SINGLE GOD's Torahs and Ten Commandments contained in these buildings. It is one thing to destroy a man made religious building. It is a vile and unforgivable sinful action to desecrate and destroy a Torah and the Ten Commandments of the ONE SINGLE GOD.

During the insane evening of Kristalnacht that initiated the Holocaust, in Germany on November 9, 1938, German Nazis, mostly almost all Christians, ran wildly amok setting fires and destroying all Jewish Synagogues and Temples. In doing so, they also destroyed the ONE SINGLE GOD's Torahs and Ten Commandments.

For destroying the ONE SINGLE GOD's Torah and Ten Commandments, their punishment from the ONE SINGLE GOD was that the Nazi destroyers all destroyed their prior living souls. These actions of destroying Jewish Synagogues, Temples, Torahs and Ten

Commandments of the ONE SINGLE GOD were also sinful actions carried out by many other Christian, non-German, Europeans.

In one very cruel insane action during the Holocaust, in Poland, all of the town's Jewish men, women and children were rounded up and taken and locked up in their wooden Synagogue that was then set afire. All of the Jewish men, women, and children were thus murdered. Because these Poles committed murder and also destroyed the Jewish Synagogue and it's Torahs and Ten Commandments, the souls of all of the destroyer murder Poles died. These destroyers and murders all have had their false prophets and false religious teachers who sinfully and ignorantly mislead them and taught them to hate Jews and to murder them. The Poles and their religious teachers did not recognize Moses as a Prophet and receiver of the ONE SINGLE GOD's Torah and Ten Commandments with specific instructions that **"You shall not Murder"**.

Moses became the First Prophet and was the first and only person ever to directly stand with and be in the presence of the ONE SINGLE GOD. While Jews recognize Moses as the Greatest Prophet, they do not address prayers to him addressing prayers only to the ONE SINGLE GOD. As recipient, from the ONE SINGLE GOD, of HIS Torah and HIS Ten Commandments, Moses became forever, the Greatest Prophet and religious teacher.

No other Prophet was ever in the presence of the ONE SINGLE GOD. No other Prophet ever received the words of the ONE SINGLE GOD in the form of a Torah (call it a bible, testament, or Koran) or in the written Words of the Ten Commandments carved into the stone tablets by the ALMIGHTY CREATOR, the ONE SINGLE GOD. The Torah and Commandments were directly given only to Moses by the ONE SINGLE GOD. They were meant to be given to the Children of Israel and to be for all of mankind forever.

Following Moses, there have been many other Prophets. But none were like Moses or as great as Moses. *Every Hebrew Prayer Book contains the statement that there will never be another Prophet as Great as Moses.*

Some later Prophets have been described as being either Major or Minor Prophets. Of those classified as being Major Prophets none reached the level of the recognized greatness of Moses. These Prophets include Isaiah, Jeremiah, Ezekiel and Samuel. The Minor Prophets, Hosea, Amos, Micah, Nahum, Nathan, Jonah and Elijah were not recognized among the greatness of the Major Prophets. While most Prophets were men, one, Deborah, was a female.

The Prophets preached the message that all of the Children of Israel had to adhere to and had to obey all of the Words and Laws of the Torah and maintain strict obedience to the ONE SINGLE GOD's Ten Commandments The Prophets tried to keep the Children of Israel on the correct path of life and preached that they were subject to and should be religiously, at all times, obeying and fulfilling each and every one of the Laws and Statutes stated in the Torah and in the Ten Commandments of the ONE SINGLE GOD.

The Prophets prophesied that there would be punishment, from the ONE SINGLE GOD, for disobedience and they also prophesied that ultimately there would be the future redemption of the Children of Israel and the future ultimate resurrection to life of the deserving dead. They prophesied that ultimately all of mankind would come to recognize, acknowledge, and pray only to the ONE SINGLE GOD and to no other god or gods.

The Children of Israel, the Jewish people, were especially strongly warned not to accept the prophecies of false prophets and to be very wary of any who claimed to be prophets even those who claimed to be prophets greater than Moses. Thus the Children of Israel, the Jews, could not accept the Jew Jesus or his disciples, or the Arab Mohammed as being true prophets of the ONE SINGLE GOD, or being prophets even greater than Moses, or as even ever really being only minor prophets.

There have been other Prophets. None ever reached the acme of greatness of the Great Chief Prophet Moses who was alone with the ONE SINGLE GOD on Mount Sinai and who received from HIM the Torah and the Ten Commandments.

THE EIGHTH PRINCIPLE OF FAITH

I believe with absolute perfect faith

that the whole LAW, now in our possession,

is the same that was given to Moses our Teacher, peace be unto

him.

There are Three sets of Laws that deal with (1) the Mother religion, the Jewish religion and the two daughter religions of (2) Christianity and (3) Islam.

The First Set of Laws are set forth in the Torah and the Ten Commandments and were given by the ONE SINGLE GOD to Moses at Mount Sinai. Moses, in turn, gave these Laws to the Children of Israel for all of mankind. That was over 3,500 years ago. These Laws are still in effect and are maintained unchanged and unaltered by the Children of Israel, the Jews of today. What the ONE SINGLE GOD declared as HIS Laws remain still today as HIS unchanged Laws and will forever remain unchanged.

With the advent of Christianity 2,000 years ago, the followers of the new daughter religion required, needed, created, and wrote a new set of Laws. They referred to the Laws of the ONE SINGLE GOD as being an old testament Laws and treated these Laws as really being an obsolete testament that could and should be cast aside and discarded. They accepted the new Laws, authored without the approval and authority of the ONE SINGLE GOD, by Christian church elders.

The new laws of Christianity became the new testament. The Ten Commandments of the ONE SINGLE GOD also became subject to becoming obsolete and requiring Christian amendments and changes. So the religiously "pious and wise" elders of Christianity meeting in Nicaea, in the common era year of 325, made the "necessary changes and improvements". Thus Christianity produced a "needed" new bible with new laws, the new testament, and also very "correctly" revised and "amended" the ten commandments,

In the seventh century of the common era, about 1,400 years ago, the daughter religion of Islam was established by Mohammed who titled himself as not only being a prophet but being the supreme greatest of all prophets. He claimed to speak for the one single god who gave him a new bible, the Koran with new laws and commandments. He was directed to convert everyone to the new faith even if this required murdering some or all of them.

Thus the followers of Islam are still today taught that it is correct and mandated that they force all to adopt their religion, or suffer as very low caste persons like slaves, or being murdered. Thus they can, in the name of their one single god, commit murder of infidels such as Christians and Jews.

The one single god of Islam, called Allah, was thus not the ONE SINGLE GOD of the Children of Israel who practiced the Mother religion of Judaism and heeded the words of the ONE SINGLE GOD, **"You shall not murder"**.

Just as the Christians, by observing their sabbath day to be on the First day, had changed the Commandment wherein the ONE SINGLE GOD had assigned, Blessed and Hallowed a special day of rest, the Sabbath, to be observed on HIS specified Seventh Day, so also did Mohammed state that Allah's sabbath day would be observed on the sixth day. The

ONE SINGLE GOD had given HIS Commandment on this subject but HE had been first overruled by the Christian church elders and then later also overruled by Mohammed and his followers.

Except for the Children of Israel, the Jewish People, mankind has never learned that the LAW (TORAH), the TEN COMMANDMENTS and the WORDS of the ONE SINGLE GOD are not ever to be altered, amended, changed or revised in any manner by man.

The ONE SINGLE GOD is the ALMIGHTY CREATOR who WAS, IS, and WILL BE the same as HIS Laws and Commandments.

The ONE SINGLE GOD does not need the stupid mentality of the "wisest" of men to tell HIM what a LAW should be or how it should be stated. Whatever ability man has to think, to comprehend, to understand, and to rationalize has been implanted within him by the ONE SINGLE GOD to think, understand, and not to ever veto or replace HIM or HIS Words. The ONE SINGLE GOD's Laws and Commandments are not ever to be revised, altered, amended or rewritten by any man.

The ONE SINGLE GOD has given man HIS Law and Commandments. This does not work in reverse. HE does not need man to tell HIM what to do or how to do something. HE does not need man to help create HIS ability to have any level of mental capability, understanding, or creative thinking.

Man is very naive if, in any manner, he believes, that with his weak thinking mind, that his small brain contains such levels of brilliant genius that he can tell the ONE SINGLE GOD what is right since he knows more than the ALMIGHTY CREATOR, the ONE SINGLE GOD.

Maimonides correctly realized that it is the ONE SINGLE GOD that is SUPREME and not man. Maimonides gave the correct words to this Eighth Principal of Faith when he stated that the ONE SINGLE GOD gave HIS Laws to Moses to give to the Children of Israel to have and to hold and that it should be forever HIS Laws for all of mankind to obey.

Moses knew that he could not change one letter or one word of the Laws of the ONE SINGLE GOD. This was also then known by all of the Children of Israel and known by today's Jewish people. They have not and are not ever to change even one small letter or one small word of the Laws and Commandments of the ALMIGHTY CREATOR, the ONE SINGLE GOD.

This message and understanding, that man is not to change any of the Laws of the ONE SINGLE GOD, has not been practiced, accepted, and acknowledged by the religious leaders and teachers of both of the daughter religions of Christianity and Islam who have instead established their own changed versions of the laws unauthorized by the ONE SINGLE GOD.

However, the daughter religions have depended, for their existence, upon their right to veto, change and rewrite the Laws and commandments of the ONE SINGLE GOD. Thus the daughter religions of Christianity and Islam also required new bibles. The Torah of the ONE SINGLE GOD had to be cast aside as obsolete and then rewritten as a Christian New Testament or as an Islamic Koran.

The result has been, that in the last 2,000 years since the advent of the daughter religion of Christianity and, in the last 1,400 years since the advent of the daughter religion of Islam, mankind has not had a "heaven on earth". Mankind rather has suffered greatly from the very many years of the increasing punishment from the ONE SINGLE GOD in the form of increasing violence and brutality and destructions resulting from murderous warfare.

Mankind has hated and murdered in the name of false religious beliefs. Every Commandment of the ONE SINGLE GOD concerning how mankind's various nations should live in peace with each other has been cast aside. Nations ruthlessly desire to conquer and rule over other nations and other religions.

Nations covet and desire to take and steal away the land and possessions of other nations. Nations will not peacefully live with and tolerate all of the peoples of all of the other nations or their different religions.

Nations and their peoples want their religion to be the dominant religion of all of the other nations and peoples. Some so-called religious leaders preach that their followers have a religious obligation and necessity to convince others to accept their belief and thus save their souls. The peoples of the nations who thus listen to and heed the hateful messages preached by these religious leaders are not obeying and adhering to the WORD and LAW of the ONE SINGLE GOD.

Is there any wonder that mankind suffers from horrible warfare? Is there any wonder that mankind still suffers from unexpected tsunamis and weather disasters and from ancient and even new illness? Is there any wonder that mankind suffers and millions perish from new and previously unknown illnesses such as AIDS?

No man, no matter from what religion, no matter how learned he appears to be, and no matter how religious or pious he may seem or appear, is ever authorized to change or revise the LAW of the ONE SINGLE GOD. That is the reason that Maimonides has stated his Eighth Principal of Faith. There is only ONE ALMIGHTY CREATOR who is the ONE SINGLE GOD and. there should be religious peace between all HIS mankind creatures.

It is the ONE SINGLE GOD who has given and provided, for all of mankind, HIS complete whole unchangeable Torah, HIS Law, and HIS Commandments. It is only HIS Torah, Law, and Commandments that all of mankind has ever needed and today urgently needs more than ever with nations of the world poised to obtain and use nuclear weapons. All Mankind must firmly retain the understanding and belief in only the ONE SINGLE GOD and HIS forever unchangeable Laws and Commandments.

THE LAWS OF THE ONE SINGLE GOD:
THE SECOND DEFINING ELEMENT

The first defining element of the definition of **"Who is a Jew"** is the requirement for one defined as a Jew to believe in the ONE SINGLE GOD. The second element is the requirement for every Jew to believe with full faith in all the Words expressed by the ONE SINGLE GOD in the Torah HE gave to Moses on Mount Sinai.

This is the Torah that Moses then gave to the Children of Israel. The Torah is also known as "the Bible". With the advent of the new daughter religions of first, Christianity, and second, Islam, the Torah has been cast aside by those who profess faith in the new daughter religions.

For these daughter religions there are new "Bibles", the New Testament and the Koran. The new "Bibles" contain many changes and do not state the Laws and Commandments of the ONE SINGLE GOD as HE stated them in HIS Torah.

The Torah consists of the First Five Books of Moses. The Torah is kept in Jewish Synagogues or Temples. It is divided into portions and each Sabbath, and during the Holydays, a portion is read. With the advent of the Jewish New Year, the reading cycle begins with the reading of the first portion from the Book of Genesis. Each subsequent week, on the Sabbath, the next following portion is read. In that manner, the entire Five Books of the Torah are completely read and repeated, from beginning to end, each year.

All who attend the weekly Sabbath services can themselves read and follow the Torah Reader's recitation of each and every word of the week's portion. It also provides an opportunity for the attendees to continue the learning and study of the Torah. The Rabbi (teacher) or another Congregation member will often recite a sermon providing additional information, explanation, and history of the weekly portion that is read.

The Torah contains the exact original version of the ONE SINGLE GOD's Ten Commandments. These are also recited and read when the Torah portion containing the Ten Commandments is recited and read.

There is no better way for one to know and learn these Ten Commandments than by reading them in the Torah. Since the Torah is hand written on scrolls that are maintained in the Synagogues and Temples, one can purchase a copy of the Five Books of Moses, the Jewish Bible, in book form, and read these original, unchanged by man, Ten Commandments.

The second element of the definition as to "who is a Jew" is contained in the Eighth Principal of Faith set forth by Maimonides. A Jew accepts and obeys the Laws and Commandments stated in the unchangeable Torah that was given by the ONE SINGLE GOD, through Moses, to the Children of Israel and through the Children of Israel to all of mankind everywhere.

THE NINTH PRINCIPLE OF FAITH

I believe with absolute perfect faith,

that this LAW will not ever be changed,

and that there will never be any other LAW from the CREATOR,

Blessed be HIS Name.

In a democracy, such as the one enjoyed by the peoples of the United States and the residents of each of the self governing Fifty States, it is the elected legislature, comprised of politically motivated, oriented, and minded individuals, that determines and enacts all of the laws of the land. As the legislatures have thus established the laws, so can they abolish the laws that they have legislated.

They can also, at any time, amend, modify, and change any laws they have previously approved and made.

The Supreme Courts, of the United States and of the Fifty States. the Highest Courts in the land, may determine that the legislated laws are unconstitutional. They may rule that the legislated laws are not complete in meaning and they may add their own varying interpretations. The decisions of the Court may then disallow and void any legislated laws or cause a changing of the meaning or intent of the laws.

These human made laws can then, at any time, by man be changed or altered by subsequent amendments, deletions, modifications, political interpretations, and abolishments. These are all appropriate and possible actions that can be taken for any and all of man made laws. But amendments, changes, modifications, political interpretations, and abolishments cannot ever be made and applied as authorized actions by man to any of the Laws and Commandments of the ONE SINGLE GOD.

HIS Laws and Commandments are given for mankind and are to be forever obeyed and to never be changed or altered as to the specific and intended meaning of the exact Words of the ONE SINGLE GOD.

There is no Court of Appeals available for mankind to appeal against any stated Law or Commandment of the ONE SINGLE GOD. There is no Court existing to over rule these Words or Commandments or to find it necessary to pronounce and enunciate an interpretation or decision as to the correct legality and constitutionality of HIS Laws.

There are no self serving personal or political considerations that are the basis for the origination and establishment of the LAWS of the ONE SINGLE GOD. No legislature is involved and there is no need for an all in favor of vote or a majority vote. There is no vote. Man is not requested to first consider, pass on, and then by vote approve any of HIS Laws and Commandments.

Once the LAWS of the ONE SINGLE GOD are made known and given to man, man cannot ever override, veto, declare the LAW unconstitutional, or in any other manner invalidate, amend, or change the LAW.

The LAW of the ONE SINGLE GOD is HIS LAW and remains unchangeable for all eternity. Thus, once given to man by the ONE SINGLE GOD, the LAWS and COMMANDMENTS HE has stated and given to man in HIS Torah and HIS Ten Commandments can never be altered, changed, modified or become subject for any need or necessity for man made improvements through alterations and interpretations.

No council of any religious body of elders, priests, prophets, or popes can ever change or amend any of the LAWS of the ONE SINGLE GOD. HE never gave approval or HIS authority or HIS right for the Nicene Council of church elders to change, modify, alter, amend or delete any to HIS Laws and any of HIS Commandments.

The ONE SINGLE GOD is very fully able to express HIMSELF without the need for help from any of mankind that HE has Created. This including any church councils of elders or religious preachers, leaders or popes that are not vested with any "rights" to amend or change HIS Words.

The ONE SINGLE GOD is fully capable of counting from one to seven without any help from church elders and religious preachers and leaders. When HE said in HIS Fourth Commandments that all were to maintain the Seventh Day as HIS established Sabbath Day, HE knew his numbers and HE could count and HE meant exactly what HE Said. The SEVENTH DAY is the SABBATH DAY of the ONE SINGLE GOD.

Similarly, when the ONE SINGLE GOD stated in HIS Second Commandment that mankind was not to make statues and images, HE knew exactly what he was saying. But again the church elders and leaders have chosen to override and veto the Words of the Second Commandment of the ONE SINGLE GOD and allow icons, statues, image and renditions of gods in art and portraits.

When the ONE SINGLE GOD states in his Sixth Commandment that man is not to murder, that is exactly what HE means. The Commandment is not word complicated and too difficult for mankind to understand. The present murders that are committed by Muslims totally and very sinfully violate the ONE SINGLE GOD's Commandment not to murder. Those who commit these crimes and also those who preach and send others to commit these crimes are, by HIM, never ever forgiven and their souls immediately die.

No human being can add to any of the Commandments that one should not murder unless the one that is to be murdered is religiously different and is therefore an infidel in which case one must, can, is required and should murder any one who is religiously believing differently. This applies to all of HIS Commandments which do not need additions, deletions, or revisions that alter and change the Commandments of the ONE SINGLE GOD.

Those who teach that it is right to murder and who instigate their followers to murder are not equally guilty of the murder. Rather, in their sinful violation of the Commandment of the ONE SINGLE GOD, they are greatly more guilty. The murderer's soul dies when the crime of murder is committed.

The soul of those, who teach and instigate others to commit the crime of murder, also dies when the teacher and instigator first speaks the words directing followers to commit the crime of murder in violation of the Commandment, not to murder, of the ONE SINGLE GOD. In speaking and teaching in the total defiance of the Sixth Commandment of the ONE SINGLE GOD, the teacher is the responsible instigator and commits a much greater sinful act than the one sent and directed to commit the actual crime of the murderer.

Thus those who teach and instigate murder, the Muslim Arab imams, mullahs, sheikhs and ayatollahs, all have themselves thus caused their own souls to immediately perish. There is no forgiveness by the ONE SINGLE GOD and no place for them in a Paradise or in the World To Come for any of these evil speakers and teachers who choose to defy the Word, the Law and Sixth Commandment of the ONE SINGLE GOD.

No priest, minister, reverend, pope, imam. mufti, mullah, sheikh, ayatollah or person who says that he speaks for any god has the right or ability to change or alter any Commandment of the ONE SINGLE GOD. They must recognize and adhere to all of the Laws and Commandments of the ONE SINGLE GOD.

Even those who preach, teach, and state that they are not changing or abolishing a Law or Commandment but rather only providing a "meaning" or an "interpretation" must be very careful to assure that they are not altering and defying the exact meaning of the Words of the ONE SINGLE GOD. There is no forgiveness that is ever given by the ONE SINGLE GOD to any person for doing this.

All of mankind has to be very careful and be very aware of all the false preachers, teachers, so called prophets, and would be interpreters of the Word, Law and Commandments of the ONE SINGLE GOD. There have been many who have often lied and falsely declared themselves to be prophets and to have "heavenly approval" to spread their sinful words and very sinfully wrong interpretations. Some are motivated only for personal profit and their desire to instill their false messages into the hearts and minds of mankind. One must not ever listen, heed, or obey the false prophets and their false statements.

The Words of the Ten Commandments were carved into stone tablets by the ALMIGHTY CREATOR, the ONE SINGLE GOD. Each person can read and study these original carved in stone Commandments contained in the Torah (Bible). Under no circumstances are they, the ONE SINGLE GOD's Words of HIS Ten Commandments, to be ever altered, amended, changed or declared obsolete by mankind. These are eternal Words, Laws, and Commandments. They should be forever always treasured, obeyed, respected, and maintained in the hearts and minds of all of mankind without any exceptions.

THE TENTH PRINCIPLE OF FAITH

I believe with absolute perfect faith,

that the CREATOR, Blessed be HIS Name,

knows every deed of all of the children of men,

and all their thoughts, as it is said,

it is HE who fashions the hearts of all,

and HE that gives heed to all their deeds.

The ALMIGHTY CREATOR is the only Creator and HE has created everything. HE is the ONE SINGLE GOD that has created each and every living thing and each and every human being. The ability and power of the ALMIGHTY CREATOR is totally beyond the comprehension of any and all human minds even those of the greatest and most intelligent of religious teachers, scientists, and mathematicians.

It is also certainly beyond the comprehension and understanding of each and every person. This includes all of those ever believed to have been, in the past, among the greatest of humanities' religious geniuses that have ever existed or who, in the future, will ever exist. No Rabbi, Priest, Pope, Imam. Mullah, Mufti, Sheik, Ayatollah, or any other so-called religious human being has ever totally known or understood the infinite abilities of the ONE SINGLE GOD.

The ALMIGHTY CREATOR, the ONE SINGLE GOD has created all of us and endowed us with life and with a soul that can, like the human body, live or die. The ALMIGHTY CREATOR has given to each of us, who may be capable of reading this, the ability to exercise a free thinking will and to be capable of the performance of good and/or evil deeds.

At all times, HE knows exactly everything that we think about, are planning, desire and want to do, have determined that we will do and we will perform. It is as if each of us were with very high technologically totally wired into a super fast hi-tech system that continually rapidly emits and at all times sends forth signals and messages of all of our thoughts and intentions to the ONE SINGLE GOD, the ALMIGHTY CREATOR. Nothing that we may at any time ever think and have thoughts about is ever hidden, remaining unknown, and concealed from the infinite knowledge of the ONE SINGLE GOD.

Since the ONE SINGLE GOD knows our every single thought, we should be using our minds and free will to think of only good thoughts and deeds. We should not, at any time, think or plan to hurt or injure any of our fellow mankind in any way. We should think about the actions that we can take that would lead only to full obedience of all of the Laws and Commandments of the ONE SINGLE GOD.

We should always give charity and needed and necessary assistance, aid, and comfort to those who require any of our help and care. We should act only in ways that always benefits and helps our fellow mankind and never do any acts that harm anyone in any way or fashion. We should deal justly and honestly with all others and give needed assistance to the poor, widows, and orphans, and also to all of those who are disabled and ill.

The ONE SINGLE GOD does not place evil thoughts into our human brains. Originally, the human brain is set to think only good thoughts and to assist in planning good actions. We all have the same ONE SINGLE GOD's given opportunity to think and plan and live good blessed lives. There are however, some who are misfortunate, because of an injurious accident or illness, and being handicapped are not able to think clearly. These individuals must and should be assisted, in all ways, in order to help them.

With our limited human intelligence, provided by the ONE SINGLE GOD, the ALMIGHTY CREATOR, we do not know, and may never know, why there are those humans who are unfortunately injured, ill and mentally handicapped individuals. But, we who are not afflicted must accept that we are therefore fully responsible and accountable to the ONE SINGLE GOD to assist each and every one of all of those less fortunate. We must and should help them in all ways to properly live and conduct themselves and enable them to lead the best of possible good lives.

Since the ONE SINGLE GOD does not Create us with brains that initiate and start our thinking process with sinful evil thoughts, it becomes our full responsibility to maintain our thoughts free of sinful evil thoughts. We should make sure that we properly keep our thoughts only on good deeds and planned accomplishments. We do not come into this life and world with evil thoughts and we should not leave this life and world leaving behind evil thoughts.

We are not born created and endowed with brains and thoughts containing built in messages of hate directed at other of the ONE SINGLE GOD'S created humans. We should therefore resist all evil messages and thoughts of hatreds that other evil humans want to teach us. We should leave behind a record of a life of good thoughts and actions that, at the time we are called to stand in after life Judgment, will testify to our complete obedience and our complete fulfillment of all of the Laws and Commandments of the ONE SINGLE GOD.

Every single word that one plans to say, and utters and ultimately states, is instantly known to the ALMIGHTY CREATOR. It behooves us to therefor be fully careful at all times in all of our thoughts and expressions. We are human and must consider and not express our thoughts in an all too swift wrongful and thoughtless manner of hateful anger. Each thought and word expressed should be carefully made to control our actions to conform to the requirements and directions given to all of us by the ONE SINGLE GOD in HIS Laws and Commandments.

It is best to first think about what one is going to say. One must not voice such furious anger that one injures another. One must not curse or make deceptive or false statements. Too many times, because man has spoken evilly, others have suffered.

As we are able to orally communicate with other persons, in a similarly manner we can also silently communicate with the ONE SINGLE GOD who at all times knows our every single thought. We can keep quiet and silent and maintain our secrets from all other human persons but there is no way, that by keeping quiet and silent, that we can ever keep our thoughts unknown as silent secrets from the ONE SINGLE GOD.

Every thought that we have, that may remain as secret silent thoughts in our minds only and are not communicated to anyone else, is nevertheless always fully and completely known to the ONE SINGLE GOD. Understanding this necessitates, mandates and requires, that at all times, our silent thoughts should and must be total thoughts of goodness, justice, charity, truth, peace, honesty, friendship and love for all of our fellow humans and all of the creatures and creations of the ONE SINGLE GOD.

There are no exceptions where one is allowed to think thoughts of hatred of other humans. Nor are there any exceptions that allow any thoughts of disobeying any of the ONE SINGLE GOD's Ten Commandments. There are absolutely no exceptions that allow, for any reason, any thoughts and plannings of actions of crime or of murder. These sinful evil thoughts are never justified and are not ever given any exception for any so called religious or any other reasons and they are not ever subject to be forgiven by the ONE SINGLE GOD.

The ONE SINGLE GOD who has created all humans knows at all times all of the deeds and thoughts of all of the humans. Each human must live a life that abides by all of the Laws and Commandments of the ONE SINGLE GOD. Not for any moment of time can one remain deep in thought about something evil and keep that thought secret and prevented from being known to the ONE SINGLE GOD.

At all times, all humans must think about that. We must keep our thoughts firmly on the righteous paths and on topics of thoughts being complete with thoughts of truth, justice, mercy, honesty, charity, and goodwill and friendship for all of your fellow human beings. Do not ever resort to biased untruthful, wrongful, unjust, and hateful thoughts. Always remember that the ONE SINGLE GOD is, at all times, an instant recipient of all of your thoughts and your plans for actions and your conduct.

Remember that there is all too often a connection between man's thoughts and man's ultimate actions and deeds. Your thoughts should result in only the deeds that produce actions that manifest, without any exceptions, truth, justice, mercy, honesty, charity, and goodwill and friendship for all of your fellow human beings.

The ONE SINGLE GOD knows all of all our thoughts and HE also knows all of all of our deeds. These thoughts and deeds cannot in any way or manner be kept as secrets from HIM. Do not listen to any of those who would lead and direct you into evil thoughts or actions. Do not listen to any of those who say that they can grant and give forgiveness, in the name of a god, for sinful thoughts and deeds that are made in disobedience of the Laws and Commands of the ONE SINGLE GOD.

THE ELEVENTH PRINCIPLE OF FAITH

I believe with absolute perfect faith,

that the CREATOR, Blessed be HIS Name

rewards all of those who keep HIS Commandments,

and punishes all of those that transgress them.

The Commandments of the ONE SINGLE GOD, the ALMIGHTY CREATOR, are very easily understood and can be obeyed by all. There is absolutely no reason to disobey any of the Commandments except if one does not believe in the ONE SINGLE GOD. **Obey all of HIS Ten Commandments. Those who do not obey the Commandments of the ONE SINGLE GOD will merit HIS Judgment and their punishments.**

The first four Commandments deal with recognizing the existence of the ONE SINGLE GOD and the relationship of mankind with the ONE SINGLE GOD

The first Three Commandments state explicitly and clearly that there is only the ONE SINGLE GOD. There are no other gods. One is not to worship or venerate any other so-called god or gods. Nor shall anyone make graven images, idols, icons, or statues that are to be used for religious worship of these gods. The ONE SINGLE GOD is to be always completely respected and HIS Laws and Commandments are to be obeyed. HIS Name is to be respected and never to be taken or stated in vain.

The Fourth Commandment clearly states that the ONE SINGLE GOD is the ALMIGHTY CREATOR who has created everything that has and still exists everywhere. This Commandment relates that HIS Creative Work was accomplished during Six Days and that the ONE SINGLE GOD then rested on the Seventh Day and that HE Blessed and Hallowed the Seventh Day and Commanded that mankind also must and should observe the Seventh Day that HE chose to be as HIS Sabbath and rest day, because HE stated that it was on that very Specific Day that he rested from HIS Creations.

The Fifth Commandment states clearly that everyone is required to respectfully honor their parents. This is understood to mean to also include having respect and honor for all of the elderly of mankind thus also including one's grandparents and ancestors and also to have respect for all and any non related elderly person.

The last Five Commandments concern one's behavior and ability to live in peace with all others and to accomplish all deeds honestly, justly and honorably. Therefore one is Commanded not to act criminally and Murder, or to Commit Adultery, Steal, Lie, Cheat, and Bear False Witness. One is not to be sinfully desirous and to jealously envy and Covet and take away any and all property, items, objects, and possessions that rightfully belong to others.

It is not difficult to live one's life in full acceptance and in accordance with each and every one of the Ten Commandments of the ONE SINGLE GOD. Those who obey and live their lives according to the Commandments are those who merit the rewards of the ONE SINGLE GOD.

Their souls remain alive in this world and also remain alive for the "World to Come" when there will be a resurrection of all of the resting dead. However, those who defy the ONE SINGLE GOD and do not live in accordance with HIS Commandments destroy their souls and will not be resurrected with all of the resting dead. Their souls have died because they had decided with their own free will and have chosen not to live and obey the Ten Commandments of the ONE SINGLE GOD.

Often, one cannot see or understand that, with obedience to the Commandments, one has been or is being blessed and rewarded by the ONE SINGLE GOD. The blessing and reward may not be apparent or understood in the mortal lifetime of the human. The blessing and reward may appear when the soul that restfully lives on after human death receives the blessing and reward of renewed resurrected life in the World to Come.

The same is true of the punishment later meted out because one does not adhere to or obey the Commandments. The greatest punishment is the soul's death which may occur even though the body is still alive. What the ONE SINGLE GOD gives HE can take away. HE Creates and gives the human a body and a soul. HE takes away the life of the body when it is time for the body to die. HE can also, at any time, take away the life of the soul of a sinner who defies and disobeys HIS Commandments.

The ONE SINGLE GOD deals justly with all of HIS Creatures and in HIS Judgment punishes all of those who with their free will choose to disobey HIS Commandments.

>   HE punishes those who accept, venerate and worship false pagan gods.

>   HE punishes those who have other gods that they religiously worship and place before the ONE SINGLE GOD

>   HE punishes those who swear and take the ONE SINGLE GOD's Name in vain.

>   HE punishes those who do not observe the Seventh Day for the Sabbatical rest.

>   HE punishes those who dishonor their parents and the elderly.

HE punishes those who murder.

HE punishes those who commit adultery.

HE punishes those who steal; those who bear false witness and those who covet the possessions of others.

After HIS Judgment with HIS Justice and HIS Mercy, all of those who by their deeds, actions and even thoughts then merit HIS Punishment are punished by the ONE SINGLE GOD either in their span of human lifetime or in the time and place that is reserved for the soul to possibly live on after death.

Those who do observe and faithfully obey the Ten Commandments of the ONE SINGLE GOD are duly and amply rewarded in their human lifetime. They are in addition also duly and amply rewarded in the time and place reserved for the soul that has earned and merited a continued life beyond the life and upon the death of the human body.

In today's world, too many do not observe the original Ten Commandments. Some observe man altered and modified commandments. Some of these altered commandments, while defying the ONE SINGLE GOD, do not appear to result in injury to other humans. However, all too often they have lead to injurious serious criminal actions including murder of other human beings. These alterations are not in agreement or accord with the original expressed Commandment Words of the ONE SINGLE GOD.

However, some of mankind heed, observe, and religiously maintain all of their conduct under such wrongly altered and modified man authored commandments. Thus they live their lives in a manner that results in actions that lead to their severely ignoring and disobeying all of the Ten Commandments of the ONE SINGLE GOD.

The worst example of the disobedience to the Commandments of the ONE SINGLE GOD is where the Sixth Commandment is modified and altered to allow those who adhere to the false commandment to actually murder other human beings.

This modified and altered version allows Muslims to commit the crime of murdering other human beings because they are "infidel" Christians or Jews. The wrath, fury and burning anger of the ONE SINGLE GOD will be expressed as HIS Punishment against all the murderers violating HIS Sixth Commandment, at the time of HIS Judgment of them. Their souls shall perish and not live in the World Beyond.

There has never been and there is now no acceptable or forgivable excuse or reason for this great disobedience to the Sixth Commandment of the ONE SINGLE GOD. Those who teach and instigate others to commit murder, to become suicide murder bombers, as well as those who actually commit the suicide murder, destroy their souls that had been given to them by the ONE SINGLE GOD.

Unlike all of the previous years of all of the many past centuries, since, at these times, in today's world there is more opportunity to be literate and knowledgeable, there is no valid excuse for any of mankind to not read, study, and understand the ONE SINGLE GOD's Ten Commandments. Therefore, each individual has a greater duty and responsibility to now read and study and acknowledge the original Ten Commandments of the ALMIGHTY CREATOR, the ONE SINGLE GOD. This will then result in greater obedience to the original Ten Commandments .

THE COMMANDMENTS OF THE ONE SINGLE GOD;
THE THIRD DEFINING ELEMENT

The first defining element of the definition of **"who is a Jew"** is the requirement to believe in the ONE SINGLE GOD.

The second defining element of the definition is to believe in, accept, and obey the Torah given by the ONE SINGLE GOD through Moses to the Children of Israel.

The third defining element is the requirement to acknowledge and obey each and every one of the Ten Commandments of the ONE SINGLE GOD.

These are the Ten Commandments that the ONE SINGLE GOD wrote and carved into the two stone tablets prepared by Moses. It does not take the brilliance and great mental capacity of a "rocket scientist" to understand the Commandments. There is really no reason why all of the Commandments, as provided to man by the ONE SINGLE GOD, cannot be obeyed.

For Commandment number One to be observed, there is no reason for not acknowledging the existence of the ONE SINGLE GOD, who as the ALMIGHTY CREATOR, Created you and me and every thing.

The mere fact, that Darwin believed that his great grandfather was a monkey or an ape and that his great great great grandmother was a one celled amoebae that came alive in a gooey mixture of muck and mud that was accidentally struck by lightening, does not eliminate the existence of the ONE SINGLE GOD.

If a person has to choose between believing in Darwin or in the ONE SINGLE GOD, there is no intelligent basis for believing in Darwin.

The reader can believe that Darwin's great grandfather, the ape, might have been his great grandfather too, or the reader can believe that like Darwin, his great great great grandmother was just another one celled amoebae, or the reader can appreciate and believe in the ALMIGHTY CREATOR, the ONE SINGLE GOD.

To be defined as a Jew, one can not and does not believe in Darwin's malarkey and must believe in the ONE SINGLE GOD. Similarly, a person who does not believe in Darwin's malarkey but nevertheless is an avowed godless secular, atheist, or so-called humanist, can not be defined or classified as a Jew.

For Commandment number Two, there is no need for anyone to "create" a god, or gods, or son of a god or another of a god. There is no reason to attempt to humanize the ONE SINGLE GOD and to create HIM in a human image. There is no reason to attempt to picture a god or make an idol, statue, or icon image for veneration and worship of a god

For Commandment number Three, there is no reason to curse or take the Name of the ONE SINGLE GOD in vain. The unknown Name of the ONE SINGLE GOD can not become a man made up name and then be subjected to vain statements.

Even without the knowledge of HIS Name, because of all due full respect for the ONE SINGLE GOD, no person should "create" a name for him and then use that made up name in vain. It must be recognized that HE gave no Name to Moses when HE was asked and, instead, HE answered that HE Was, HE Is, and HE Will BE.

It must also be recognized and observed that by this Commandment Three, the ONE SINGLE GOD has forever commanded that HIS Name should not be ever stated in vain.

For Commandment number Four, it is not at all difficult in any manner or way to obey the Commandment to refrain from daily work and activity and only to rest and worship on the Seventh Day that the ONE SINGLE GOD Hallowed and Blessed.

HE did not choose another day to hallow and bless as HIS Sabbath Day. HE did not state that man could at any time choose any other day than the Seventh Day as the day to be forever observed and maintained as HIS Blessed and Hallowed Sabbath Day.

For Commandment number Five, there is no reason for not teaching children to always properly respect their parents, grand parents and the elderly. This conduct should form the basis to bring peace within families, nations and all of mankind. But to assure this conduct by children, parents have the responsibility to diligently always teach this Commandment to their children.

They can not rely only upon teachers or "holy men and women" to teach their children this Commandment. As they expect their children to honor and respect them as parents, they must also assure that their children express and have, for all of their elders, the proper conduct, respect, and honor.

For Commandments numbering Six through 10, that govern mankind's needed behavior, there is no excusable or forgivable reason to violate these Commandments, of the ONE SINGLE GOD, to never commit murder, or to never commit adultery, or to never steal, or to never lie and give false witness and testimony, or to never covet.

Because all of these Ten Commandments are very easily understood and can be easily obeyed, there is no reason for disobedience. All of mankind is directed by the ONE SINGLE GOD to obey HIS Ten Commandments. This is the complete essence of the Third Element defining **"Who is a Jew"**.

A Jew acknowledges his treasured beliefs in all three of the required elements that define the Jew. First, in accord with element number one, he must, in full faith, believe in the existence of the ALMIGHTY CREATOR the ONE SINGLE GOD. Second, in accord with element number two, he must, in full faith, believe in the Commandments and Laws of the ONE SINGLE GOD as they are written and stated in HIS Torah. Third, in accord with element number three, he must specifically, in full faith, believe in and obey each of the Ten Commandments of the ONE SINGLE GOD. The total belief in these first three basic elements, define and classify the believer as being Jewish. A non believer is not Jewish.

THE TWELFTH PRINCIPLE OF FAITH

**I believe with absolute perfect faith
in the coming of Messiah,
and although he may delay his coming,
I will wait for his coming.**

A good friend, who was a writer of poetry, was a very observant Catholic. He had been born in Scotland and stated that he would never return there even for a visit. He explained that as a child he had been a student in a Catholic parochial school and had to take a long walk, from his home, across his town and walk through a Christian Protestant district to get to his school. On several occasions, he had been stopped and struck and severely beaten by angry Protestant youngsters.

He would always explain that he strongly believed that the true messiah was the Jew Jesus and that he would again return a second time. He would discuss his firm belief in Jesus as the messiah and state, "You will see when Jesus, who was Jewish, comes again for the second time, I will then say here comes the messiah once again for a second time and all of the Jews will then proclaim him as the messiah and they will then very loudly state "Look there, here he comes the messiah we have waited for, here he comes for the first time".

But the good Scottish American friend was very wrong. To date, no Messiah has ever appeared and all of the many predictions concerning all of the wondrous events that would then occur worldwide with peace among all peoples and nations everywhere, with the appearance of the Messiah, have not happened.

Men still know tragic and hateful warfare and there still has not ever been peace and brotherhood of mankind everywhere or anywhere on this ONE SINGLE GOD'S Created Earth. Indeed, man is now capable and can now destroy the entire Created World with his horrible murderous Nuclear, Biological, and Chemical (NBC) weapons of mass destruction.

The wolf and lamb, and the leopard and the kid, still can not and do not lay down to rest together in peace. Bows and arrows and swords and spears have graduated and been upgraded to now become the horrible NBC weapons of mass destruction and the means to kill and destroy many millions of humans.

Indeed man is now capable of destroying the entire world that the ONE SINGLE GOD Created. The swords have not been and are not being changed into peaceful pruning hooks or farm implementation tools. Men still hate one and another and violate each and every one of the ONE SINGLE GOD's Commandments as they engage in warfare and sinfully murder of each other.

For thousands of years and continuing still today, tragic events still strike at all humans. There are floods, fires, earthquakes, mud slides, hurricanes, tornadoes, tsunamis, and numerous illnesses including many new illnesses that were completely unknown in years past. These tragic events were not created by natural evolution or any of Darwinistic chance happenings of nature. These events were all created by the ALMIGHTY CREATOR as punishments, for all of the disobedient human races, by the ONE SINGLE GOD.

Has the Messiah ever appeared? Has the Messiah ever been sent to bring man to an age of paradise on this earth? Has any Messiah appeared that caused mankind to cease making war and killing innocent men, women, and children? No!

The Messiah has not ever appeared to man because man has not merited and deserved the appearance of the Messiah to be sent by the ONE SINGLE GOD. Man has sadly continued to disobey the ONE SINGLE GOD and all too often scorn and not fulfill HIS stated Laws and Commandments.

The Torah, the Bible, relates that the Children of Israel cried out and groaned, to the ONE SINGLE GOD of their patriarch Abraham, because of their slavery, servitude, bondage and bitterness of their lives as slaves to the Egyptians. They cried out because the evil Pharaoh decreed that all of the new male infants born to the Children of Israel had to be thrown into the Nile River and drowned.

The ONE SINGLE GOD heard their cries and groans and sent his agent messenger, Moses, to free them from their evil and bitter bondage and slavery and take them out of Egypt to the Promised Land of the Covenant. Moses, as a messenger appeared in the eyes of the Children of Israel, to be a Messiah of those times.

Moses did all that the ONE SINGLE GOD asked him to do. But he was human and not a deity or a Messiah. Therefore he was not a perfect being and erred and was not allowed to take the Children of Israel into the Land promised by the ONE SINGLE GOD to be HIS eternal gifted inheritance to the Children of Israel.

No human being can ever be totally one hundred percent perfect in all ways in his life and in complete obedience to the Commandments and Laws of the ONE SINGLE GOD. Not man, but only the ONE SINGLE GOD is totally perfect at all times in all ways. The Messiah also will not be a perfect being and may humanly err since the Messiah will not be a god or a son of god or any kind of deity and only the ONE SINGLE GOD is ever and always a Perfect Being. The Messiah will be sent, as HIS Agent Moses was, only to carry out all of the instructions and directions of the ONE SINGLE GOD and bring peace and HIS Blessing to all mankind. This will be done at a time as and when determined by the ONE SINGLE GOD.

The Messiah as Moses will not be a perfect being. He will not be sent to mankind to be worshipped by man or to stand in place of the ONE

SINGLE GOD. The Messiah will only be a servant, agent, and messenger under instructions and guidance of the ONE SINGLE GOD.

When the Messiah shall appear, at the time set by the ONE SINGLE GOD, all of mankind will know of the arrival of the Messiah. His arrival will not be concealed or made known only to certain nations and peoples. Upon the arrival of the Messiah sent to all mankind by the ONE SINGLE GOD, the world will be a better place for all mankind. All nations will exist in peace and without warfare and the never again ever have need for weapons. Indeed, as it has been stated, nations will turn swords into plowshares.

All of mankind's sinfully evil ones will perish and not exist. The evil ones will all bodily die and there will not be any resurrection of the dead souls of any of the evil mankind. There will be continued peace all over the lands of the world among all of the surviving nations where people are not sinful and evil. Men will no longer know or think of war and they will be without thoughts of any hatreds or biases.

All of the Commandments and Laws of the ONE SINGLE GOD shall be obeyed by all of mankind. And the wolf and the lamb, and the leopard and the kid, will be the best of friends. Isaiah's prophecy will come true. At the time of the Messiah, all of mankind will acknowledge and know only the ONE SINGLE GOD and will not know of any other gods or deities. All prayers and worship will be addressed only to the ONE SINGLE GOD. Lest man maintain sinful violation of the Commandments of the ONE SINGLE GOD, all statutes, idols, icons and other displays that are man made, to represent any deities or gods, will be destroyed.

With the appearance of the Messiah, and as all of mankind ceases to deny and defy all of the Laws and Commandments of the ONE SINGLE GOD, the ALMIGHTY CREATOR, the storms and punishments of the ONE SINGLE GOD will cease. There will be no more tornadoes, hurricanes, floods, massive forest fires, volcanic explosions, blizzards, tsunamis, earthquakes, and mudslides. There will be no more famines and droughts.

Every man will greet each and every one of all of his neighbors with respect and friendship. No man shall have any hatred for his neighbors even for those who are not of his race, color, or ethnicity. Each shall willingly give any aid and help necessary to any of his neighbors. Peace shall be wonderful for all of mankind. There will be no illnesses.

With the appearance of the Messiah, the ONE SINGLE GOD shall cause the resurrection of the dead. All souls who are sleepily resting shall awake to the new dawn of mankind. But only those, who have deserved to have their souls sleep and rest and await the resurrection, shall be awaked and revived. All of the lost dead souls will remain as lost dead souls and not be capable of being awakened and revived.

Until the appearance of the Messiah, all mankind must, while waiting his arrival, be patient, just, charitable, righteous and obedient to all of the Commandments and Laws of the ONE SINGLE GOD. The time for the appearance of the Messiah will be determined by the ONE SINGLE GOD who is watching and waiting for mankind to merit and be worthy of the Messiah being sent to appear and bring salvation to all of mankind.

THE THIRTEENTH PRINCIPLE OF FAITH

I believe with absolute perfect faith

that there will be a revival of the dead

at a time which will please the CREATOR.

Blessed and praised be HIS Name forever and ever.

In the beginning, in the Torah, the Bible, it is written that man is made in the image of the ONE SINGLE GOD. That image of the ONE SINGLE GOD is not the image of the human body.

The image of the ONE SINGLE GOD is rather the unseen and indescribable soul of man that is in the image of the ONE SINGLE GOD. Just as no man has ever seen and therefore cannot describe the ONE SINGLE GOD, no man has ever seen the soul of a human and no man can describe the human soul.

The body of man does not live forever. Some of mankind have long lives of many years and some do not live long lives of many years. Some are well and healthy in body and mind while others are sickly, crippled, and in other ways not well.

Some slip away in death very peacefully while others may painfully die as a result of serious illness, accident, or are killed in warfare or are murdered.

While the human body dies and is buried, or some are cremated, only the soul has a possible ability to be able to live on eternally. That possibility depends upon whether the deceased has led and lived a life of justice, kindness, charity, and in the obedience to the Commandments and Laws of the ONE SINGLE GOD. Thus man alone has a free will and may in his actions and deeds control the outcome decision of the ONE SINGLE GOD's Judgment as to the eternal destiny of his soul. Man, by his lifetime actions can give continued life to his soul or he can destroy his own soul.

Those souls that the ONE SINGLE GOD, in HIS Judgment, determines as deserving and meriting continued existence after the death of the human body will be allowed and awarded an after life. The ultimate resurrection and the awakening to life of the soul, after the period of the sleeping and resting after the death of the body, will occur upon decision of the ONE SINGLE GOD as to the time of resurrection.

Until the resurrection of the dead, at the time of the appearance of the Messiah sent by the ONE SINGLE GOD, the souls of humans that are determined to merit an after life, sleep peacefully and await the resurrection. There is no paradise or heaven for the souls that are alive while they still are peacefully asleep and slumber. After death, immediate living soul life in a Paradise and Heaven does not exist. After the human body dies, those souls that are still alive peacefully sleep continually until the time of resurrection.

It is written that King Saul of Israel was faced with a very serious coming battle of war with the Pagan Philistines. He was very concerned and wanted to know the battle outcome. Would he survive the battle being victorious or would he be slaughtered and defeated by the Philistines?

It is written that there had been "witches" that were believed to be able to communicate with the dead. King Saul earlier had all of the "black magic witches" put to death. However, one witch survived and King Saul found her and then took her to the grave of the Prophet Samuel who had anointed him the first King over the Children of Israel.

The "witch", it is written, brought forth the spirit of the soul of the Prophet Samuel from the grave. The spirit of Samuel, awakened, then asked. "Why have you awakened me from my rest and my sleep?"

Saul questioned the spirit of Samuel as to the outcome of the next day's battle with the Philistines and was then informed by the awakened spirit of the soul of Samuel that, on the following day of the battle with the Philistines, Saul and his sons would all be killed. The events of the battle the next day were as the spirit of Samuel had stated when he was aroused from the sleep of the dead. Saul was very severely wounded and fell upon his sword and died so that he would not be captured, tortured, and killed by the Philistines.

The anointed David, who had as a youngster killed the gigantic Philistine Goliath using a sling shot, then became the new King over the Children of Israel. It was also prophesied and is still believed that the Messiah, who would be later eventually be sent by the ONE SINGLE GOD, would be a descendant of the psalmist King David.

The Prophet Samuel had died and his buried body was left to ultimately return to the dust of his original creation. However, as it is written, Samuel's soul was not dead. Neither was his soul in a Paradise or Heaven. His soul was resting and asleep. The soul of Samuel had been disturbed in its rest and sleep and was awakened. His soul then, after the revelation made to King Saul, returned to the rest and sleep to wait for the time when the ONE SINGLE GOD would cause the resurrection of the dead.

Those who by their lifetime actions and deeds deserve to have their souls live on beyond the death of their body will be resurrected only when the ONE SINGLE GOD is ready to cause the dead to come alive. But, there will not then be present all of the humans who have ever lived. Many who have died will not have earned, merited, and deserve have living sleeping souls that are to be resurrected.

ONE: HIS NAME SHALL BE ONE · 225

Too many have lived lives being evil, unjust, uncharitable, cruel, unkind, and disobedient of the Commandments and Laws of the ONE SINGLE GOD. By their own self destruction of their souls, they will be dead both in body and soul and will not be resurrected at the time of the Messiah. Too many wrong acts and deeds of man, performed with his free will, are so very sinful and have so violated the Laws and Commandments of the ONE SINGLE GOD that they themselves have caused the destruction and death of their souls.

Each human being is blessed with a life that is breathed into his body by the ONE SINGLE GOD. It is then the responsibility of each human being to protect and shelter his soul and keep it alive by the manner of how the human being lives. Man is vested with a free will by the ONE SINGLE GOD who does not force, compel, or direct any person in any way, shape, or manner as to how to live.

Evil beings, such as evil rulers of nations or evil religious leaders, who teach and instigate followers to murder and kill, do not merit the reward of having living souls that can awake at the time of resurrection. Men like Hitler, Himmler, Eichman and all of their followers have exercised their free will, and by their unforgivable sinful acts, destroyed and killed their souls. The same has been true of religious leaders of any religion that have ever sent their followers to murder during crusades, inquisitions, pogroms, and holocausts.

Muslim men like the Imams, Muftis, Mullahs, Sheiks. Emirs, and Ayatollahs who totally violate the ONE SINGLE GOD's Commandment and teach and preach murder, and who then instigate and send others to commit murder, have likewise then murdered their own souls. They kill their souls immediately when they utter their vile first words of hatred and direct others to commit the criminal actions of murder.

Those who instruct and send others to be suicide murderer bombers, and also the suicide murderer bombers themselves, do not wind up in any eternal Paradise. It is utter nonsense to believe that they will be blessed with an existence in a Paradise of Heaven. Rather, by divine Judgment of the ONE SINGLE GOD, their souls instantly die when they first plan, urge and instigate others to go forth and commit murder. There are no exceptions for any of those defying the ONE SINGLE GOD's Commandment not to murder as being by "a Koranic exception".

The souls of all of those who commit murders also instantly die. There will be an after life and a resurrection of the dead but only for those whom the ONE SINGLE GOD determines as meriting the resurrection. Murderers do not merit resurrection.

For each of the Laws and Commandments that are ignored and defiantly cast aside and not obeyed, the human will suffer the absolute Judgment of the ONE SINGLE GOD. There is no Court to appeal to for overruling this Judgment. Therefore it should be known and understood that it is the duty and the responsibility of each human being to take all of the necessary moments of time necessary to read and learn all of the original Ten Commandments of the ONE SINGLE GOD. Once this is accomplished and learned, it is then not difficult to live a life in total obedience of all of these Ten Commandments.

Each human being should commence reading the Torah, the "Bible", starting with the first words **"IN THE BEGINNING GOD"** written in the first paragraph of the first page of the original "bible", the Torah that was given to mankind by the ONE SINGLE GOD. Then every one should continue reading the rest of the Torah, the "Bible". Reading, knowing, fulfilling, and obeying the Laws and Commandments written into the Torah will assure survival and ultimate revival of their resurrected souls after death.

THE TWO STATED REASONS

In the Preface, it was stated that there are two reasons for this writing.

The first reason was that too many have harbored hatreds against their fellow man.

Thus herein there is explanation of the Jewish Religious beliefs.

The second reason was to define and explain "Who is a Jew".

Thus herein there is the definition of the three required elements that define a Jew .

As to the first reason, all too often the hatreds of man have been based on untruths, false and fraudulent information, and lies. These hatreds have been inserted into the minds and hearts of individuals who never really knew or understood who, what, and why they hated.

Many have been purposely instructed, misinformed, and misguided into these hatreds. Thus, similar to a virus infection, the vicious hatred illness of anti-Semitism has been allowed to fester for almost the two millenniums of the religion of Christianity and also during the following era of the religion of Islam.

The Christian religion has been always said to be a religion of love. But this love has very sinfully produced horrible murderous crusades, murderous inquisitions, murderous pogroms, and the more recent murderous Holocaust that resulted in the murder of over six million men, women, and included over one and a half million murdered infants and children.

Similarly, the religion of Islam is said to be a true monotheistic religion of belief in the one single god who has created not only the Muslims but who has created all humans who are all his creations. But, now we are to understand and believe that this one single god has amended his "You shall not Murder" Commandment and instructed and wants the believers in Islam to all become murderers and kill all infidels who are described as being Christians and Jews.

Muslims are now, today, especially to murder all of the Jews. They accept the "fact" that the one single god wants Muslims to murder, in his name, for him. This has caused Muslims to believe that the one single god allows Jihad murder and suicide murderous attacks and blesses the suicide murderers.

Thus the Muslims today are injected with the illness of anti-Semitism, the virus of the hatred of Jews. They receive this message of hate on a daily basis in their Mosques, newspapers, television programs and in teachings in their schools and colleges.

This has very tragically resulted in too many violent murderous Muslim actions that are still continuing in these days. It is now even tragically resulting in Muslims murdering Muslims in Iraq, Afghanistan and in Jordan. Once taught to murder and to believe that these actions are blessed by the one single god, it has now resulted in Muslims also murdering each other.

The first reason and purpose of this writing was to tell all of the haters exactly what the Jews religiously believed since the Jews were hated because of their religion, their beliefs, and because they would not convert and accept either of the Christian or Islamic religions. What was it in the Jewish religion that required hatred and murder of Jews by Christians and Muslims? If the reader is one who hates Jews, what is it he or she hates?

Simply stated, the Jews have been, for almost four thousand years, very guilty of loyally and stubbornly maintaining and keeping their belief in their monotheistic religion founded by Abraham the first Jew, with their belief being in the belief in the ONE SINGLE GOD, the ALMIGHTY CREATOR, who has created everything and all of mankind including those who have professed their religious beliefs in Christianity and Islam and also, of course, including those who have manifested hatred of Jews.

The Jews faithfully believe in the Torah (their Bible) that they believe was given to them by the ONE SINGLE GOD through Moses. They accept, in full belief, the exact stated words of the Ten Commandments that are contained in the Torah and described therein as having been carved by the ONE SINGLE GOD into the stone tablets prepared by Moses on Mount Sinai.

Although the Jews have been subjected to murderous attacks by those obsessed with hatred, the Jews have never conducted murderous crusades, murderous inquisitions, murderous pogroms, and murderous Holocausts against Christians. They have also not massacred and murdered Arabs and Muslims. They do not condone, encourage, and send murderous suicide bomber attackers to murder Arab and Muslim men, women and children.

The ONE SINGLE GOD looks down at all of the actions of the entire human race. HE knows of all the sinful hatreds that some have against their fellow man. HE sees all of the murderous attacks that take place. These attacks are against HIS Commandment not to murder. HIS Judgment and punishment is and always will be against all who with their own free will violate HIS Commandment and commit murder.

All who ever harbor or who will harbor hatred against any of their fellow human beings, the creations of the ONE SINGLE GOD, the ALMIGHTY CREATOR, will be brought to Justice under HIS Judgment and punished by HIM. No individual can profess and maintain belief, in any so-called religion of love, that orchestrates and inspires the individual to hatred and to commit murderous actions and not be subject to HIS Judgment and HIS Punishment.

The ONE SINGLE GOD does not ever bless and reward those who, for any reason, commit murder. This applies even more so for those who murder in the name of any religion and even more so for those who are committing murder doing and saying that they are doing so in HIS Name. For many centuries innocent men, women, infants and children have been intentionally and willfully tortured and painfully murdered by murderers who say they are committing the violent murder in HIS Name. All who harbor hatred in their hearts, minds, and souls are ignorant of the ONE SINGLE GOD's Commandment not to murder and very sinfully believe that they can violate HIS Commandment by murdering in HIS Name.

So then why do some many hate the Children of Israel, the Jews? Why do so many undertake anti-Semitic actions? Why have so many violated the Sixth Commandment of the ONE SINGLE GOD and committed the murder of innocent men, women and children?

Upon what is their hatred based?

Why do they hate?

They hate the Jews because the Jews have very faithfully and stubbornly, for Four Thousand Years, maintained their monotheistic religious belief in only the ONE SINGLE GOD, the ALMIGHTY CREATOR.

They hate the Jews because the Jews have faithfully and stubbornly maintained their belief in the TORAH, the Original "Bible", given to them, that they believe was given not only for them, but was given for all of mankind, by the ONE SINGLE GOD through Moses and the Children of Israel.

The stubborn Jews refuse to accept any other man written bibles, testaments, or Korans. They also hate the Jews because the Jews faithfully and stubbornly maintain the belief that the Seventh Day is the Sabbath Day chosen for all mankind by the ONE SINGLE GOD as was stated to have been so commanded by the ONE SINGLE GOD is HIS Original "Bible ", the TORAH.

They hate the Jews because the Jews religiously celebrate different Holydays that are those stated to be celebrated as commanded by the ONE SINGLE GOD in HIS Original "Bible", the TORAH. The Jews believe that there are not any different religious Holydays to be recognized and celebrated as stated in any other man written bibles, testaments, or Korans.

They detest and hate the Jews because the Jews have faithfully and stubbornly maintained the dietary Laws as commanded by the ONE SINGLE GOD in His Original "Bible", the TORAH and stubbornly and differently refused to eat the foods, commanded not to be eaten. The Jews believe that if the ONE SINGLE GOD has said not to eat certain foods, they are not to question HIS Commandment and Decision.

They hate the Jews because their religions of "love" have taught them to hate and even to murder Jews.

They are taught and told that the Jews caused the evil murderous Romans to kill the Jew Yeshua Ben Yosef, Jesus. This has lead to many mass murderous attacks upon Jews because Christians were taught that Jews were Christ killers and god killers. Christians also falsely were told that Jews killed Christians because they had to use their blood for the Passover Matzos. Did the Christians also then believe that their Jesus, the Jew, in his celebrations of the Passover Holyday, known as the Last Supper, made, served, and ate matzos baked with pagan's pre-Christian's blood? This false Blood Libel has repeatedly been stated time and time again and was raised in many lies expressed and taught by high ranking Catholic priests.

The Russian rulers, to prompt their people toward anti-Semitic pogrom actions, produced the false tale of the "Protocols of the Elders of Zion" accusing the Jews of wanting and plotting to control all nations and all the world's monitory matters. They printed this libel and it still exists and is today taught to Moslem students. Along with Hitler's Mein Kampf, the Protocols ranks as a best selling books in Arab and Muslim countries. These books, Muslim Best Sellers, will soon be joined with Jimmy Carter's new book as the Muslim best sellers.

Arabs are to believe that Jews want to control and dominate them and take and rule over all of their lands. Imagine the tremendous size and magnitude of the lie. Five and a Half Million Jews desire to conquer Three Hundred Million Arabs and increase the land size of their minute State of Israel from 8,400 Square Miles by seizing in conquest the over Six Million Square Miles of Arab owned lands. Utter nonsense and a disgrace that some of mankind's minds are so ignorant.

These published lies have been believed by haters to be true. The haters believe each of the false untruths about Jews. They believed and still believe that it was the Jews, and not the evil and pagan murdering Romans, that killed the Jew Jesus. They believed the false untruth that Jews murdered Christians for their blood. They believed the false untruth that Jews, few in number compared to the billions of Christians and Muslims, plot and intend to overwhelm all of the worlds peoples and nations and conquer and rule the world and all sources of monitory wealth.

All of the carefully and purposely taught lies of hatred has resulted in many millions of murders being committed by Christians and Muslims in very intentional, ruthless, sinful, and utter defiance of the Sixth Commandment of the ONE SINGLE GOD not to commit murder.
Throughout all the centuries of Christianity and Islam, preachers and priests of these faiths have lied and told many untruths in order to inspire and instigate their followers and believers to hate and murder Jews. This tragically culminated in the Holocaust of the last century and the current, almost daily, murders of Jews living in Israel. This has resulted in "recognition" that Jews should not be allowed to have even one very tiny country while the Twenty One Arab League nations, having millions of square miles of land need more land and should have a Twenty Second country. This also culminates in the Muslim belief that the more than Fifty Muslim nations also need and should and must have more lands. They do not have more lands because of the guilty desire of Christians and Jews to live, adhere to their religious beliefs, and exist.

The call to hatred and to murder Jews has often been made by leaders of the nations who Covet the property of the Jews. During the crusades, the mobs who were the crusaders often entered Jewish communities to rob, steal and murder. These actions were condoned by the "holy" men and the crusader Pope who encouraged them onward to fight the Islamic occupiers of the Holy Land. The Spanish rulers, Isabella and Ferdinand, wanted the property and all of the wealth or possessions of the Jews of Spain. So, with full Papal blessings and encouragement, began the murderous "holy inquisitions". Jews were either to convert and accept the religion of Christian Catholicism or leave the country and go into exile. Of course they would have to leave their homes, lands, and possessions behind. Jews that had lived peacefully in Spain for many hundreds of years and many generations had to choose between staying in Spain and giving up their Jewish faith or remaining Jewish and leaving their homes and lands to go into exile without any possessions.

Some Jews decided to stay and openly convert to Catholicism but still secretly adhered to their true beliefs in Judaism. When they were caught maintaining their true Jewish belief, the love religion of Christianity, with total and full approval and blessings of the Pope and the Vatican, would have them "good, properly, and very painfully" tortured and then burned alive at the stake. The Spanish public, as onlookers, applauded the public torture and killing of the Jews.

Then, how surprised today many who are Spanish or called Hispanic, and believe that their ancestors were always Catholic, would be to discover that they have inherited Jewish blood and DNA from ancestors who were forcibly "converted" to Catholicism but remained secret Jews or Marranos (Spanish meaning " pigs") and intermarried with Spanish Catholics.

The Germans and Europeans, before, during, and after World War II, also coveted and wanted the homes, property, and whatever wealth or possessions the Jews had. So they too were not totally unhappy that Jews were rounded up and taken to death concentration camps by the Nazi Germans and their fellow European cohorts who existed in almost ever country conquered by the Nazi Germans.

As soon as the Jews, men, women, children and infants were taken away and transported to the death concentration camps, their loving Christian neighbors immediately took all of the property and homes of the Jews. Their few artistic paintings of value, were taken by the Nazis to be given to Goering's collection. After the war, many of the Jewish owned paintings of value wound up in Art Galleries throughout the world. Some of these renown Galleries still, to this date, have refused to return these stolen paintings to their rightful owners, the survivors of the Nazi death camps or the families of the non-survivors.

In some European countries, it was not the Nazi Germans who rounded up the Jews. In all too many times, in many countries, it was their long time Christian neighbors that rounded them up and turned them over to the Nazi Germans. Sometimes they did not turn them over to the Nazi Germans but instead murdered their Jewish neighbors to steal and take their homes and possessions. These actions, of having their Jewish neighbors murdered by the Nazis, or doing the murders themselves, to steal the possessions of the Jews, was done in many European countries and in most of these crimes against humanity, the criminal stealers have never since then sought to return the stolen possessions to any Jewish survivors or their descendants who may have survived the Holocaust.

In one instance, for example, Polish neighbors, **in the Town of Jedwabne,** rounded up all their Jewish neighbors, men, women, children, infants, the young and the elderly, everyone Jewish. They locked them up inside the wooden synagogue of the Jews and then set fire to the synagogue and burned to death all of the Jewish men, women, children and infants of their community who had lived with them for centuries. Their Polish neighbors then took, and still have retained all the land, homes, and possessions of the murdered Jews.

This is sadly very true elsewhere in Poland where coveted Jewish properties were taken and kept as their Jewish neighbors were being murdered by the Nazi's or by the Poles themselves.

The Jews, the inheritors of the title of Children of Israel, still pray in the Hebrew language of the Original Bible, the TORAH, and the original language of the Ten Commandments of the ONE SINGLE GOD. They do not pray in Latin. Rather, the language of the idol worshipping pagan Romans became the first of the Christian prayer languages and is still the language of the Roman Catholics and the

Vatican. For the most part, Christians do not understand the Hebrew language and have not taken time to study the language and cannot read Hebrew. Jesus did not pray in Roman Latin. He prayed in Hebrew.

In the past some have tried to translate the Hebrew TORAH and the translations have been faulty and incorrect. The prime example often given is the translation that Moses came down from the presence of the ONE SINGLE GOD with the Ten Commandments and that there were "horns" on his head. The correct translation should be that there was radiation around his head.

The Jewish Star of David has been defiled in many ways. It is a symbol of Judaism and was once the symbol on the sheath of King David, the Psalmist, and the man whom the Prophets predicted would be the ancestor of the Messiah. Christians can accept the fact that there was a man of the Children of Israel who was anointed and became the King and his name was David. They can even recite some, but not all, of King David's psalms. Perhaps the most known of King David's psalms is the Twenty Third Psalm that begins with "The Lord is My Shepherd, I shall not want."

The Christians agree and recognize that the Messiah would be a descendant of the Jewish King David. They religiously state that the Jew, Yeshua Ben Yosef, was that descendant of the Jewish King David and was the Messiah. But they cannot accept the Star of David and all too often have had hatred and defiling contempt for the Star of David symbol. The International Red Cross and Red Crescent have repeatedly refused to recognize the Jewish equivalent, the Red Star of David (the Mogen David Adom) even though the Jewish organization is often the first to provide medical services, equipment, and doctors to those anywhere in need.

The Red Star of David was among the first to respond to the needs of the tsunami victims even though most were Muslims. And they were among the first non US organizations to come and respond to the needs of the victims of Hurricanes Katrina and Rita. Recently, a hidden Star of David inside a red square, will be allowed and recognized by the International Red Cross.

While the Star of David is often held in contempt, not so for the cruel vicious murderous symbol of the pagan Roman murder device, the cross. This murder device, an outstanding contempt to the ONE SINGLE GOD's Commandment "You Shall Not Murder" is venerated and worshipped as the religious symbol of Christianity. The symbol of pagan violation of the ONE SINGLE GOD's Commandment not to murder is mounted on the tops of churches and on church steeples. It is almost like pointing upwards, heavenly, a finger in disgusting contempt of the ONE SINGLE GOD. The Pope proudly walks about with his staff bearing the symbol of the murdering deadly cross with a statue of a man, murdered by the pagan Romans, mounted on the cross.

A comedian, Lenny Bruce, remarked, "It is a good thing the Romans did not have electricity or all Christians ladies would be walking around with little electric chairs on their necklace chains" and electric chairs would be mounted on the peaks of all church steeples and the Pope would walk around with an electric chair on his staff containing the statue of a man electrocuted and chained into the chair.

The Jews have never believed in or tried to force conversions upon Christians or Muslims. The Jews have never sought to "save the Christians or Muslims and their souls even if they had to kill them to save them." The Jews have never desecrated the Churches of Christians or the Mosques of the Muslims. Today, there are many ancient Churches and ancient Mosques. But where are the ancient Synagogues of the Mother Religion?

Since Judaism preceded Christianity and Islam for millenniums, one would expect and believe that there would be a great number, many, ancient synagogues. But in the past two thousand years since Christianity and the past fourteen hundred years of Islam, the followers of the Daughter Religions have destroyed all of the ancient several thousand year old synagogues.

So there are many reasons to hate Jews because they are still, after all the centuries of being hated, persecuted, and murdered, still very stubbornly faithful to the belief of the Children of Israel in the ONE SINGLE GOD and HIS Torah and HIS Ten Commandments.

Today, it is not the Jews who, while wanting only a small country small in size, covet the twenty-one Arab League countries and many millions of square miles of land territory of the Muslim Arabs. Rather it is the more than Billion Muslims who covet and want all of the very tiny land of the Jews in Israel. Please take the time to look upon and review a map and notice all of the Muslim Arab and other Muslim lands. Note their land sizes. Then note the land size of Israel. Compare all the land sizes. Note that Israel can hardly be seen on the map.

The Jews do not hate or despise the Muslims. It is too bad, and a very grievous unforgiven sin against the ONE SINGLE GOD, that the Muslims must have hatred for the Jews and have strong desires to murder them.

To answer the question as to where are the ancient Jewish Synagogues, one has only to look back a few years ago when the Old City, the Walled City of Jerusalem, was under the total control and domination of the Arab Muslims (the ones who titled themselves as Jordanians). The Arab Muslims who captured and occupied the Old City of Jerusalem intentionally desecrated and destroyed each and every one of the ancient Synagogues that had existed in the Old City of Jerusalem. Desecrating the ancient Jewish Cemetery, Memorial Headstones for deceased Jews, were torn away and then moved and used as side walk pieces and also as urinal splash blocks by and for the Arabs.

More recently, the Arab Muslims have run amok and destroyed the Jewish Tomb of Joseph, the Biblical Joseph who explained the dreams of the Pharoh and saved the Egyptians from the seven years of famine and requested that he be taken from Egypt after his death and buried in the Land of Israel. The Arabs have also violated the religious sanctity of the Christian Church of the Nativity in Bethlehem when terrorists seized possesion during a battle with the Israelis. Given full control of all of the land now governed by Israel, the Arab Muslims would destroy every Jewish Synagogue and every Christian Church. How many Christian Churches are there in all of the Arab countries???? Try to enter Saudi Arabia with a copy of the New Testament and see what happens to you, and you will never find a Christian Church in that country or in most Arab Muslim countries.

There are many other invented lies and reasons given to hate the Jews and be anti-Semitic.

The second reason and purpose of this writing was to define "Who is a Jew". There has been no finite definition established and accepted. For past centuries it sufficed to say and declare that the Jewish Rabbinical Law had provided the definition that anyone whose mother was Jewish, and whose father did not have to be Jewish, was therefore automatically Jewish since the mother was Jewish.

Today, Jews are separated by the strength and depth of their religious belief into "denominations" known mainly as Orthodox, Conservative, and Reform. There are some lesser "denominations" also. Accordingly, there are new thoughts and new declarations and definitions by some Conservative and Reform Rabbis who no longer represent the Orthodox Jews who have maintained and taught the sternest and greatest religious considerations and religious depth of belief.

The previously followed and adhered to religious laws and beliefs have been revised by each of the latter two denominational divisions. Thus the prior accepted Rabbinical definitions are not followed by all Jews. There is then need for a new Rabbinical definition that can be accepted by all who are Orthodox, or Conservative, or Reform.

The Reform Jewish Rabbis have already now changed the previous definition by the inclusion that anyone whose father was Jewish, even if the mother was not Jewish, is also therefore Jewish. The problem with the old definition, the Orthodox definition, and the new Reform definition is that no consideration was given to the fact that the child is not allowed a free will for self determination and might not desire to be Jewish.

It was an automatic "you are" definition. It completely eliminated the recognition that the ONE SINGLE GOD had given all human beings the freedom of will to think, act, and to determine what and who they wanted to be and which religion they would choose to accept and believe as being the "true religion". Each person is, after all, personally answerable to the ONE SINGLE GOD concerning his or her life choices and actions. Thus each person can choose the religion to follow and accept. No person is marked as belonging to a religion decided and chosen by others be they parents, family, or friends. This is a very personal choice and selection. Thus merely having or not having one or both parents, who have chosen to be Jewish, does not result in a child being automatically Jewish and staying Jewish. The same free will choice exists for a child born to Christian or Muslim parents. It is for the child to decide which religion to follow when the child reaches the mental age to have the capability of free will decision.

When then reaching the age of capability to make life decisions, the child who desires to be Jewish must understand and recognize that he/she must first believe in the existence of the ONE SINGLE GOD, and then secondarily believe in HIS Torah and HIS Ten Commandments.

The author, Naomi Ragen, in her novel, "The Covenant", on Page 151, states the questions and problem of defining "who is a Jew?" She states that Jews are not a race because there are "beautiful black Ethiopian immigrants coming to Israel who are Jewish". She asks whether Jewishness involves and is a religion?

The answer to all of these and similar questions begins with the definitions most important basic first element requirement. To be Jewish one must absolutely believe in the existence of the ONE SINGLE GOD who created everything and everyone and is the ALMIGHTY CREATOR. One who does not believe in the ONE SINGLE GOD, a secularist, atheistic, humanistic, or in any way a non-believer can not be defined as being and is not a Jew. There is not a so-called Jewish denomination that can be Jewish without the belief in the ONE SINGLE GOD. The new denomination of Humanistic Judaism is non Jewish and the very title is an incorrect oxymoron

Once it is established that a person believes in the first element of the definition and believes in only in a ONE SINGLE GOD, then the second and third defining elements must be positively answered. The person must also believe in the ONE SINGLE GOD's original unchangeable "Bible", the Torah, given to Moses to give to the Children of Israel and thus also given for all of mankind. The Torah contains the exact words, word by word, of the ONE SINGLE GOD's Ten Commandments as given to Moses to give to the Children of Israel and thus also given for all of mankind.

The requirements, of the second and third elements of the definition, to believe in the Torah (the second element) and Ten Commandments (the third element) of the ONE SINGLE GOD, eliminates Christians who believe in a trinity of gods and who believe in an amended and altered ten commandments.

It also eliminates all Muslims who believe in their version of the one single god but do not believe in the original "bible" the Torah and believe instead in their Koran that does not contain and include the ONE SINGLE GOD'S original Ten Commandments.

In summation, the Jewish people, the Children of Israel, believe today, as they have for many thousands of centuries, in the existence of the ONE SINGLE GOD. This belief existed when the world of mankind consisted of mostly pagan believers and worshippers.

After two millennium of Jewish religious belief, the Christian religion came to exist among mankind and then many centuries later, the Muslim religion of Islam came to exist among mankind. Throughout the ages, Jews, the Children of Israel did not ever persecute and murder Christians or Muslims. Rather it has been the other way with Christians and Muslims persecuting and murdering Jews.

The murder of six million Jewish men, women and children in the last century and the murder of Jewish men, women and children in the last and this current young new century attests to the results of the hatred that have been preached and taught to Christians and Muslims who have violated the ONE SINGLE GOD's Ten Commandments.

Those who, no matter how and under what banner of a religion, have destructive hatred that exists within them, in total defiance of the ONE SINGLE GOD, and results in persecution and murder, will never ever be forgiven by the ONE SINGLE GOD.

All of mankind, not only the Jewish Children of Israel, must be completely and totally obedient to the ONE SINGLE GOD and adhere to each and every one of all of HIS original unaltered Ten Commandments.

Mankind is not to follow and heed the words and messages of false men who claim to be HIS priests and prophets and who claim to speak in HIS Name and thus teach and instigate their followers to defile HIS Commandments and specifically to go out and murder other men, women, and children, including elders who are aged and infants, who are innocent. Think and consider all of your thoughts and actions. Are your thoughts and actions those that can stand and exist before the Judgment of the ONE SINGLE GOD???

THE DEFINITION OF WHO IS A JEW

The Three basic elements that define and give the total answer, as to who is a Jew, have herein been stated to be that:
1. A Jew believes in the ONE SINGLE GOD, and
2. A Jew believes in the Torah of the ONE SINGLE GOD, and
3. A Jew believes in the Ten Commandments of the ONE SINGLE GOD.

Jews today are said to be divided into several different religious categories or denominations. The mostly known divisions are said to be Ultra Orthodox, Modern Orthodox, Conservative, Reform, Reconstructionist, Secular, Atheistic, and Humanistic.

Of these divisions only the Ultra and Modern Orthodox, Conservative, Reconstructionist, and Reform Jews can and should be defined as Jews since they meet the three basic element requirements. They recognize the existence and have belief in the ONE SINGLE GOD. They believe in and maintain the Torah in their Synagogues and Temples. They adhere to recognition and belief of the Ten Commandments. However, there are differences among these Jews respecting intensity and interpretations of the Laws and Commandments causing the divisions.

The Secular, Atheistic, and Humanistic divisions do not qualify for being defined as Jewish divisions. Therefore their followers are not, by their own definition Jews. They do not believe in the ONE SINGLE GOD. They do not believe in the HIS Torah and do not believe in the Laws and Commandments of the ONE SINGLE GOD stated in HIS Torah. They do not acknowledge all of the Ten Commandments starting with the most important First Four Commandments.

Some have held the firm belief that one could disavow himself from all three required elements and still be included and considered a Jew if he was a child of a Jewish mother. Lately this has been modified to include being considered a Jew if one had a Jewish father.

Thus today, the Catholic Cardinal Jean-Marie Lustiger, whose parents were both Jewish and murdered in the Holocaust, is considered to be a Jew even though he had long ago renounced Judaism and converted to Catholicism. By this same definition, if Jean-Marie ever becomes the Pope, Catholics will have a Jew as their Pope.

Some foolishly believe that Jews are a distinct and separate race or people. They forget that the wife of Moses was the daughter of the pagan priest Jethro. They do not acknowledge the fact that besides the Children of Israel, there were some Egyptians who fled Egypt with Moses and merged into the families of the escaping Children of Israel. They seem to intentionally forget that the pagan Ruth came to Israel with her mother-in-law when Ruth's Jewish husband died. Ruth then married Boaz and from this marriage came their descendant, King David. And from the descendants of King David, it is written and believed that the messenger from the ONE SINGLE GOD, HIS selected Messiah, will come to save and bring a new dimension to the world. Jews are not a distinct race or a distinct people. Tomorrow, the Pope could decide to be Jewish and by adherence and full belief in the three required elements be, by definition, Jewish.

Evolution??? or Intelligent Design????

THE ANSWER IS ADAPTOLUTION!!!!

THE THEORY OF ADAPT·O·LUTION

We, you and I, did not evolve from absolutely nothing. We, you and I, did not have a monkey for an uncle and our great great great great grandfather was not an ape.

Of course I am speaking about you and I. I am not speaking for Darwin who more than likely, for sure absolutely, did have a monkey for an uncle and a great great great grandfather who was an ape. At least Darwin's uncle, the monkey, and his great great great grandfather, the ape, probably had the same intelligence as their descendent Darwin.

It has been written that Darwin's Theory of Evolution came about when Darwin noted that turtles of a specie of turtles on one Island, had some different features than other turtles of the same species who lived on a far distant Island.

Yes, indeed, the turtles had adapted to living on different Islands with a different climate and with many other differences. Darwin also noticed that birds of a particular specie on one Island had longer beaks than the same specie of birds who lived on the other far remote Island.

The birds on both Islands made their meals the worms that lived under the earth. On the one Island the worms lived close to the surface. On the other Island, because of the earth's differences, the worms lived much further down under the top surface.

Lacking forks, knifes and spoons, the birds on that Island adapted by growing longer beaks to reach deeper to their food supply meals of worms. The turtles and birds just adapted to their surroundings just as Polar Bears and Penguins adapt to their world of harsh cold arctic winter.

In summary, all species of man, animal, insects, turtles, birds, fish, viruses, bacteria, and plant life ADAPT to the nature of their surrounding world and its environment and climate. If they fail to do so, they will not survive. The turtles and birds seen by Darwin did not evolve, they adapted and they survived.

The theory of ADAPT O LUTION is not in conflict with the Theory called the Theory of Intelligent Design. **{We are not supposed to call the Theory of Intelligent Design the Theory of the Existence of the ONE SINGLE GOD.}** The Theory of ADAPT O LUTION confirms that the Intelligent Designer, the ONE SINGLE GOD, provided and allowed for all living creatures, including you and me, and of course including the turtles and birds, to survive by adapting to the surrounding world and changes in nature, environment and climate.

Recently, much has been written about the two opposing Theories, the Theory of Intelligent Design and the Theory of Evolution.

The one Theory is that some believe there is some unknown Intelligent Designer who has created everything in the multitude of Universes. And that the Intelligent Designer created you and me. This sounds like a religious Theory with the Intelligent Designer being a GOD. So of course, the liberal atheists do want this Theory recognized, or heaven forbid , taught to children in school.

Others, the liberal atheists, seculars and humanists, believe that everything just happened by sheer chance and that you and I were created because our prior ancestors originally were one celled creatures that were resulted from nothing and Evolved into us. They believe that our ancestors Evolved from the one celled creatures into monkeys and apes before becoming us. This has now lead to legal controversy as to whether our children should be taught that we were all created by an Intelligent Designer, a GOD, or whether we just evolved from Darwin's nothing that came from out of nowhere.

Should our children be taught only Darwin's Theory of Evolution and told that this Theory was based upon one hundred percent absolute and certain Scientific evidence? Should our children be taught the other Theory of Intelligent Design? If this second Theory were to be taught, would that be like teaching religion in school, Heaven Forbid? Or, possibly, should both Theories be taught in our schools?

The truth of the matter is that those Scientists, who declare and profess that they have the complete ultimate wisdom and truthful proof that all and everything, including of course themselves, you, and me, were just here by some mere chance and that we came from out of nothing from out of nowhere and we all have monkeys as uncles and apes as great great great grandparents and ancestors, are fools. But maybe not, I can easily believe that those Scientists who espouse the Theory of Evolution are, themselves, very truly, really, evolved and descended from some of nothing from nowhere that became monkeys and then apes and then themselves. Indeed, it may be that some of the evolutionized monkeys and apes have much greater mental capacity and wisdom then the Darwinized Scientists.

Each of us were created by an Intelligent Designer, the ALMIGHTY CREATOR, the ONE SINGLE GOD. None of us have been the result of any evolution. Nor has any plant, insect, animal, virus, fish, bacteria or substance of any matter been the result of any evolution. Rather, the same Intelligence that Designed us, you and me, and all of the matter that exists in all of the infinite Universe and beyond, had the Supreme Intelligence and Design capability to have all matter designed and created to be capable of adaptation to any changes of our climate, environment, world and the universe.

Why is it that we just happen to live on a world that can provide us with air to breath, water to drink, and food and nourishment? How come our planet world allows life? Why is it placed in its orbit around the energy giving sun in the exact place. space, and distance from the sun so that we can survive on this planet and enjoy the sun without burning to death or freezing to death.

I look about me and I see the evidence, not of evolution but of the infinite Intelligent Design of the ONE SINGLE GOD that allows us to live on this planet. I see the walls, floor and ceiling of my room and I know that while this was all made by man it was made from materials created by the Intelligent Designer, the ONE SINGLE GOD, and provided for man's use. None of the materials were provided by chance from nothing from nowhere as stated by the whims of Darwin's Theory. None of these inorganic materials evolved from inorganic one celled nothings from nowhere.

Recently, the Dover Area School Board in Pennsylvania wanted to have 9th grade students taught by their biology teachers concerning the Other Theory, the Theory of Intelligent Design, as an alternative to the Darwin Theory of Evolution. However, that was overruled by a not so very intelligently designed or evolved Judge John Jones. He believed that the teaching would violate the requirement of separation of Church and State by violating the Establishment Clause of the First Amendment to the United States Constitution. He went along with the scientific experts who testified that Darwin's Theory of Evolution certainly, without any doubt, represented good, valid, and absolutely true science.

Since then. there has been many other open controversies regarding teaching our children whether only Darwin's Theory should be taught. To most believers who believe that they are themselves the absolute results and the scientific evidence of evolution, Judge Jones ruling was the perfect solution. However, I find it in conflict with the more truthful scientific Theory of Intelligent Design. Indeed, the Intelligent Designer, the ONE SINGLE GOD, has provided a better answer than Judge Jones. The Intelligent Designer has an underlying Theory that allows for understanding that changes to living creatures are permissible and that all living creatures can change by adapting to their environment and its changes without so called evolution.

This underlying Theory is the Theory of "Adapt o lution." Under this Theory, all creatures can adapt and change to address and overcome changing and new world conditions of climates and environments. They can change themselves as it is required of them to survive. Those who do not undertake to adapt themselves will not survive. It has been said, the strongest and the fittest will survive. If another ice age came, those creatures who would, when required, change themselves and adapt to the cold would survive. Those who did not change and adapt themselves would not survive.

Viruses are said to mutate when they are threatened by extinction by new vaccines. Indeed the weakest who cannot adapt to the new vaccines do not survive. However, some of the strongest viruses will adapt and survive. ***That which is called mutation is really adaptation.*** The evidence that the human race adapted to very cold northern climates can be seen by the existence of the Eskimos. Humans have also adapted to other climates and environments such as deserts and climatic locations that manifested itself in diverse protective skin pigmentation and facial design. Other creatures also have found reason to adapt themselves to environmental changes. One can replace the Theory of Evolution with the Theory of Adaptolution explaining away the falsity of Evolution while being subordinately compatible to the Theory of Intelligent Design and existence of the ONE SINGLE GOD without need for the nonsense of the Theory of Evolution.

CONCLUSION

The reader should understand that there has not been any valid reason for those who hate to really harbor any hatred for any of mankind and particularly against those who adhere to their Jewish religious beliefs. Not all Christians and Muslims are possessed with the hatreds that are expressed below. But all too often, in history, too many have been thus possessed.

The hater of the Jews hates the ONE SINGLE GOD that Jews believe in and worship. The hater of the Jews also **hates the original first bible, the Torah,** that states the initial monotheistic origin and essence of the recognized existence of the ONE SINGLE GOD that is somewhat in some manner also attempted to be recognized in the Christian and Muslim religions. The hater of the Jews also dislikes and **hates the Ten Commandments** of the ONE SINGLE GOD and therefore must alter, change, and amend these Commandments.

Jews have never forced others to accept their Judaic religion and beliefs and the choice of conversion or the thrust of the sword. Jews have tried to live peacefully without hatred with the many peoples of many nations. But the peoples of the many nations have, because of their vile and very wrongful and sinful hatred, all too often murdered their neighbor Jews and stolen their possessions.

Many times their neighbors have tragically forced the Jews to chose between conversion to their religious beliefs or being murdered.

This hatred has existed throughout all of the past millenniums and centuries of years . It existed in the Nazis of Germany and with many other German and European Christians who were their willing evil cohorts. Today this hatred still strongly exists in the Christian and Muslim world.

Jews have never ever called for murderous extermination of Muslim Iranians; but some Iranians, as they are taught and understand their faith, have called upon the world to murder and exterminate all of the Jewish people Those Iranians are doing this while the ONE SINGLE GOD looks down upon them. Those Iranians may be believers in a daughter religion but they have nothing but contempt and hatred for the MOTHER RELIGION. Their punishment for this murderous sinful hatred will surely come from the ONE SINGLE GOD.

Those who possess hatred against Jews and the Judaic religion must know and need to know that they also hate (1) the ONE SINGLE GOD, (2) they hate HIS Bible, the TORAH, and (3) they hate HIS TEN COMMANDMENTS.

There is today much dispute about whether the Ten Commandments shall be posted on the walls of our Courts of Justice and made known to all persons Some believe that the Ten Commandments are statements of religion and thus interfere with the reasoning and beliefs of those who have no religious beliefs. Others believe that only their version of the Ten Commandments must be posted. There is no valid reason not to post those of the Ten Commandments that certainly are addressed to all of mankind and are not religious statements but apply to all mankind. These are the Commandments that, in the name of Justice, must apply to, and must be obeyed by, all of the mankind created by the ONE SINGLE GOD.

The following of the Ten Commandments, lest we offend Darwinist, do not favor any single one of the worlds religions, and should and must be posted on the walls of all of the Courts of Judgment and Justice and even in all of our homes.

Commandments For All Of Mankind

HONOR YOUR MOTHER AND FATHER.
You shall honor and respect your parents, your mother and your father. You shall likewise honor and respect your grandparents and all who are your elders. Make each day a day that you act according to this Commandment and cause your mother and father to know that you love, honor and respect them. Be the object of praise by all who are your elders. **You shall not hate anyone, your parents or any persons who are your elders.**

YOU SHALL NOT MURDER.
You shall not harm. injure, maim or murder any of your fellow mankind, your neighbors, or any person who does not agree with you for any reason or over any matter of differences. At all times, you shall not possess, harbor or teach any hatred against any of mankind. **You shall live without any hatreds and thus eliminate any thoughts or actions of hatreds and murder.**

YOU SHALL NOT COMMIT ADULTERY.
You shall not bring shame and dishonor upon yourself and your family by being sexually unfaithful to your spouse, children, parents, and family by committing adultery or any other sinful sexual act. You shall always merit and earn the respect of your spouse, children, family, neighbors, and community by the honorably life you live. **You shall not commit a sinful harmful injurious sexual act against any person because of hatred.**

YOU SHALL NOT STEAL.
You shall not steal and wrongfully take away from any one, for your own possession, anything that does not belong to you. You shall not defraud anyone or keep and maintain, without permission, anything that belongs to some one else. You must return and give back to the owner anything that you have taken into your possession that does not belong to you. **You shall not take anything into your possession through theft or stealing or because you harbor hatred against the rightful owner.**

YOU SHALL NOT BEAR FALSE WITNESS.

You shall not testify falsely, be untruthful, or lie. All your words, oral or in writing, shall not cause any wrongful harm to anyone. You shall not ever state or make a false oath. **Your words shall be true and never purposely be false causing harm and injury because of hatred.**

YOU SHALL NOT COVET.
You shall not wrongfully desire anything that is not yours and that belongs to some other person. You shall not wrongfully desire any of their possessions. You shall want only and desire those items and materials that you can buy and pay for or merit and earn through your good and honest labor. **You shall not allow hatred to govern your actions and cause coveting thoughts that may lead to wrongful actions against, or takings from, your neighbor or anyone else.**

The above six commandments can be inscribed on metal tablets and placed upon the walls of the Courts of Judgment and Justice and in you home. They do not reflect a choice of one religious belief over another and indeed do not reflect anything that even an atheist could or would fault.

These six commandments mounted on the walls of our Courts, and even upon the walls of our homes and schools, would be an inspiration for adults to behave like honorable adults and would especially teach and inspire all of our youth. They would lessen the happenings of hatreds, crimes, and wrongful and illegal behaviors. They would also strongly defy any and all the wrongful reasons given and stated for one to have and justify hatreds against any of mankind.

There are three bibles that cover the religions of the Judaism, Christianity, and Islam. The first, the oldest, is the Torah of the Mother religion of Judaism. It was and is written in the Hebrew Language. The second oldest is the New Testament of the oldest of the Daughter Religion of Christianity. The New Testament was first written and expressed in Latin. The youngest is the Koran of the youngest of the Daughter Religion of Islam. and was and is written in Arabic.

The first that should be studied by all is the Torah. This should be done before one studies the bibles of the younger daughter religions.

The best study would be accomplished by a study in the Hebrew language. After completing this study, one could study the New Testament. The best study would be accomplished by a study in the Latin language After completing this study, one could study the Koran. The best study would be accomplished by a study in the Arabic language. After the study of all three Bibles, one could reason and determine the values of each of the Bibles, their differences, and the one best representative of the religion of the ONE SINGLE GOD that should be recognized and adhered to by the reader.

The great problem has been that, all too often, the individual who is born into and believes one of the Daughter religions, does not commences his or her belief by knowing and understanding the Mother religion that gave birth and life to the Daughter religion. It is important to commence the understanding of all three religions with the beginning words of the first bible, the Torah. These four words are **"IN THE BEGINNING GOD"**. These words compel the reader to continue to read the entire Torah. Then, and only then, can anyone understand the words that follow in the other bibles, the New Testament and the Koran. In the Torah, the reader learns about the ONE SINGLE GOD and HIS Ten Commandments. This can result and lead to very serious questions as to the other beliefs promulgated and contained in the Daughter religions.

While study in the original languages of the three religions is the best way to study, all three religions can be studied using recognized, accurate, acceptable translations into English or other languages. Care must be taken not to utilize translations made to justify one religion while condemning other religions and the study of Mother and Daughter religions, must challenge and question beliefs that are opposite of each other and change the Commandments and Laws of the ALMIGHTY CREATOR, the ONE SINGLE GOD. **Let it also be understood that a Jew can be defined as one who believes in the ALMIGHTY CREATOR, the ONE SINGLE GOD, and believes in HIS Torah, and believes in HIS Ten Commandments. This is not reason to harbor hatreds of Jews and defy the ONE SINGLE GOD by murdering and maiming Jews.**

Each person, man or women, is the creation of the ONE SINGLE

GOD. This is the ONE SINGLE GOD that has created everything. Any person, man or women can look about themselves and see the evidence of the existence of the ONE SINGLE GOD. Even a person, man or women, who is blind can feel and touch upon the evidence of the existence of the ONE SINGLE GOD.

I see the evidence when I look about me. I see other humans. I look outside through the window and I see trees, grass, ants, butterflies, birds, squirrels, and other living creatures. I look about in the room I am in. The walls are man made, and also the floor, ceiling, doors, windows, and light fixtures. Man made from substances that man did not create and make. All of the substances that make up the floor, ceiling, doors, windows and light fixtures were created by the ONE SINGLE GOD. Without the creations of the ONE SINGLE GOD, man could not make anything and certainly not the building and room that I am in.

I go outdoors and enjoy a day of beauty and sunshine. The flowers of all shapes and colors are mine to view and enjoy. The sun is shining in a blue sky and there are soft cotton like small clouds that are slowly drifting by. The ONE SINGLE GOD has presented me with his beautiful world of this earth and HIS heaven above. It would be a blessing if all mankind could take the time to think this way and give thanks to the ONE SINGLE GOD. This should be a requirement of all religions of mankind. Perhaps if all men and women took the time to do this, there would not be time for thought of hatreds nor time and thought or necessity for wars.

I look again at the tree with its beautiful branches and leaves. I give my personal thanks to the ONE SINGLE GOD for HIS CREATIONS. I look at the tree and think of the poet, Joyce Kilmer, who best expressed it when he said:

I THINK THAT I SHALL NEVER SEE

A POEM AS LOVELY AS A TREE.

FOR POEMS ARE MADE BY FOOLS LIKE ME.

BUT ONLY GOD CAN MAKE A TREE.

Thank you, Joyce Kilmer, for your very wise Poem.

Thank YOU, my ONE SINGLE GOD, for all of YOUR BEAUTIFUL WORLD that YOU ENDOWED for me and all of mankind with all of YOUR CREATIONS.

Thank YOU, my ONE SINGLE GOD, for providing me with the ability to think and to appreciate all of YOUR ENDEAVORS.